# Q and A
# in
# Pharmacology

**(Part 1—General Pharmacology)**

## Author

**Dr Shiva Murthy N**

Professor, Department of Pharmacology
Dr Chandramma Dayananda Sagar Institute of Medical Education
and Research, Kanakapura Road, Devarakaggalahalli,
Near Harohalli, Ramanagara District,
Karnataka India

**Published in 2024**

**Book Title:** "Q and A in Pharmacology (Part-1 General Pharmacology)"

**Authored by:** Dr Shiva Murthy N

**Contact email ID:** shivuindia@gmail.com

**Copyright©** Dr. Shiva Murthy N

**Editor:** Mrs. Sowmya Nataraj

**Address for communication/Office address:**

Dr Shiva Murthy N,
Shree SowmyaShiva Sadana, No 57, 1$^{st}$ cross, 4$^{th}$ main,
Kothanur Dinne, JP Nagar 8$^{th}$ Phase,
Bangalore – 560078, Karnataka, India
Phone: +91 8884328275
Email: shivuindia@gmail.com

We do not have any other office.
For sales, please write to shivuindia@gmail.com

**First Edition:** March 2024

**Paper Size:** A4 size

**No of Pages:** 194 pages including cover pages

**Original soft copy prepared, designed and maintained by:** Mrs. Sowmya Nataraj

**Disclaimer:**

Dedicated to


All my teachers and students.

(including medical, dental, pharmacy, physiotherapy,

Nursing, Allied Health Science courses, and all possible courses!)


Dr. Shiva Murthy N

**Preface to Q and A in Pharmacology (part-1) first edition**

Pharmacology is the science that deals with various classes of drugs, their pharmacological properties, adverse drug reactions, drug-drug interactions, indications, and contraindications. Understanding general pharmacology and basic concepts is very important. This forms the basis for better understanding different therapeutic classes of drugs and their properties. In this handbook, I have made an attempt to provide answers to the most common questions.

This book does not replace the standard prescribed text books of pharmacology that are mentioned in the university curriculum. This effort is just to augment the learning and improve the ability of the students to read, retain, and answer the most common questions that may be asked in formative assessments such as class tests and internal examinations and in final summative assessments such as university examinations and NEXT examination.

I wish the best for the students who supported my efforts and helped me improve the book through their feedback.

**Dr Shiva Murthy N**

**About the Author**

**Dr. Shiva Murthy N, MBBS, MD, MBA.**

He is currently working as a professor (with 22 years of post-MD experience) at the Department of Pharmacology, CDSIMER Medical College, Ramanagara. He is also the founder and president of the Medical Pharmacologists Society and the managing editor of the JPADR journal. He is the recipient of several awards, such as the INSC Research Excellence Award (2023), the Best Research Paper Awards (Hyperpiesia Conference (2021), and KSMPCON (2023). He is also the author of five other books, namely Pharmacovigilance Reflective Writing E-Book, Clinical Trials Management, Arogya Janapada, Molehalu-Navajaatha Shishuvina Amrutha, and Practical Pharmacology Record Book.

## Acknowledgements

I would like to thank all my colleagues, friends, teachers, and students who directly or indirectly supported or helped me understand the need of the hour and lacunae in current teaching and learning methods. This helped me bring out this book after gaining a decade of teaching experience, which helped me arrive at some important conclusions and answers to the unanswered questions.

I would also like to thank all the MEU members, senior faculty members, and administrative staff of both DMWIMS Wayanad and CDSIMER, Ramanagara who helped me successfully transform myself into a successful teacher and an author too. I also want to thank my family members, who are constantly supporting me in achieving various milestones, including this book. I also thank the my wife Mrs Sowmya Nataraj for doing proof reading and supporting me in editing this book.

I would like to thank the various authors of pharmacology text books and research/review articles for their best efforts in bringing the information together. By reading their articles, I learned a lot and gained knowledge about the pharmacology subject. I was able to summarise the information gained from these articles and books and successfully put it in the form of Q&A in pharmacology through this book.

Lastly, I would like to thank Notion Press for providing the platform for designing the cover pages, publishing my book, and marketing in global markets.

**- Dr. Shiva Murthy N**

**Table of Contents**

| Sl No | Questions | Page No |
|---|---|---|

**Table of Contents contd...**

| Sl No | Questions | Page No |
|---|---|---|

**Table of Contents contd...**

# Table of Contents contd...

## 1. What is Pharmacology?

Pharmacology is the science that deals with drugs and its properties
The word *Pharmacon* means *drugs* and *logos* means *discourse* (study) in Greek. All aspects of drugs including their actions, interactions with biological systems and use in medicinal conditions are dealt in Pharmacology subject.

## 2. What is drug?

*Drug word is derived from Drogue*. It means a dry herb. Drug is defined as "*single active chemical entity present in a medicine that is used for diagnosis, revention, treatment/cure of a disease*".

As per WHO definition, *Drug is any substance or product that is used or is intended to be used to modify or explore physiological systems or pathological states for the benefit of the recipient*".

## 3. Who is the father of pharmacology?

Oswald Schmiedeberg is regarded as the 'father of pharmacology'. He proposed the many fundamental concepts in pharmacology.

Based on his recommendations many drugs were purified, and chemically characterized. Many highly potent and selective new drugs have been developed. In addition, mechanism of action including molecular target of these drugs were elucidated. This lead to the growth of pharmacology which forms the backbone of rational therapeutics.

## 4. Enumerate the some of the important branches of Pharmacology?

Some of the important branches pharmacology are mentioned below:

**Pharmacokinetics (PK)** - means movement of the drug and its alteration in the body. PK includes absorption, distribution, storage or binding or localization, metabolism (biotransformation) and excretion of the drug

**Pharmacodynamics (PD)** - PD means actions of drugs on physiological and biochemical processes. It also deals with the mechanism of action at receptors (macromolecular)/ organ system/ subcellular sites.

**Clinical pharmacology** - Scientific study (Pharmacodynamic and/or pharmacokinetic investigation) of old/new drugs in healthy volunteers and/ or in patients.

**Chemotherapy** - Deals with selective toxicity of the drugs towards the infecting organism/malignant cell with minimal or no action on the host cells.

**Pharmacy** - means it is the science and art of preparing suitable dosage forms, storage and dispensing of drugs for the purpose of administration of drugs to man or animals.

**Pharmacotherapeutics** - Means Rational application of pharamcological information based on the evidence for the purpose of treatment/ prevention/ eradication of the disease.

**Toxicology**- means the study of drugs/poisons/ chemicals (household chemicals, environmental pollutant, industrial chemicals, agricultural fertilizers/ insecticides) regarding their actions, methods of detection, prevention and treatment of poisonings.

## 5. What are the sources of drugs?

Drugs are found through various sources. Some of the important sources are discussed below:

### 1. *Plants*

- One of the most important and oldest sources of drugs.
- Many biologically active substances are obtained from plants.
- Traditional systems of medicine provides clues to initiate research activities and identify the active principle.

- Some of the plant extracts like opium, bella-donna, ephedra, cinchona, curare, foxglove, sar-pagandha, qinghaosu are described in Egyptian, Greek, Aztec, Ayurvedic, Chinese and other systems of medicine.

- Based on Chemical structure, the drugs extracted from plants are divided into several categories:

### *Alkaloids:*

- *Eg.* morphine, atropine, ephedrine, nicotine, ergotamine, reserpine, quinine, vincristine, etc
- Chemical structure contain alkaline nitrogenous

- They are formulated as water soluble hydrochloride/ sulfate salts.

### *Glycosides:*

- Cardiac glycosides (digoxin, ouabain) - Glycosidic drugs - Chemically they have heterocyclic nonsugar moiety (Aglycone) linked to a sugar moiety
- Senna - plant purgatives are Anthraquinone glycosides
- Aminoglycosides (Gentamicin and other antibiotics) - have an aminosugar in place of a sugar moiety

### *Oils: -*

*Fixed* (nonvolatile) oils –
- eg. Groundnut oil, Coconut oil, Sesame oil, etc.
- Viscous, inflammable liquids, insoluble in water
- Triglycerides yield calorie with high amount of fatty acids
- Used for food and as emollients

*Essential* (volatile) oils
- Eg. Eucalyptus oil, Pepermint oil, Nilgiri oil, etc.
- Aromatic (fragrant) terpene hydrocarbons

- Source- flowers or leaves by steam distillation
- Are of no food value.
- used as flavouring agents, carminatives, counter-irritants and astringents;
- Clove oil used to allay dental pain examples are is
- Volatile oils - Menthol, thymol, camphor - are solids at room temperature.

*Mineral oils*
- Source petroleum;
- Eg. liquid paraffin – used as  lubricant laxative,
- Soft and hard paraffin - used as emollient and as ointment bases. cough mixtures.
- Sesquiterpene endoperoxide – eg. Artemisinin - obtained from a Chinese plant – used as antimalarial drug

### *2. Animals*

- e.g. adrenaline, thyroxine, insulin, liver extract (vit. B12).
- Antisera and some vaccines
- animal are developed as medicine,

### *3. Microbes*

- e.g. penicillin, gentamicin, tetracycline, erythromycin, polymyxin B, actinomycin D (anticancer).
- Source - fungi, actinomycetes and bacteria,
- e.g. diastase from a fungus and streptokinase - streptococci – used as therapeutic enzymes,
- Vaccines – produced using microbes.

### *4. Minerals*

- e.g. iron salts, calcium salts, lithium carbonate, magnesium/aluminium hydroxide, iodine
- used as medicinal substances.

### *5. Synthetic chemistry*

- *Eg.* Atropine substitutes, adrenergic b2 agonists, synthetic glucocorticoids/ progestins/ cephalosporins, etc.

- Largest source
- Purity and uniformity of the product
- Diverse congeners of naturally obtained drugs
- Achieve greater selectivity of action or even novel type of activity
- Entire families are synthetic - e.g. benzodiazepines, thiazides, benzimidazoles, fluoroquinolones, etc

- Newer Target specific biomolecules - e.g. ACE inhibitors, glycoprotein IIb/IIIa receptor antagonists, HIV-reverse transcriptase inhibitors, etc.
- Chiral form - single active enantiomer products, which may be therapeutically superior.

## *6. Biotechnology*

- e.g. human growth hormone, human insulin, altaplase, interferon, etc
- Produced by recombinant DNA technology
- Peptides and proteins - newer drugs of biotechnological origin
- eg. Monoclonal antibodies, regulator peptides, erythropoietin and other growth factors
- Proteomics - protein therapeutics
- New development - designed and customized proteins synthesized .

## 6. Explain the methods used to name the drugs? What is brand name, generic name, and chemical name?

It is important to use same name to identify a particular drug throughout world to avoid confusion. In general drugs are named using chemical names, generic names and brand names.

## Chemical name:

Chemical names are prepared based on the chemical structure of the molecule. It is very difficult to remember and identify a particular drug using chemical name.
Eg. Atenolol's chemical name is as follows: 4-[2-hydroxy-3-[(1-methylethyl) amino] propoxy] benzene acetamide.

This name is generally included in drugs dossier filed for registration with regulatory authorities.

## Generic Name (Also called as Non-Proprietary Name):

These are the names accepted by competent scientific authority either appointed by the government of a particular country or World Health Organizaiton (WHO). WHO is having the responsibility to harmonize/enforce the practices throughout the world/ member countries for the benefit of mankind.

Following are the examples of agencies authorized to issue Generic Names to the new drugs.

- United States Adopted Name (USAN) by the USAN council
- British Approved name (BAN)
- Recommended International Nonproprietary Name (rINN) – by WHO

Some old drugs are still called with different generic names as it was not harmonized at the time of their invention and registration.
Eg. Norepinephrine = Noradrenaline, Adrenaline = Epinephrine

Other names for generic names are – official name, approved name etc.

## Brand Names (Also known as Proprietary Names):

This name is provided by manufacturer or marketing agency. It is the property or trade mark of a particular company for a particular molecule/formulation.

One molecule may be formulated differently / similarly by different manufacturers. They will use the brand name to promote their product to generate revenue. Therefore it is having a commercial angle to the pharmaceutical product.

Generally generic drugs are less costly. But branded drugs cost more than their generic counterparts.

Same product may be marketed with different brand names in different countries. This will add the complexities

Pfizer's Azithromycin is called with different brand names in different counties.

Eg.  ZITHROMAX in USA, TRULIMAX in Europe

Government of India is promoting generic drugs to reduce the cost of treatment. To ensure the quality of medications issued to patients in generic stores, Bio-equivalence studies should be mandatory. These studies helps us to compare the plasma concentration achieved by generic drugs in comparison with innovator's brand. If the concentration achieved should be within the acceptable limits. Then only the patient will get the therapeutic benefits.

## 7. What are the sources of Drugs information?

Sources of drugs information can be divided into

Primary source of drugs information

- Research papers, conference presentations

Secondary source of drugs information

- Review articles, Meta-analysis publications

Tertiary source of drugs information

- Text books, *Pharmacopoeias* and *Formularies*

### *Pharmacopoeias:*

Published by the Government in a country

*Contain information* - chemical structure, molecular weight, physical and chemical characteristics, solubility, identification and assay methods, and standards of purity, storage

conditions and dosage forms of officially approved drugs in a country
Eg. Indian pharmacopoeia (IP), British pharmacopoeia (BP), European pharmacopoeia (Eur P), United States pharmacopoeia (USP)

### *Formularies:*

Published by the Government in a country

*Contain information* - indications, dose, dosage forms, contraindications, precautions, adverse effects and storage of selected drugs that are available for medicinal use in a country.
Eg. British National Formulary (BNF), the National Formulary of India (NFI)

### *Martindale:*

*The Complete Drug Reference (Extrapharmacopoeia):* non-official compendium

*Published by* Royal Pharmaceutical Society of Great Britain

Contains information - on medicines used/registered all over the world.
The information included new launches, their pharmaceutical, pharmacological and therapeutic information on drugs.

Other sources of information are *Physicians Desk Reference (PDR)* and *Drug:Facts and Comparisons.*

## 8. What are Essential Drugs? Add a note on Essential Drugs Concept?

*Essential Medicines (drugs) are defined by WHO as* "Drugs that satisfy the healthcare needs of the population on priority basis".

This concept helps to prioritise the health care needs of a particular population based on the prevalence/incidence of the diseases in a particular region.

Essential drugs are selected into the list based on

- Public health relevance,
- Evidence on efficacy and safety (quality, including bioavailability, and stability on storage can be assured)
- Comparative cost effectiveness.
- Be available within the context of functioning health systems
- Available at all times in adequate amounts,
- Available in appropriate dosage forms,
- Available with assured quality and adequate information,
- Available at a price the individual and the community can afford.
- Helps to optimum utilization of resources by the governments (especially in developing countries)
- Availability of facilities and trained personnel, financial resources; genetic, demographic and environmental factors.
- If two or more drugs having similar indication, in such situation choice should be made based on their relative efficacy, safety, quality, ease of manufacturing, storage, cost and readily availability in the country.
- Generally single compounds should be included. But fixed ratio combination products may be included only when ingredient meets the requirements of a defined population group, and when the combination found to have special advantage in therapeutic effect, safety, compliance or in reducing the emergence of drug resistance.
- Essential drugs list is revised time to time based on the changing priorities for public health action, and epidemiological conditions.
- List should be developed rationally based on standard treatment guidelines.
- Latest revision of "National Essential Drugs List (India)" was done in 2023. Current list contains 384 drugs. It contains 3 categories for being available at primary, secondary and tertiary levels of health care facility.

## 9. What are "Over The Counter" drugs? What are "Prescription Drugs"?

**Over The Counter:**

Some drugs are considered relatively harmless and are made available for purchase without need of prescription issued by a registered prescription. These are 'non-prescription' or 'over-the-counter' (OTC) drugs.

Eg. Antacids, laxatives like senna, lactulose, analgesics like paracetamol aspirin, vitamins, ferrous salts, etc.

These allowed to for sale even in grocery stores.

**Prescription Drugs:**

According to *schedule H* of Drugs and Cosmetic Rules (1945), majority of drugs are included under prescription drugs. As per this rules prescription drugs must be sold on retail basis at a registered pharmacy only against a prescription issued to a patient by a registered medical practitioner.

Eg. Most of the drugs including those used for the treatment of infections, cancers, hypertension, diabetes etc.

The list prescription drugs and over the counter drugs are amended from time to time.

## 10. Define Orphan Drugs? Write a note on drugs for rare diseases?

Orphan drugs are medications developed to diagnosis/treatment/ prevention rare diseases, often referred to as orphan diseases.

- Orphan diseases - affect a small percentage of the population.
- No reasonable expectation that the cost of developing and marketing it will be recovered from the sales of that drug.
- Development and availability of orphan drugs have been gaining attention due to the increasing recognition of rare diseases

- In 2013, the Indian government introduced the Orphan Drug Policy, which aimed to promote the development and accessibility of orphan drugs in India
- India: Orphan drugs are defined as those intended to treat diseases or conditions that affect fewer than 20,000 people in the country
- USA: Orphan Drug Amendment (1983) Act of USA, a rare disease/ condition is one that affects less than 0.2 million people in the USA
- incentives to encourage the development of orphan drugs - incentives include tax benefits, fee waivers for clinical trials and regulatory filings, expedited review processes, and extended market exclusivity periods.
- International organizations and pharmaceutical companies plays a crucial role in advancing orphan drug development and access in India
- Examples: Imatinib is used to treat chronic myeloid leukemia (CML) and gastrointestinal stromal tumors (GIST, Eculizumab is used to treat paroxysmal nocturnal hemoglobinuria (PNH) and atypical hemolytic uremic syndrome (aHUS), Defibrotide is used to treat hepatic veno-occlusive disease (VOD), a rare and life-threatening condition.

## 11. Mention commonly used dosage forms with few salient features?

Drugs can be formulated into various dosage forms. They are designed to deliver the medication to the body in a specific manner based on the clinical condition and route of administration. Here are some common dosage forms are discussed below:

**Tablets:**

- Solid dosage forms designed to be swallowed orally.
- Prepared in various shapes, sizes, and colors and contain the active pharmaceutical ingredient (API) along with other excipients.
- Typically compressed powders,

**Capsules:**

- Capsules are shells containing either powder, granules, or pellets

**Liquid Formulations:** Solutions, Suspensions, Syrups

### *Solutions*

- Are homogeneous mixtures of the drug dissolved in a liquid solvent (e.g., water).

### *Suspensions*

- Contain finely divided drug particles suspended in a liquid vehicle.

### *Syrups*

- Are concentrated solutions of sugar and water with the drug dissolved or suspended in them

**Topical Preparations:**

- Dosage forms are applied to the skin or mucous membranes
- Used for local or systemic effects.
- Examples include creams, ointments, gels, lotions, patches, and aerosols.
- Used for conditions such as dermatitis, infections, pain relief, and hormone replacement

**Injectables:**

- Dosage forms include solutions, suspensions, and emulsions
- Administered via intravenous (iv), intramuscular (im), subcutaneous (sc), or other routes.
- Used when rapid onset of action, precise dosing, or bypassing the gastrointestinal tract is necessary.

**Inhalation Products:**

- Dosage forms deliver drugs directly to the lungs for local or systemic effects.
- Examples include
- Metered-dose inhalers (MDIs),

- Dry powder inhalers (DPIs),
- Nebulizers, and
- Nasal sprays.
- They are commonly used for
- Asthma,
- Chronic obstructive pulmonary disease (COPD), and
- Nasal allergies

## Suppositories:

- Solid dosage forms
- Inserted into the rectum, vagina, or urethra,
- They melt or dissolve at the site of insertion and release the drug for absorption.
- Used for local or systemic effects and
- Particularly useful when oral administration is not feasible

## Implants:

- Devices containing drug formulations
- Surgically inserted into the body.
- Release the drug over an extended period,
- Providing sustained therapeutic effects.
- Examples- contraceptive implants, hormone-releasing implants, and drug-eluting stents

## Dermal Patches:

- Are adhesive patches applied to the skin,
- Deliver drugs through the skin's layers for systemic absorption.
- Provide controlled release
- Used for - pain management, hormone replacement therapy, and smoking cessation

## 12. Mention advantages and their disadvantages of Tablets?

Tablets are a common method of drug dosage delivery.

## Advantages
## Convenience:

- Tablets are
- Easy to handle,
- Easy to transport,
- Easy to administer,

- More convenient for both patients and healthcare providers

## Accurate Dosage:

- Tablets allow for
- Precise dosing,
- The amount of active ingredient in each tablet can be carefully controlled during manufacturing.

## Stability:

- Tablets can provide
- Stability to the active pharmaceutical ingredient (API),
- Protect API from degradation caused by environmental factors such as light, moisture, and air.

## Ease of Production:

- Tablet manufacturing
- Processes are well-established
- Can be easily scaled up for mass production,
- Also Cost-effective in production.

## Taste Masking:

- Tablets can be formulated to
- Mask the taste of bitter or unpleasant-tasting drugs,
- Improving patient compliance,
- Helpful in pediatric and geriatric populations.

## Extended Release Formulations:

- Tablets can be designed as
- Extended-release formulations,
- Allow for sustained drug release over an extended period,
- Reduce the frequency of dosing
- Improve patient adherence.

## Patient Compliance:

- Tablets offer
- Convenience and familiarity to patients,
- Contribute to better compliance with prescribed medication regimens

## 13. Discuss on solid dosage formulations with their advantages and disadvantages?

**Solid dosage forms**

- are pharmaceutical formulations that exist in a solid state and are intended for oral administration.
- **Examples:** tablets, capsules, powders, granules, and lozenges.

**Advantages:**

- **Stability**: Solid dosage forms generally offer better stability compared to liquid formulations.
- They are less prone to degradation caused by factors such as light, moisture, and temperature fluctuations, which can extend the shelf life of the medication.
- **Accurate Dosage:** Solid dosage forms allow for precise dosing, as the amount of active pharmaceutical ingredient (API) in each unit can be accurately measured and controlled during manufacturing.
- This helps ensure consistent therapeutic outcomes and reduces the risk of dosing errors.
- **Convenience:** Solid dosage forms are convenient to store, transport, and administer.
- They do not require special handling or refrigeration, making them suitable for self-administration by patients in various settings.
- **Taste Masking:** Solid dosage forms can be formulated to mask the taste of bitter or unpleasant-tasting drugs, improving patient acceptance and compliance, especially in pediatric and geriatric populations.
- **Extended Release Formulations:** Solid dosage forms can be designed as extended-release or sustained-release formulations, allowing for controlled and prolonged drug release.
- This can reduce the frequency of dosing, improve patient adherence, and maintain steady plasma drug concentrations over time.
- **Ease of Manufacturing:** Solid dosage forms are relatively easy to manufacture on a large scale using well-established and cost-effective processes.
- This scalability facilitatesmass production, reduces manufacturing costs, and ensures consistent product quality.
- **Packaging Flexibility:** Solid dosage forms offer flexibility in packaging options, including bottles, blister packs, and unit-dose packaging.
- This allows for convenient dispensing, storage, and administration according to patient needs and preferences.

**Disadvantages:**

- **Swallowing Difficulty:** Some patients, particularly children, the elderly, and individuals with swallowing disorders, may have difficulty swallowing solid dosage forms such as tablets and capsules.
- This can lead to poor compliance and adherence to medication regimens.
- **Slow Onset of Action:** Solid dosage forms may have a slower onset of action compared to liquid formulations, as they need to disintegrate and dissolve in the gastrointestinal tract before absorption can occur.
- This delay may be problematic for drugs requiring rapid therapeutic effects.
- **Gastric Emptying Variability:** The absorption of drugs from solid dosage forms can be affected by factors such as gastric emptying rate, gastrointestinal pH, and food interactions.
- This variability may lead to inconsistent drug absorption and efficacy.
- **Not Suitable for Certain Patients:** Patients with dysphagia, gastrointestinal motility disorders, or conditions affecting gastrointestinal absorption may not be able to take solid dosage forms.
- Alternative dosage forms such as liquids, suspensions, or injectables may be required.
- **Size and Shape Constraints:** Some patients may have difficulty swallowing large or oddly shaped tablets or capsules, which can affect medication compliance and adherence.
- Manufacturers should consider patient preferences and ease of administration when designing solid dosage forms.

**14. Write about the Liquid dosage forms and their advantages and disadvantages?**

**Liquid dosage forms**
- are pharmaceutical formulations that exist in a liquid state and are intended for oral, topical, or parenteral administration.

- **Examples:** solutions, suspensions, syrups, emulsions, and elixirs.

- These are liquid pharmaceutical preparations that contain a process of dissolving or suspending a drug substance and excipients in a suitable solvent or mixture of solvents.

- The tablets are designed to produce rapid therapeutic effects in the absence of gastrointestinal problems and/or provide maximum therapeutic response.

- Medications can be given as solutions or dispersions in liquid form.

- The dispersion of an active compound is a multiphase or a two-phase process in which another component is added to the formula, whereas pharmaceutical solutions are clear and homogeneous liquids that contain an active substance and a solvent.

- Liquid Dosage Forms are useful for people who find it **difficult to swallow solid forms** of medication.

- Several additive ingredients are required for the preparation of liquid dosage forms.

- The list includes vehicles, stabilizers, and preservatives.

- Along with this, it also includes suspending agents, emulsifiers, solubilizers, colors, and Flavors in liquid dosage forms.

- There are many types of liquid dosage forms, including syrup, suspension, eardrops, eye drops, etc.

- Ingestion or administration of a liquid medicine dose,

- Various routes of administration are available, including orally, intravenously, intramuscularly, topically, subcutaneously, etc.

- Oral and parenteral routes of administration are available for liquid dosage forms (injections, inhalations, ophthalmic, nasal, optic, and topical).

**Advantages**

- Children and the elderly may struggle to swallow tablets or capsules, so liquid dosage forms may be a better choice than tablets and capsules.

- Their appearance is attractive and they provide psychological benefits. Sweetened, colored, and flavored vehicles can be used to deliver bitter and unpleasant medicines.

- Dosage is more flexible with liquid dosage forms compared with solid dosage forms like tablets and capsules.

- Measurement of a different volume can easily and conveniently adjust the dose of the drug substance. It is more difficult for tablets and capsules to be absorbed than liquid dosage forms if they are taken orally.

- Liquid dosage forms are absorbed at a much faster rate than solid dosage forms. Liquid dosage forms are suitable for the administration of hydrophobic and deliquescent medicines that are not suitable for solid dosage forms.

- Adsorbents and antacids deliver more intense effects in liquid dosage form than they do in tablet form. Solid dosage forms are more difficult to take correctly than liquid dosage forms. In certain types of medicines, such as cough preparations, liquid dosage forms are expected.

**Disadvantages**

- The chemical degradation of liquid dosage forms is typically more pronounced than solid dosage forms.

- Bulky and not convenient to transport or store, they take up a lot of space. If the container is accidentally broken, the entire dosage form is lost.

- Because liquid dosage forms are inherently unstable, their shelf-life is very often shorter than that of their corresponding solid dosage forms.

- It is not uncommon for a solution to provide an ideal environment for microbial growth. For this reason, preservatives are often required.

- Vaccines, for instance, need to be stored in special conditions due to their liquid form A solid form of a drug has an unpleasant taste that is always more apparent when the drug is dissolved.

- The patient's measurement of the correct volume determines whether the dose is given correctly, which increases the chance for variability.

- For patients with vision impairments, arthritis, or struggles with reading numbers on their oral dosing syringe and medicine cup, this can be a significant issue.

- Breakage of containers is an issue. Instable compared to other forms.

- Liquid dosage forms are the solution that contains vehicles, stabilizers, preservatives, emulsifying agents, suspending agents, solubilizers, sweetening agents, flavoring agents, coloring agents, etc.

## 15. Discuss various routes of drug administration.

A medication administration route is often classified by the location at which the drug is applied, such as **Oral or Parenteral.**

- The choice of routes in which the medications are applied depends not only on convenience but also on the drug's properties and pharmacokinetics.
- Therefore it is crucial to understand the characteristics of the various routes and associated techniques.

- Many interprofessional healthcare team members are involved in administering medications to patients.
- Each medication administration route has unique contraindications, and the healthcare team members need to recognize them.
- This activity describes medication administration routes and explains the interprofessional team's role in improving care for patients who undergo medication administration.
- A medication administration route is often classified by the location at which the drug is administered, such as oral or intravenous.
- The choice of routes in which the medication is given depends not only on convenience and compliance but also on the drug's pharmacokinetics and pharmacodynamic profile.
- Therefore it is crucial to understand the characteristics of the various routes and associated techniques.

## Enteral Route of Medication

- Oral administration of medication is a convenient, cost-effective, and most commonly used medication administration route.
- The primary site of drug absorption is usually the small intestine, and the bioavailability of the medication is influenced by the amount of drug absorbed across the intestinal epithelium.
- The first-pass effect is an important consideration for orally administered medications.
- It refers to the drug metabolism whereby the drug concentration is significantly diminished before it reaches the systemic circulation, often due to the metabolism in the liver.
- A sublingual or buccal route is another form of the enteral route of medication administration that offers the benefit of bypassing the first-pass effect.
- By applying the drug directly under the tongue (sublingual) or on the cheek (buccal), the medication undergoes a passive diffusion through the venous blood in the oral cavity, which bypasses the hepatic portal vein and flows into the superior vena cava.

- Compared to sublingual tissue, which has highly permeable mucosa with rapid access to the underlying capillaries, buccal tissue is less permeable and has slower drug absorption.
- A rectal route is another enteral route of medication administration, and it allows for rapid and effective absorption of medications via the highly vascularized rectal mucosa.
- Similar to sublingual and buccal routes, rectally administered medications undergo passive diffusion and partially bypass the first-pass metabolism.
- Only about half of the drug absorbed in the rectum directly goes to the liver.

**Parenteral Route of Medication**

- Intravenous injection is the most common parental route of medication administration and can bypass the liver's first-pass metabolism.
- Given their superficial location on the skin, peripheral veins provide easy access to the circulatory system and are often utilized in the parenteral administration of medications.
- The upper extremity is usually the preferred site for intravenous medication as it has a lower incidence of thrombophlebitis and thrombosis than the lower limbs.
- The median basilic or cephalic veins of the arm or the metacarpal veins on the hand's dorsum are commonly used. In the lower extremity, the dorsal venous plexus of the foot can be used.
- An intramuscular medication route can be administered in different body muscles, including the deltoid, dorsogluteal, ventrogluteal, rectus femoris, or vastus lateralis muscles.
- Although the dorsogluteal site, or the buttock's upper outer quadrant, is a common site chosen traditionally for intramuscular injections by healthcare professionals, it poses a potential risk of injury to the superior gluteal artery and sciatic nerve.
- On the other hand, the ventrogluteal site, or the anterior gluteal site, targets the gluteus medius muscle and avoids these potential complications; thus, it is recommended.

- Subcutaneous injections are another form of the parental route of medication and are administered to the layer of skin referred to as cutis, just below the dermis and epidermis layers.
- Subcutaneous tissue has few blood vessels; therefore, the medications injected undergo absorption at a slow, sustained rate.
- Subcutaneous medication can be administered to various sites, including the upper arm's outer area and abdomen, avoiding a 2-inch circle around the navel, the front of the thigh, the upper back, or the upper buttock area behind the hip bone.
- The intraarterial route is not commonly used for drug administration.
  - Injection of contrast material after an arterial puncture is done for angiography.
  - The other uses of this route are for administering regional chemotherapeutic agents and treating malignant tumors of the brain.

**Other Routes of Medication**

- A transnasal drug route facilitates drug absorption by passive diffusion across the single-layered, well-vascularized respiratory epithelium directly into the systemic circulation.
- An inhaled medication is delivered rapidly across the large surface area of the respiratory tract epithelium.
- Drugs absorbed into the pulmonary circulation enter directly into the systemic circulation via the pulmonary vein, bypassing the first-pass metabolism.
- The particle size of the inhaled medication is usually 1 to 10 µm for effective delivery. The efficacy of drug delivery to the lungs depends not only on the drug particle size and morphology but also on the patient's respiratory physiology, such as tidal volume and tracheal inspiration velocity.
- A vaginal route is an underexplored drug delivery route that is not commonly used but has the advantage of bypassing the first-pass effect and can serve as an effective method for local and systemic therapy.

- The venous plexuses from the vagina communicate with the vesical, uterine, and rectal venous plexuses and drain into the internal iliac veins.
- The veins from the middle and upper vagina drain directly into the inferior vena cava and bypass the hepatoportal system.
- The transdermal route can deliver drugs through the skin.
- This route uses common administration methods: local application formulations like transdermal ointments and gels, drug carriers like nanoparticles and liposomes, and transdermal patches.
- The intraosseous route is useful, especially in neonates, for administering fluids and drugs when both peripheral and central venous accesses have failed.
- Clinical trials are now being conducted on its usefulness in administering medications in out-of-hospital cardiac arrest.
- It is also used for the administration of prophylactic antibiotics for regional surgeries.

## 16. Discuss the advantages and disadvantages of oral route of drug administration?
**Oral route**

This is convenient and indicated for patients who can ingest and tolerate oral medication. Some medications with short half-lives are administered orally as timed-release or sustained-release forms that get absorbed over several hours.

**Advantages:**
- Ease of administration
- Widespread acceptance by the patients.

**Disadvantages:**
- Variable absorption rates
- Degradation of some drugs before reaching the site of absorption into the bloodstream
- The inability of many compounds to effectively traverse the intestinal epithelial membrane cells to reach the bloodstream.
- The insolubility of many drugs at low pH levels is prevalent in the digestive tract.
- The inactivation of the drug in the liver on its way to the systemic circulation
- Irritation of the mucous lining of the gastrointestinal tract. This can be prevented to some extent by coating.

## 17. Discuss the advantages and disadvantages of sublinguial and buccal route of drug administration?

**Sublingual and Buccal Routes**

- These are indicated for medications with high first-pass metabolism that need to avoid clearance by the liver. For instance, nitroglycerin is cleared more than 90% during a single pass through the liver; therefore, it is given in a sublingual form.

**Advantages:**

- Rapid absorption is due to the abundant mucosal network of systemic veins and lymphatics, thereby leading to a rapid onset of action.

- If there is any untoward event, the tablet can be removed.

- Avoids first-pass hepatic metabolism.

- A tablet can be kept for a long time in the buccal cavity, which helps develop formulations with a sustained-release effect.

- This route is useful in patients having swallowing difficulties.

- Low risk of infection

- Convenience

**Disadvantages:**

- The tablet must be kept in the buccal cavity and neither chewed nor swallowed.

- Excessive salivation may cause quick dissolution and absorption of the tablet.

- Patients may find it difficult to accept an unpalatable tablet. Hence some drugs are applied as a patch or a spray.

**18. Discuss the advantages and disadvantages of rectal route of drug administration?**

**Rectal Route**

This route is useful for patients with gastrointestinal motility problems such as dysphagia or ileus that can interfere with delivering the drug to the intestinal tract. The rectal route is also often utilized in patients near the end of life undergoing hospice care.

**Advantages:**

- A relatively large amount of the drug can be administered.
- Those drugs destroyed by the acidic medium in the stomach and those metabolized by pancreatic enzymes can be administered effectively.
- Safe and convenient for infants and the elderly.
- It can be used in emergency situations, such as in infants having seizures when the intravenous route is unavailable.
- The rate of absorption is uninfluenced by the ingestion of food or the rate of gastric emptying.
- Bypasses hepatic metabolism
- Less degradation of drugs compared to that in the upper gastrointestinal tract.

**Disadvantages:**
- Some hydrophilic drugs like antibiotics and peptide drugs are unsuitable for rectal administration as they are not readily absorbed.
- Some drugs can cause rectal irritation and proctitis, leading to ulceration and bleeding.

**19. Discuss the advantages and disadvantages of Intravenous route of drug administration?**

**Intravenous Route**

- This directly administers the medications to the systemic circulation. It is indicated when a rapid drug effect is desired, a precise serum drug level is needed, or when drugs are unstable or poorly absorbed in the gastrointestinal tract.
- It is also the route utilized in patients with altered mental status or severe nausea or vomiting, unable to tolerate oral medications.

**Advantages:**

- Rapid onset of action
- Predictable way of action and almost complete bioavailability
- The problems of oral drug administration can be eliminated by avoiding the gastrointestinal tract
- The best way of administration in very ill and comatose patients who cannot ingest anything orally

**Disadvantages:**

- Causes pain
- Chance of infection
- The delivery of protein products that require sustained levels can be difficult.

**20. Discuss the advantages and disadvantages of Intramuscular route of drug administration?**

**Intramuscular Route**

- This can be utilized when oral drug absorption occurs in an erratic or incomplete pattern, the drug has high first-pass metabolism, or the patient is not compliant.
- A depot preparation of the drug can be given intramuscularly, and the medication dissolves slowly into the circulation to provide a sustained dose over a more extended time.

**Example:**
- Haloperidol decanoate.
- Vaccines are also administered via the intramuscular route.

**Disadvantages:**

- Injection site pain
- The amount of drug administered has to be adjusted according to the mass of the muscle available.
- Peptides get degraded locally.
- Complications - hematoma, abscess, peripheral nerve injury, puncture of a blood vessel leading to inadvertent intravascular administration.

**21. Discuss the advantages and disadvantages of subcutaneous route of drug administration?**

**Subcutaneous Route**

- This is used when the drug's molecular size is too large to be effectively absorbed in the intestinal tract or when better bioavailability or a faster absorption rate is needed than the oral route. It is easy to administer and requires minimal skills, so patients can often self-administer the medication.
- Common medications administered subcutaneously include insulin, heparin, and monoclonal antibodies.
- The rate of absorption of drugs through this route can be enhanced by infiltration with the enzyme hyaluronidase.
- The major factors that affect the rate of absorption by this route include the size of the molecules (large molecules having slow penetration), viscosity, and the anatomical characteristics of the site of injection (vascularity and amount of fatty tissue).

**Disadvantages:**

- The rate of absorption is difficult to control.
- Local complications - irritation and pain.
- Injection sites must be changed frequently to prevent the buildup of unabsorbed medication, which could lead to tissue injury.

**22. Discuss the advantages and disadvantages of Intranasal route of drug administration?**

**Intranasal Route**

- This can be utilized in administering nasal decongestants for cold or allergy treatment.
- Other uses include desmopressin for the treatment of diabetes insipidus or intranasal calcitonin for the treatment of osteoporosis.

Factors that affect the rate of absorption of drugs via the nasal route are:

- **The rate of nasal secretion** - The rate of secretion is inversely proportional to the bioavailability of the drug.
- **Ciliary movement** - The speed of ciliary movement is inversely proportional to the bioavailability of the drug.
- **Vascularity of the nose** - The volume of blood flow is directly proportional to the rate of drug absorption.
- **Metabolism of drugs in the nasal cavity** - The enzymes present in the nasal tissues alter the absorption of some compounds, especially peptides that are disintegrated by aminopeptidases.
- **Diseases affecting nasal mucous membrane.** Common colds can affect nasal drug absorption.
- **Enhancement of nasal drug delivery**:
- Rapid mucociliary clearance can lead to poor bioavailability of the drug. This can be overcome by in situ gelling drug delivery.
- **Chitosan** is a natural bioadhesive polysaccharide obtained from crustacean shells that can be used as an absorption enhancer. Chitosan binds to the nasal mucosal membrane and facilitates drug absorption through paracellular transport and other mechanisms.

**Advantages:**
- Increased permeability of the nasal mucosa compared to the gastrointestinal mucosa.
- Highly vascularized subepithelial tissue.
- Quick absorption, usually within thirty minutes
- Avoids the first-pass effect.
- Avoids the effects of gastric stasis and vomiting.
- Ease of administration.
- Higher bioavailability of the drugs than in the case of the enteral route or inhalational route.

**Disadvantages:**
- Nasal cavity diseases and conditions may result in impaired absorption.
- The dose is limited due to the small area available for absorption.
- The time available for absorption is limited.
- This route does not apply to all drugs.

**23. Discuss the advantages and disadvantages of Inhalational route of drug administration?**

- The inhalational route of drug administration involves the delivery of medications directly to the respiratory tract via inhalation, typically through the nose or mouth.
- This route is commonly used for the treatment of respiratory conditions such as asthma, chronic obstructive pulmonary disease (COPD), and cystic fibrosis.

**Advantages:**
- **Rapid Onset of Action:** Inhalational drugs often have a rapid onset of action because they are delivered directly to the site of action in the lungs.
- This can lead to quicker relief of symptoms compared to oral medications.

- **Targeted Delivery:** Inhalational drugs target the respiratory tract, allowing for localized therapy and minimizing systemic side effects.
- This targeted delivery can enhance drug efficacy while reducing the required dose.

- **High Bioavailability:** Inhalational drugs bypass the gastrointestinal tract and liver metabolism, leading to higher bioavailability compared to orally administered drugs.
- This can result in lower doses required to achieve therapeutic effects.

- **Noninvasive Route:** Inhalational administration is noninvasive and generally well-tolerated, making it suitable for patients who have difficulty swallowing pills or injections.
- **Patient Convenience:** Inhalational medications are often delivered using portable devices such as metered-dose inhalers (MDIs) or dry powder inhalers (DPIs), allowing for convenient self-administration by patients.

**Disadvantages:**
- **Device Related:** Proper administration of inhalational medications requires the use of specialized devices such as inhalers or nebulizers.
- Patient education and training are necessary to ensure correct technique and optimal drug delivery.
- **Technique Related:** Inhalational drug delivery requires coordination between inhalation and actuation of the device.
- Poor technique can result in inadequate drug deposition in the lungs and reduced efficacy.
- **Risk of Systemic Side Effects:** While inhalational drugs target the respiratory tract, systemic absorption can still occur, leading to potential systemic side effects.
- Care must be taken to minimize systemic exposure, especially with potent medications.
- **Limited Compatibility:** Not all drugs are suitable for inhalational administration due to their physicochemical properties or potential for airway irritation.
- Formulation challenges may limit the availability of inhalational options for certain medications.
- **Infection Risk:** Inhalational devices can become contaminated with bacteria or fungi, posing a risk of respiratory infections, particularly in immunocompromised individuals.
- Proper device cleaning and maintenance are essential to reduce this risk.
- **Environmental Concerns:** Some inhalational medications, particularly those delivered using propellant-based MDIs, may contribute to environmental pollution.
- Increasing emphasis on environmentally friendly propellants and device technologies is addressing this concern.
- 
- **Conclusion:** The inhalational route of drug administration offers several advantages, including rapid onset of action, targeted delivery, high bioavailability, and patient convenience.
- However, it also has limitations such as device related and technique related issues, risk of systemic side effects, and environmental concerns.
- Careful consideration of these factors is necessary when selecting inhalational therapy for patients with respiratory conditions

## 24. Add a note on Vaginal route of drug administration?

- The vaginal route of drug administration involves the delivery of medications directly to the vaginal mucosa for local or systemic effects.

- This route is primarily used for the treatment of various gynecological conditions, including vaginal infections, contraception, hormone replacement therapy, and certain reproductive health issues.

- **Key points regarding the vaginal route of drug administration :**

- **Localized Therapy:** The vaginal route allows for targeted delivery of medications to the vaginal mucosa, leading to localized therapy with minimal systemic exposure.
- This can reduce the risk of systemic side effects and improve the efficacy of treatment for vaginal conditions such as infections and inflammation.

- **Drug Absorption:** The vaginal mucosa is highly vascularized, allowing for rapid absorption of drugs into the systemic circulation.
- This can be advantageous for delivering medications with systemic effects, such as hormone replacement therapy or emergency contraception.

- **Dosage Forms:** Vaginal medications are available in various dosage forms, including creams, gels, tablets, suppositories, and inserts.
- Each dosage form offers unique advantages in terms of ease of administration, retention within the vaginal cavity, and duration of drug release.

- **Patient Acceptability:** The vaginal route of drug administration is generally well-tolerated by patients and may be preferred over other routes, particularly for conditions affecting the female reproductive system.
- Patients may find vaginal dosage forms convenient, discreet, and easy to use.

- **Factors Affecting Drug Absorption:** Several factors can influence drug absorption from the vaginal mucosa, including pH, vaginal secretions, blood flow, and the presence of infection or inflammation.
- Formulation characteristics such as viscosity, solubility, and bioadhesion can also affect drug release and absorption.

- **Clinical Applications:** The vaginal route is commonly used for the treatment of vaginal infections, including bacterial vaginosis, yeast infections (e.g., candidiasis), and sexually transmitted infections (e.g., trichomoniasis).
- It is also utilized for hormone replacement therapy, contraception (e.g., vaginal rings), and the induction of labor (e.g., prostaglandin E2 gel).

- **Precautions and Considerations:** Healthcare providers should consider potential contraindications, precautions, and patient preferences when prescribing vaginal medications.
- Proper patient education regarding administration techniques, potential side effects, and follow-up care is essential to ensure optimal treatment outcomes.

### Conclusion:
- The vaginal route of drug administration offers advantages such as localized therapy, rapid drug absorption, and patient acceptability for the treatment of various gynecological conditions.
- Healthcare providers should carefully consider the clinical indications, dosage forms, and patient factors when prescribing vaginal medications to optimize therapeutic efficacy and patient satisfaction.

## 25. Add a note on Transdermal route of drug administration?

- The transdermal route of drug administration involves the delivery of medications through the skin for systemic effects.

- This route offers several advantages, making it suitable for a variety of therapeutic applications.

**Key points regarding the transdermal route of drug administration :**

- **Direct Absorption:** Transdermal drug delivery allows for direct absorption of medications through the skin into the systemic circulation.
- This bypasses the gastrointestinal tract and hepatic first-pass metabolism, resulting in enhanced bioavailability and reduced potential for gastrointestinal side effects.
- **Controlled Drug Release:** Transdermal delivery systems are designed to provide controlled and sustained release of medications over an extended period.
- This can lead to more stable plasma concentrations, improved patient compliance, and reduced frequency of dosing compared to oral medications.
- **Convenience and Comfort:** Transdermal patches are convenient and easy to use, requiring simple application to the skin.
- Patients may prefer transdermal delivery over other routes due to its noninvasive nature, minimal discomfort, and lack of needles or injections.
- **Avoidance of Hepatic First Pass:** By bypassing hepatic first-pass metabolism, transdermal drug delivery can improve the bioavailability of certain medications and reduce the risk of metabolic degradation in the liver.
- This can be particularly beneficial for drugs with high first-pass metabolism or low oral bioavailability.
- **Prolonged Duration of Action:** Transdermal patches can provide prolonged duration of action, allowing for continuous drug delivery and steady plasma concentrations over an extended period.
- This can improve therapeutic efficacy and reduce fluctuations in drug levels compared to oral medications.
- **Suitable for Lipophilic Drugs:** Transdermal delivery is particularly well-suited for lipophilic drugs that can penetrate the skin barrier and reach systemic circulation.
- However, the molecular size, lipophilicity, and potency of the drug can influence its permeability and effectiveness through the transdermal route.
- **Clinical Applications:** Transdermal patches are commonly used for the management of chronic conditions such as pain (e.g., fentanyl patches), hypertension (e.g., nitroglycerin patches), hormone replacement therapy (e.g., estrogen patches), and smoking cessation (e.g., nicotine patches).
- They may also be used for the delivery of certain medications in pediatric or geriatric populations.
- **Considerations and Precautions:** Healthcare providers should consider factors such as skin integrity, site of application, drug characteristics, and patient compliance when prescribing transdermal medications.
- Proper patient education regarding application techniques, rotation of application sites, and potential side effects is essential for optimal treatment outcomes.

**Conclusion:**

- The transdermal route of drug administration offers several advantages, including controlled drug release, convenience, prolonged duration of action, and improved patient compliance.
- Healthcare providers should consider the clinical indications, drug characteristics, and patient preferences when prescribing transdermal medications to optimize therapeutic efficacy and patient satisfaction .

**26. Add a note on Drug Delivery to the Cardiovascular System.**

- Drug delivery to the cardiovascular system involves the administration of medications to treat various conditions affecting the heart and blood vessels.
- This route of drug delivery is essential for managing cardiovascular diseases, including hypertension, coronary artery disease, heart failure, arrhythmias, and thromboembolic disorders.

**Key points regarding drug delivery to the cardiovascular system :**

- **Oral Medications:** Many cardiovascular medications are administered orally, allowing for convenient and noninvasive drug delivery.
- Oral medications include antihypertensives (e.g., angiotensin-converting enzyme inhibitors, beta-blockers, calcium channel blockers), lipid-lowering agents (e.g., statins), antiplatelet agents (e.g., aspirin, clopidogrel), and anticoagulants (e.g., warfarin, direct oral anticoagulants).

- **Intravenous Administration:** Some cardiovascular medications require rapid onset of action or precise dosing, necessitating intravenous administration.
- Intravenous drugs include vasodilators (e.g., nitroglycerin, nitroprusside), inotropic agents (e.g., dobutamine, milrinone), antiarrhythmics (e.g., amiodarone, lidocaine), and thrombolytics (e.g., alteplase) used for acute myocardial infarction or ischemic stroke.

- **Transdermal Delivery:** Transdermal patches can deliver medications directly into the systemic circulation through the skin.
- Transdermal delivery systems are used for certain cardiovascular medications, such as nitroglycerin patches for angina pectoris, providing continuous and controlled drug release over an extended period.

- **Intra-arterial Delivery:** Intra-arterial drug administration involves the direct infusion of medications into specific arteries using catheter-based techniques.
- This route of drug delivery is used for localized treatment of conditions such as peripheral artery disease, pulmonary arterial hypertension, and intra-arterial thrombolysis for acute ischemic stroke.

- **Intracoronary Delivery:** Intracoronary drug delivery involves the direct injection of medications into the coronary arteries during cardiac catheterization procedures.
- This route is used for delivering vasodilators (e.g., adenosine, verapamil) or anticoagulants (e.g., heparin) to treat coronary artery spasm or prevent thrombotic complications during percutaneous coronary interventions.

- **Drug-Eluting Stents:** Drug-eluting stents are used in percutaneous coronary interventions to deliver antiproliferative drugs (e.g., sirolimus, paclitaxel) directly to the coronary artery wall to inhibit neointimal hyperplasia and reduce the risk of restenosis.
- These stents are coated with a polymer matrix that releases the drug over time to prevent renarrowing of the treated artery.

- **Targeted Drug Delivery:** Emerging technologies aim to enhance drug delivery to specific sites within the cardiovascular system using targeted drug delivery systems.
- These systems may include nanoparticles, liposomes, micelles, or conjugates designed to deliver medications selectively to diseased tissues or cells while minimizing systemic exposure and off-target effects.

**Conclusion:**
- Drug delivery to the cardiovascular system encompasses various routes and technologies aimed at treating a wide range of cardiovascular conditions.
- Healthcare providers must consider factors such as drug efficacy, safety, pharmacokinetics, and patient preferences when selecting the most appropriate route of drug delivery for individual patients with cardiovascular diseases.

**27. Add a note on Drug Delivery to the Central Nervous System (CNS)**
- Drug delivery to the central nervous system (CNS) presents unique challenges due to the blood-brain barrier (BBB), which restricts the passage of most drugs from the bloodstream into the brain and spinal cord.
- Overcoming this barrier is crucial for treating neurological disorders such as Alzheimer's disease, Parkinson's disease, epilepsy, and brain tumors.

**Key points regarding drug delivery to the CNS:**
- **Blood-Brain Barrier (BBB):** The BBB is a highly selective barrier composed of specialized endothelial cells that line the brain's blood vessels.
- It limits the passage of hydrophilic and large-molecule drugs from the bloodstream into the brain parenchyma, protecting the CNS from potentially harmful substances.
- However, it also poses a significant challenge for drug delivery to the brain.

**Strategies to Cross the BBB:**
- **Lipophilic Drugs:** Lipophilic drugs have a higher propensity to cross the BBB due to their ability to dissolve in the lipid bilayer of the endothelial cells.
- Examples: Antidepressants, antipsychotics, and anesthetics.

- **Active Transport Systems:** Some drugs can utilize specific transport systems at the BBB to facilitate their transport into the brain.
- These include carrier-mediated transporters for essential nutrients such as glucose, amino acids, and nucleosides.

- **Disruption of the BBB:** Certain techniques, such as osmotic disruption, focused ultrasound, or pharmacological agents (e.g., bradykinin analogs), can transiently disrupt the BBB's integrity, allowing for increased drug permeability.

- **Nanoparticle Delivery:** Nanoparticles can be engineered to encapsulate drugs and facilitate their transport across the BBB through receptor-mediated endocytosis or passive diffusion.

## Route of Administration:
- **Intravenous Injection:** Intravenous administration is the most common route for systemic delivery of CNS drugs.
- However, many drugs struggle to cross the BBB, limiting their effectiveness.

- **Intrathecal Injection:** Intrathecal administration involves direct injection of drugs into the cerebrospinal fluid (CSF) via lumbar puncture or implanted catheters.
- This route bypasses the BBB and allows for higher drug concentrations in the CNS.

- **Intranasal Delivery:** Intranasal administration can bypass the BBB through olfactory and trigeminal nerve pathways, providing direct access to the brain.
- This route is being explored for delivering drugs to treat neurodegenerative diseases and psychiatric disorders.

- **Intracerebral Implantation:** Implantable devices or reservoir systems can be surgically implanted into the brain to deliver drugs directly to the target site, bypassing the BBB.

## Clinical Applications:
- **Treatment of Neurological Disorders:** Drug delivery to the CNS is essential for managing neurological disorders such as Alzheimer's disease, Parkinson's disease, multiple sclerosis, epilepsy, and brain tumors.

- **Pain Management:** Intrathecal drug delivery systems are used for the management of chronic pain conditions such as cancer-related pain, neuropathic pain, and spasticity.
- **Diagnostic Imaging:** Contrast agents can be administered intravenously or intrathecally to enhance visualization of CNS structures in diagnostic imaging modalities such as magnetic resonance imaging (MRI) and computed tomography (CT).

## Conclusion:
- Drug delivery to the CNS requires overcoming the challenges posed by the blood-brain barrier to ensure adequate drug concentrations at the target site.
- Various strategies and routes of administration are being explored to improve drug delivery efficiency and efficacy for the treatment of neurological disorders and diagnostic purposes.

## 28. Discuss the factors modifying drug absorption?
- Several factors can modify drug absorption, influencing the rate and extent of drug absorption into the bloodstream.
- Understanding these factors is crucial for optimizing drug therapy and ensuring consistent therapeutic outcomes.

**Key factors that can modify drug absorption:**

**Physicochemical Properties of the Drug:**

- **Lipophilicity:** Lipophilic drugs tend to be absorbed more readily across biological membranes than hydrophilic drugs due to their ability to dissolve in lipid bilayers.
- **Molecular Size:** Small molecules are generally absorbed more efficiently than larger molecules due to their greater ability to penetrate biological barriers.
- **Ionization State:** The degree of ionization of a drug at physiological pH can affect its lipid solubility and therefore its ability to cross membranes.
- Weak acids and bases may undergo ion trapping in compartments of different pH, affecting their absorption.

**Formulation Characteristics:**

- **Dosage Form:** The formulation of a drug (e.g., tablet, capsule, solution, suspension) can significantly impact its dissolution and subsequent absorption.
- For example, immediate-release formulations may be absorbed more rapidly than extended-release formulations.

- **Excipients:** Excipients used in drug formulations can affect drug absorption by altering drug solubility, stability, and dissolution properties.

**Gastrointestinal Factors:**

- **Gastric Emptying:** The rate of gastric emptying can influence drug absorption, particularly for drugs absorbed in the stomach. Factors such as food, pH, and gastrointestinal motility can affect gastric emptying rates.
- **Intestinal Transit Time:** The time spent in the small intestine, where most drug absorption occurs, can affect the extent of drug absorption. Factors such as intestinal motility and disease states may alter transit time.

**Physiological Factors:**

- **pH Gradient:** Variations in pH along the gastrointestinal tract can affect drug ionization and solubility, impacting absorption.
- For example, weak acids may be more readily absorbed in the acidic stomach environment.

- **Surface Area and Blood Flow:** Increased surface area and blood flow in the gastrointestinal tract can enhance drug absorption.
- Conditions such as diarrhea or inflammatory bowel disease may increase surface area but reduce absorption due to impaired barrier function.

**Patient-Specific Factors:**

Age: Age-related changes in gastrointestinal physiology, such as decreased gastric acid secretion and intestinal motility, can affect drug absorption, particularly in the elderly.

- **Disease States:** Gastrointestinal diseases such as inflammatory bowel disease, celiac disease, and gastroesophageal reflux disease can impair drug absorption by altering gastrointestinal physiology or mucosal integrity.

- **Genetic Variability:** Genetic polymorphisms in drug transporters, metabolizing enzymes, or drug targets can influence drug absorption and disposition, leading to interindividual variability in drug response.

**Drug Interactions:**
- Drug interactions can affect drug absorption by altering gastrointestinal pH, intestinal motility, or the activity of drug transporters and metabolizing enzymes.
- For example, drugs that inhibit gastric acid secretion may reduce the absorption of weakly acidic drugs.

**Conclusion**
- Drug absorption is a complex process influenced by multiple factors, including the physicochemical properties of the drug, formulation characteristics, gastrointestinal factors, physiological factors, patient-specific factors, and drug interactions.
- Healthcare providers must consider these factors when prescribing medications to ensure optimal drug absorption and therapeutic outcomes.

**29. What is the clinical significance of bioavailability of the drug?**

- The clinical significance of bioavailability lies in its impact on the efficacy and safety of drug therapy.
- Bioavailability refers to the fraction of an administered dose of a drug that reaches systemic circulation in its active form.
- Understanding and optimizing bioavailability are crucial for ensuring consistent and predictable drug responses in patients.

**Key aspects of the clinical significance of bioavailability:**

- **Efficacy:** Bioavailability directly influences the therapeutic efficacy of a drug.
- A higher bioavailability ensures that a larger proportion of the administered dose reaches the systemic circulation, leading to greater pharmacological effects.
- Conversely, drugs with lower bioavailability may require higher doses to achieve therapeutic concentrations.
- **Dose Selection:** Knowledge of a drug's bioavailability is essential for determining the appropriate dosage regimen.
- Drugs with low bioavailability may require higher doses or alternative routes of administration to achieve therapeutic concentrations.
- Conversely, drugs with high bioavailability may be dosed less frequently or at lower doses to avoid adverse effects.
- **Interchangeability of Formulations:** Bioequivalence studies are conducted to demonstrate that different formulations of the same drug produce equivalent systemic exposure.
- This information allows healthcare providers to interchangeably prescribe generic and brand-name formulations with confidence, provided they are bioequivalent.
- **Therapeutic Monitoring:** For drugs with a narrow therapeutic index, maintaining consistent plasma concentrations is critical to avoid subtherapeutic or toxic effects.
- Knowledge of bioavailability allows healthcare providers to monitor drug levels and adjust dosing regimens accordingly to optimize therapeutic outcomes while minimizing adverse effects.
- **Variability in Patient Response:** Interindividual variability in drug absorption can significantly impact patient responses to therapy. Factors such as gastrointestinal motility, disease states, genetic polymorphisms, and drug interactions can influence bioavailability and contribute to variability in drug response among patients.
- **Safety and Tolerability:** The bioavailability of a drug can affect its safety profile and tolerability.
- Drugs with erratic or low bioavailability may exhibit unpredictable pharmacokinetics, leading to increased risk of adverse effects or treatment failure. Optimizing bioavailability helps ensure consistent drug exposure and reduces the risk of adverse events.

**Conclusion:**

- Bioavailability plays a crucial role in determining the efficacy, safety, and tolerability of drug therapy.
- Understanding and optimizing bioavailability are essential for selecting appropriate dosing regimens, monitoring therapeutic responses, and ensuring optimal outcomes for patients receiving pharmacotherapy.

**30. Discuss the factors affecting drug distribution?**

- Drug distribution refers to the process by which a drug is distributed throughout the body's tissues and fluids after absorption into the bloodstream.
- Several factors influence drug distribution, impacting the extent and pattern of distribution within the body.

**Key factors affecting drug distribution:**

- **Blood Flow to Tissues:** Blood flow plays a critical role in drug distribution, as it determines the rate at which drugs are delivered to various tissues and organs.
- Organs with high blood flow, such as the heart, liver, kidneys, and brain, typically receive larger amounts of drug compared to tissues with lower blood flow.
- **Protein Binding:** Many drugs bind to plasma proteins, primarily albumin, upon entering the bloodstream.
- Protein-bound drugs are less available for distribution to tissues and organs, as only the unbound (free) fraction of the drug is pharmacologically active and able to diffuse across cell membranes.
- **Tissue Perfusion and Permeability:** The permeability of cell membranes and the degree of vascularization in different tissues influence drug distribution.
- Drugs must be able to cross cell membranes to reach their target sites within tissues.
- Additionally, the presence of tight junctions

between endothelial cells in the blood-brain barrier and other selective barriers can limit drug penetration into certain tissues.

- **Lipid Solubility:** Lipophilic drugs tend to distribute more readily into adipose tissue and tissues with high lipid content due to their ability to dissolve in lipid membranes.
- Conversely, hydrophilic drugs may have limited distribution into lipid-rich tissues.
- **Tissue pH:** The pH of tissues can influence the ionization state of drugs and affect their distribution.
- Weak acids tend to accumulate in acidic tissues, while weak bases may accumulate in alkaline tissues.
- This phenomenon, known as ion trapping, can impact the distribution and elimination of drugs in various tissues.
- **Drug-Metabolizing Enzymes:** Enzymes present in tissues can metabolize drugs, leading to local inactivation or conversion to active metabolites.
- The activity of drug-metabolizing enzymes in specific tissues can affect the distribution and pharmacological effects of drugs.
- **Disease States:** Pathophysiological conditions such as edema, inflammation, infection, or tissue damage can alter tissue perfusion, protein binding, and membrane permeability, affecting drug distribution.
- In some cases, disease-related changes in tissue physiology may result in altered drug distribution kinetics.
- **Physiological Factors:** Individual variability in factors such as body composition, age, gender, and genetic polymorphisms can influence drug distribution.
- For example, differences in body fat percentage, muscle mass, and organ size can affect the volume of distribution of lipophilic and hydrophilic drugs.

**Conclusion:**

- Understanding the factors that affect drug distribution is essential for predicting drug concentrations in target tissues, optimizing dosing regimens, and ensuring therapeutic efficacy while minimizing the risk of adverse effects.
- Pharmacokinetic studies and clinical observations help elucidate the complex interplay between these factors and their impact on drug distribution in vivo.

## 31. What is the clinical significance of drug distribution?

- The clinical significance of drug distribution lies in its impact on the pharmacokinetics, efficacy, and safety of drug therapy.
- Understanding and optimizing drug distribution is essential for achieving therapeutic outcomes and minimizing adverse effects.

**Key aspects of the clinical significance of drug distribution:**

- **Target Tissue Delivery:** Drug distribution determines the extent to which a drug reaches its target tissues and sites of action within the body.
- Effective distribution ensures that therapeutic concentrations of the drug are attained at the desired sites, allowing for the pharmacological effects to occur.
- **Therapeutic Efficacy:** Proper drug distribution is critical for achieving therapeutic efficacy.
- Drugs must be distributed to the target tissues in concentrations sufficient to exert their intended pharmacological effects.
- Inadequate distribution may result in suboptimal therapeutic outcomes or treatment failure.
- **Pharmacokinetic Parameters:** Drug distribution influences pharmacokinetic parameters such as volume of distribution (Vd), which reflects the apparent volume into which a drug distributes in the body relative to its plasma concentration.
- Knowledge of Vd helps guide dosing regimens and predict drug distribution in different patient populations.
- **Duration of Action:** The distribution of a drug to tissues with slow elimination rates can prolong its duration of action.
- This is particularly relevant for drugs with prolonged half-lives or extended-release formulations, where distribution to peripheral tissues contributes to sustained therapeutic effects.
- **Adverse Effects:** Drug distribution can also contribute to the occurrence of adverse effects.
- Distribution of drugs to off-target tissues or organs may result in unintended pharmacological effects or toxicity. Understanding the

tissue distribution profile of a drug helps identify potential adverse effects and monitor for their occurrence.

- **Drug Interactions:** Drug distribution may be affected by interactions with other drugs or substances.
- Competition for protein binding sites or alterations in tissue perfusion can influence the distribution of co-administered drugs, leading to changes in pharmacokinetics and potentially affecting therapeutic outcomes.
- **Individual Variability:** Variability in drug distribution among individuals can impact drug response and susceptibility to adverse effects.
- Factors such as body composition, organ function, genetic polymorphisms, and disease states can influence drug distribution and contribute to interindividual variability in drug response.
- **Therapeutic Monitoring:** Monitoring drug concentrations in plasma or target tissues can provide valuable information about drug distribution and guide dosing adjustments to optimize therapeutic outcomes.
- Therapeutic drug monitoring is particularly important for drugs with narrow therapeutic windows or complex distribution kinetics.

Conclusion:
- Drug distribution plays a crucial role in determining the pharmacokinetics, efficacy, and safety of drug therapy.
- Understanding the factors influencing drug distribution and optimizing dosing regimens based on individual patient characteristics are essential for achieving therapeutic goals while minimizing the risk of adverse effects.

## 32. Write a note on biotransformation or drug metabolism.

- Biotransformation, also known as drug metabolism, refers to the process by which the body chemically alters drugs or xenobiotics to facilitate their elimination from the body.
- This transformation typically involves enzymatic reactions occurring primarily in the liver but can also take place in other tissues such as the intestine, kidneys, and lungs.
- Drug metabolism is crucial for the conversion of pharmacologically active compounds into inactive or less active forms, as well as for the generation of metabolites that are more readily excreted from the body.

**Following are the phases of drug metabolism with examples:**

**Phase I Metabolism:**
- Phase I metabolism involves functionalization reactions that introduce or unmask functional groups on the drug molecule, typically through oxidation, reduction, or hydrolysis reactions.
- These reactions often make the drug more polar and facilitate subsequent elimination.
- **Example:** Cytochrome P450 enzymes (CYP450) catalyze many phase I reactions.
- For instance, CYP3A4 is involved in the metabolism of a wide range of drugs, including the antihypertensive drug amlodipine.
- CYP3A4 oxidizes amlodipine to its major metabolite, which is less pharmacologically active and more readily eliminated.

**Phase II Metabolism:**
- Phase II metabolism involves conjugation reactions in which the drug or its phase I metabolites are conjugated with endogenous molecules such as glucuronic acid, sulfate, amino acids, or glutathione.
- Conjugation makes the drug more water-soluble and facilitates renal or biliary excretion.
- **Example:** Glucuronidation is a common phase II reaction catalyzed by UDP-glucuronosyltransferase (UGT) enzymes.
- For example, acetaminophen (paracetamol) undergoes glucuronidation to form a water-soluble metabolite that is excreted in the urine.
- However, when acetaminophen is overdosed, the glucuronidation pathway becomes saturated, leading to the formation of a toxic metabolite that can cause liver damage.

**Other Metabolic Pathways:**
- In addition to phase I and phase II reactions, drugs can undergo other metabolic pathways such as methylation, acetylation, and amidation.
- These pathways may also contribute to drug elimination and detoxification.

- **Example:** Methotrexate, a chemotherapy drug used to treat cancer and autoimmune diseases, undergoes polyglutamation, a process in which it is conjugated with glutamate residues.
- Polyglutamated methotrexate is less prone to efflux from cells and has a longer intracellular half-life, enhancing its pharmacological activity.

**Genetic Variability:**
- Genetic polymorphisms in drug-metabolizing enzymes can lead to interindividual variability in drug metabolism, affecting drug efficacy, safety, and pharmacokinetics.
- Poor metabolizers may require lower doses to achieve therapeutic effects, while ultrarapid metabolizers may require higher doses.
- Example: Genetic variations in the CYP2D6 gene can result in poor, intermediate, extensive, or ultrarapid metabolizer phenotypes.
- Poor metabolizers of CYP2D6 substrates may have reduced efficacy or increased toxicity when prescribed drugs such as codeine, which requires CYP2D6-mediated activation to its active metabolite morphine.

**Conclusion:**
- Drug metabolism is a crucial process that influences the pharmacokinetics, efficacy, safety, and individual response to medications.
- Understanding the metabolic pathways involved, genetic variability, and potential drug interactions is essential for optimizing drug therapy and minimizing the risk of adverse effects in clinical practice.

### 33. Discuss the importance of drug metabolism in relation to prescribing by clinical practitioners?

- The importance of drug metabolism in relation to prescribing by clinical practitioners lies in its significant impact on the pharmacokinetics, efficacy, safety, and individual response to medications.
- Clinical practitioners need to consider various aspects of drug metabolism when prescribing medications to optimize therapeutic outcomes and minimize the risk of adverse effects.

**Key points highlighting the importance of drug metabolism in prescribing:**

- **Pharmacokinetic Variability:** Drug metabolism contributes to interindividual variability in drug response due to genetic differences, environmental factors, age, gender, and concurrent medications.
- Understanding the metabolic pathways involved and potential variations in metabolism among patients is essential for individualizing drug therapy.
- **Drug Interactions:** Drug metabolism can lead to pharmacokinetic interactions between medications, affecting their metabolism, bioavailability, and plasma concentrations.
- Clinical practitioners need to be aware of potential interactions, such as enzyme inhibition or induction, when prescribing multiple medications to avoid therapeutic failure or toxicity.
- **Therapeutic Drug Monitoring (TDM):** Drug metabolism influences the pharmacokinetic parameters of medications, such as clearance, half-life, and steady-state concentrations.
- Therapeutic drug monitoring involves measuring drug levels in the blood to optimize dosing regimens and ensure therapeutic efficacy while minimizing the risk of adverse effects.
- **Personalized Medicine:** Genetic polymorphisms in drug-metabolizing enzymes can result in interindividual variability in drug metabolism and response.
- Pharmacogenomic testing can help identify genetic variants that may affect drug metabolism, allowing for personalized prescribing and dosing adjustments to optimize therapeutic outcomes.
- **Drug Safety:** Drug metabolism plays a crucial role in the detoxification and elimination of xenobiotics and endogenous compounds, reducing their pharmacological activity or toxicity.
- Clinical practitioners need to consider metabolic pathways and potential toxic metabolites when prescribing medications, particularly in patients with impaired organ function or genetic predispositions.
- **Dose Adjustments:** Knowledge of drug metabolism enables clinical practitioners to make appropriate dose adjustments based on factors such as hepatic or renal function, age, and concurrent medications.
- Patients with impaired metabolism may require

lower doses or extended dosing intervals to achieve therapeutic effects while minimizing the risk of adverse reactions.

- **Avoiding Drug Allergies and Idiosyncratic Reactions:** Drug metabolism can contribute to the formation of reactive metabolites or immunogenic compounds, leading to allergic reactions or idiosyncratic adverse effects.
- Understanding metabolic pathways and potential metabolite-mediated reactions can help clinical practitioners identify and avoid drugs with a higher risk of adverse reactions in susceptible individuals.

**Conclusion:**

- Understanding of drug metabolism is crucial for clinical practitioners when prescribing medications to ensure safe, effective, and individualized pharmacotherapy.
- Consideration of metabolic pathways, genetic variability, drug interactions, and patient factors can help optimize therapeutic outcomes and minimize the risk of adverse effects in clinical practice.

## 34. What is the clinical importance of drug metabolism?

- Drug metabolism plays a crucial role in pharmacokinetics, influencing the pharmacological effects, efficacy, safety, and duration of action of medications.
- Understanding drug metabolism is essential for predicting drug interactions, optimizing dosing regimens, and ensuring safe and effective pharmacotherapy.

**Following are some examples illustrating the clinical importance of drug metabolism:**

- **Activation of Prodrugs:** Prodrugs are inactive or less active drug precursors that require metabolic activation to exert their pharmacological effects.
- Drug metabolism converts prodrugs into their active forms, enhancing bioavailability and therapeutic efficacy.
- Example: Codeine, a weak opioid analgesic, is metabolized by the liver enzyme CYP2D6 to morphine, its active metabolite, which provides the pain-relieving effects.
- This metabolic activation enhances the analgesic potency of codeine.
- **Inactivation and Detoxification:** Drug metabolism can lead to the inactivation and detoxification of xenobiotics and endogenous compounds, facilitating their elimination from the body and reducing their pharmacological activity or toxicity.
- Example: Acetaminophen (paracetamol) is primarily metabolized in the liver by sulfation and glucuronidation to inactive metabolites that are excreted in the urine.
- However, a minor metabolic pathway involving CYP2E1 leads to the formation of a toxic metabolite, N-acetyl-p-benzoquinone imine (NAPQI), which can cause hepatotoxicity if not detoxified by glutathione conjugation.
- **Drug Clearance and Elimination:** Drug metabolism plays a crucial role in drug clearance and elimination from the body, particularly through renal or biliary excretion of metabolites or parent drugs.
- Metabolism influences the pharmacokinetic parameters of drugs, such as clearance, half-life, and steady-state concentrations.
- **Example:** Warfarin, an oral anticoagulant, undergoes extensive hepatic metabolism by multiple cytochrome P450 enzymes, primarily CYP2C9 and CYP3A4.
- Metabolism of warfarin influences its clearance and therapeutic anticoagulant effects, requiring careful monitoring of international normalized ratio (INR) to prevent bleeding or thrombotic complications.
- **Drug Interactions:** Drug metabolism can lead to pharmacokinetic interactions between medications, affecting their metabolism, bioavailability, and plasma concentrations.
- Inhibition or induction of drug-metabolizing enzymes can alter the metabolism of co-administered drugs, leading to therapeutic failure or toxicity.
- **Example:** Grapefruit juice contains compounds that inhibit intestinal CYP3A4 enzymes, leading to increased bioavailability of certain medications metabolized by this enzyme, such as statins (e.g., simvastatin) and calcium channel blockers (e.g., felodipine).

This can result in elevated plasma concentrations and enhanced pharmacological effects, increasing the risk of adverse effects or toxicity.

- **Genetic Variability:** Genetic polymorphisms in drug-metabolizing enzymes can result in interindividual variability in drug metabolism, leading to differences in drug efficacy, safety, and therapeutic response among patients.
- **Example:** Genetic variations in the CYP2D6 gene can affect the metabolism of various medications, including antidepressants (e.g., fluoxetine, venlafaxine) and antipsychotics (e.g., haloperidol).
- Poor metabolizers of CYP2D6 substrates may require dose adjustments or alternative medications to achieve optimal therapeutic outcomes.

**Conclusion:**
- Drug metabolism plays a critical role in determining the pharmacokinetics and pharmacodynamics of medications, influencing their efficacy, safety, and clinical outcomes.
- Understanding the mechanisms and implications of drug metabolism is essential for optimizing drug therapy, minimizing adverse effects, and ensuring personalized pharmacological management in clinical practice.

## 35. What is drug elimination and factors affecting drug elimination?

- Drug elimination refers to the removal of drugs or their metabolites from the body, typically through routes such as renal excretion, hepatic metabolism, biliary excretion, respiratory excretion, or other pathways.
- Elimination is a crucial aspect of pharmacokinetics, influencing the duration and intensity of drug effects, as well as the overall pharmacological profile of a medication.
- Several factors can affect drug elimination, including:
- **Renal Function:** Renal excretion is a primary route of elimination for many drugs and their metabolites.
- Factors such as glomerular filtration rate (GFR), renal blood flow, and tubular secretion or reabsorption can influence renal clearance.

- Impaired renal function, as seen in renal insufficiency or chronic kidney disease, can lead to reduced drug clearance and prolonged elimination half-life.
- **Hepatic Function:** Hepatic metabolism is another major route of drug elimination, involving enzymatic transformation of drugs into metabolites that are more easily excreted.
- Liver disease, hepatic dysfunction, or impaired hepatic blood flow can affect drug metabolism and elimination rates.
- Genetic polymorphisms in hepatic enzymes, such as cytochrome P450 (CYP) enzymes, can result in variable rates of drug metabolism and elimination among individuals.
- **Biliary Excretion:** Biliary excretion contributes to the elimination of certain drugs and metabolites via secretion into bile and subsequent excretion into the intestine.
- Obstructive liver diseases or biliary tract disorders can impair biliary excretion and lead to drug accumulation.
- Drugs with high biliary excretion rates may undergo enterohepatic circulation, where they are reabsorbed from the intestine back into the bloodstream, prolonging their elimination half-life.
- **Gastrointestinal Motility:** Gastrointestinal motility can affect drug absorption, distribution, and elimination.
- Changes in gastric emptying time, intestinal transit time, or absorption from the gastrointestinal tract can influence the rate and extent of drug elimination.
- Conditions affecting gastrointestinal motility, such as gastroparesis or intestinal obstruction, can alter drug absorption and elimination kinetics.
- **Respiratory Excretion:** Some drugs, particularly volatile or gaseous compounds, may be eliminated through respiratory excretion via exhalation.
- Factors affecting pulmonary function, such as respiratory rate, lung capacity, or ventilation-perfusion mismatch, can influence drug elimination via this route.
- Changes in respiratory function, such as in patients with pulmonary disease or altered respiratory physiology, may affect the rate of drug elimination through the lungs.

- **Age, Gender, and Body Composition:** Age-related changes in renal and hepatic function, as well as alterations in body composition (e.g., lean body mass, fat distribution), can affect drug elimination rates.
- Gender differences in drug metabolism and elimination have been reported, partly attributed to variations in hepatic enzyme activity and renal function between males and females.

**Conclusion:**

- Overall, drug elimination is a complex process influenced by multiple factors, including renal and hepatic function, gastrointestinal physiology, respiratory function, and patient demographics.
- Understanding these factors is essential for optimizing drug therapy, minimizing the risk of adverse effects, and ensuring safe and effective pharmacological management in clinical practice.

## 36. What is the clinical significance of drug elimination?

- Drug elimination is a critical process in pharmacokinetics, referring to the removal of drugs or their metabolites from the body through various routes, such as renal excretion, hepatic metabolism, or other pathways.
- Understanding drug elimination is crucial for determining dosing regimens, predicting drug interactions, and assessing drug safety and efficacy.

**Following are some examples highlighting the clinical significance of drug elimination:**

- **Renal Clearance:** Renal clearance plays a significant role in the elimination of many drugs and their metabolites.
- Impaired renal function can lead to reduced drug clearance, resulting in drug accumulation and potential toxicity.
- **Example:** Patients with renal impairment may require dose adjustments or extended dosing intervals for medications excreted primarily by the kidneys, such as antibiotics (e.g., vancomycin, gentamicin) or anticoagulants (e.g., enoxaparin, dabigatran).
- **Hepatic Metabolism:** Hepatic metabolism, particularly via cytochrome P450 enzymes, is a major route of drug elimination for many medications.
- Drug interactions involving inhibition or induction of hepatic enzymes can affect drug metabolism and elimination rates.
- Example: Concurrent administration of a potent cytochrome P450 inhibitor, such as ketoconazole, with a drug metabolized by the same enzyme pathway, such as simvastatin, can lead to increased plasma concentrations of the statin, potentially increasing the risk of adverse effects such as myopathy or rhabdomyolysis.
- **Biliary Excretion:** Biliary excretion contributes to the elimination of certain drugs and their metabolites, particularly those that undergo enterohepatic circulation.
- Biliary obstruction or dysfunction can impair drug excretion and lead to drug accumulation.
- **Example:** Patients with obstructive jaundice or cholestasis may experience delayed clearance of drugs excreted via the bile, such as opioids (e.g., morphine) or certain antibiotics (e.g., erythromycin), potentially increasing the risk of adverse effects or toxicity.
- **Enterohepatic Circulation:** Enterohepatic circulation involves the reabsorption of drugs or metabolites from the intestine back into the bloodstream via the liver, prolonging their elimination half-life.
- Interrupting enterohepatic circulation can accelerate drug elimination.
- **Example:** Administration of bile acid sequestrants, such as cholestyramine, can disrupt enterohepatic circulation by binding bile acids in the intestine, reducing their reabsorption and promoting their fecal excretion.
- This mechanism is exploited in the treatment of hyperlipidemia and certain types of diarrhea.
- **Respiratory Excretion:** Some volatile or gaseous drugs may be eliminated through respiratory excretion via exhalation.
- Alterations in pulmonary function, such as impaired ventilation or increased respiratory rate, can affect drug elimination via this route.

- **Example:** Inhalation anesthetics, such as sevoflurane or nitrous oxide, are eliminated primarily via respiratory excretion.
- Changes in pulmonary function, such as in patients with chronic obstructive pulmonary disease (COPD), may affect the rate of elimination of these agents.

**Conclusion:**

- Understanding the mechanisms of drug elimination is essential for optimizing drug therapy, minimizing the risk of adverse effects or toxicity, and ensuring safe and effective pharmacotherapy in clinical practice.
- Various patient factors, including renal and hepatic function, as well as the presence of comorbidities or concurrent medications, can influence drug elimination processes and guide therapeutic decision-making.

## 37. Discuss the methods of prolongation of drug action by changing the type of formulation?

- Prolongation of drug action refers to the extension of the duration of therapeutic effect or the sustained release of a medication over an extended period.
- Various methods and technologies can be employed to achieve this goal, enhancing patient compliance, reducing dosing frequency, and optimizing therapeutic outcomes.

**Following are some methods commonly used to prolong the action of drugs:**

- **Sustained Release Formulations:** Sustained release formulations are designed to release the active drug gradually over an extended period, maintaining therapeutic concentrations in the bloodstream and minimizing fluctuations in drug levels.
- **Examples**: Extended-release tablets or capsules, which utilize special coatings, matrices, or osmotic pumps to control the rate of drug release.
- These formulations allow for once- or twice-daily dosing and provide a more constant drug concentration over time.
- **Controlled Release Systems:** Controlled release systems use advanced drug delivery technologies to regulate the release of medication in response to specific physiological or environmental cues.

- **Examples:** Microspheres, liposomes, and nanoparticles, which encapsulate drugs and release them in a controlled manner based on factors such as pH, temperature, or enzymatic activity at the target site.

- **Implantable Devices:** Implantable devices or drug-eluting implants are inserted into the body to deliver controlled doses of medication over an extended period.
- These devices offer sustained release and localized drug delivery to target tissues or organs.
- **Examples:** Drug-eluting stents used in interventional cardiology to prevent restenosis in coronary arteries.
- These stents release antiproliferative drugs locally to inhibit the growth of scar tissue.

- **Transdermal Delivery Systems:** Transdermal delivery systems deliver medications through the skin for systemic absorption, providing sustained release and prolonged drug action.
- These systems offer advantages such as noninvasive administration, avoidance of first-pass metabolism, and improved patient compliance.
- **Examples:** Transdermal patches containing reservoirs or matrices that release drugs slowly over several hours to days.
- These patches are used to deliver medications such as opioids for pain management, nicotine for smoking cessation, and hormonal contraceptives.

- **Depot Injections:** Depot injections involve the administration of long-acting formulations of medications via intramuscular or subcutaneous injection, resulting in slow and sustained release of the drug into the bloodstream.
- **Examples:** Depot formulations of antipsychotic medications, such as haloperidol decanoate and fluphenazine decanoate, used in the treatment of schizophrenia.
- These injections provide therapeutic blood levels of the drug for several weeks to months.

- **Prodrug Strategies:** Prodrugs are inactive or less active drug derivatives that undergo enzymatic or chemical conversion in the body to release the active drug.
- By modifying the chemical structure of the drug, prodrug strategies can prolong the duration of action, improve drug stability, and enhance drug absorption.
- **Examples:** Oseltamivir phosphate (Tamiflu), which is a prodrug of the antiviral medication oseltamivir.
- Oseltamivir phosphate is converted to its active form in the body, prolonging its duration of action and improving oral bioavailability.

## Conclusion:

- These methods of prolonging drug action offer diverse approaches to achieve sustained release, controlled delivery, and extended therapeutic effects.
- The selection of an appropriate drug delivery strategy depends on factors such as the pharmacokinetics of the drug, the desired duration of action, patient preferences, and the specific clinical indication.

## 38. Discuss novel drug delivery concepts? give examples?

- Novel drug delivery concepts refer to innovative approaches and technologies designed to enhance the delivery of medications to target sites within the body, improve therapeutic efficacy, reduce adverse effects, and optimize patient outcomes.
- These advancements in drug delivery systems aim to overcome challenges associated with conventional dosage forms and offer new strategies for drug administration.

## Following are some examples of novel drug delivery concepts:

- **Nanotechnology-Based Drug Delivery:** Nanotechnology involves the manipulation of materials at the nanoscale (1-100 nanometers) to create nanosized drug carriers or nanoparticles.
- These nanoparticles can encapsulate drugs, protect them from degradation, and facilitate targeted delivery to specific tissues or cells.
- **Examples**: Liposomes, polymeric nanoparticles, dendrimers, and carbon nanotubes.
- Liposomal formulations of chemotherapy drugs, such as Doxil (pegylated liposomal doxorubicin), enhance drug delivery to tumor tissues while minimizing systemic toxicity.

- **Targeted Drug Delivery Systems:** Targeted drug delivery systems are designed to deliver medications selectively to specific tissues, organs, or cells, thereby maximizing therapeutic efficacy and minimizing off-target effects.
- **Examples:** Antibody-drug conjugates (ADCs), which combine monoclonal antibodies with cytotoxic drugs to target cancer cells expressing specific antigens.
- ADCs such as Adcetris (brentuximab vedotin) and Kadcyla (ado-trastuzumab emtansine) are used in cancer therapy.

- **Stimuli-Responsive Drug Delivery:** Stimuli-responsive drug delivery systems are designed to release drugs in response to specific environmental stimuli, such as changes in pH, temperature, or enzyme activity at the target site.
- **Examples:** pH-sensitive nanoparticles that release drugs in response to acidic conditions found in tumor microenvironments.
- These systems can enhance drug accumulation in tumors while minimizing systemic exposure.

- **Implantable Drug Delivery Systems:** Implantable drug delivery systems involve the insertion of devices or implants into the body to deliver controlled doses of medication over extended periods.
- These systems offer advantages such as sustained release, reduced dosing frequency, and improved patient compliance.
- **Examples:** Drug-eluting stents used in interventional cardiology to prevent restenosis following angioplasty.
- These stents release antiproliferative drugs locally to inhibit the growth of scar tissue in coronary arteries.

- **Microneedle-Based Drug Delivery:** Microneedle-based drug delivery systems utilize tiny needles or microneedles to administer medications through the skin, bypassing the stratum corneum and enhancing drug absorption.
- **Examples:** Transdermal patches containing microneedles for the delivery of vaccines, insulin, or other therapeutics.
- These patches offer painless, noninvasive drug delivery and can improve patient adherence.

- **Gene Delivery Systems:** Gene delivery systems are designed to deliver nucleic acids, such as DNA or RNA, to target cells for gene therapy or genetic modulation.
- These systems can be used to treat genetic disorders, cancers, and other diseases at the molecular level.
- **Examples:** Viral vectors (e.g., adenoviruses, lentiviruses) and nonviral vectors (e.g., lipoplexes, polyplexes) used to deliver therapeutic genes or RNA interference (RNAi) molecules for gene silencing.

**Conclusion:**

- Research is continuing in identifying various novel drug delivery systems by applying novel drug delivery concepts in improving drug efficacy, safety, and patient outcomes.
- Continued research and development in this field are essential for advancing drug delivery technologies and addressing unmet medical needs.

## 39. What is the importance of plasma protein binding of drugs?

- Plasma protein binding of drugs refers to the extent to which medications bind to proteins in the blood, primarily albumin and alpha-1 acid glycoprotein.
- This process affects the distribution, metabolism, and elimination of drugs in the body.

**Following are some key points regarding the importance of plasma protein binding:**

- **Distribution**: Only the unbound fraction of a drug is free to distribute to its target tissues and exert pharmacological effects.
- Bound drugs remain in the bloodstream and are not able to interact with receptors or exert their therapeutic actions.
- Thus, the extent of plasma protein binding influences the effective concentration of the drug at its site of action.
- **Pharmacokinetics**: Plasma protein binding affects the pharmacokinetic properties of drugs, including their volume of distribution, clearance, and half-life.
- Highly protein-bound drugs tend to have a smaller volume of distribution and longer half-life because they are confined to the vascular compartment for a longer duration.
- **Drug-Drug Interactions**: Drugs that bind extensively to plasma proteins may compete for binding sites, leading to displacement interactions when co-administered with other highly protein-bound drugs.
- This can increase the concentration of the unbound fraction of the displaced drug, potentially leading to increased pharmacological effects or toxicity.
- **Clinical Significance**: Knowledge of a drug's plasma protein binding characteristics is important in clinical practice for optimizing dosing regimens.
- Drugs with high protein binding may require dosage adjustments in patients with hypoalbuminemia (low albumin levels) to avoid toxicity, as more of the drug will be in its unbound, pharmacologically active form.
- **Drug Development**: Understanding the plasma protein binding of drugs is crucial in drug development and formulation.
- It helps in predicting drug distribution, designing optimal dosing regimens, and assessing potential drug-drug interactions during the development process.

**Conclusion:**
- The plasma protein binding significantly influences the pharmacological effects, distribution, metabolism, and elimination of drugs in the body, making it an essential consideration in both clinical practice and drug development.

## 40. Write a note on blood brain barrier and its clinical importance?

- The blood-brain barrier (BBB) is a highly selective semipermeable membrane barrier that separates the circulating blood from the brain extracellular fluid in the central nervous system (CNS).
- It is composed of endothelial cells that line the capillaries in the brain, along with astrocytes and pericytes, which provide structural and functional support to the BBB.

### Structure and Function:
- **Endothelial Cells:** The endothelial cells of the BBB are tightly joined together by tight junctions, which prevent most molecules from passing between them.
- This tight sealing restricts the movement of substances from the bloodstream into the brain tissue.

- **Astrocytes:** Astrocytes are star-shaped glial cells that surround the blood vessels in the brain.
- They contribute to the structural integrity of the BBB and regulate its permeability by releasing chemical signals that influence the tightness of the junctions between endothelial cells.

- **Pericytes:** Pericytes are contractile cells located within the basement membrane of blood vessels.
- They play a role in regulating blood flow and maintaining the integrity of the BBB.

### Clinical Importance:
- **Protection of the Brain:** One of the primary functions of the BBB is to protect the brain from harmful substances present in the bloodstream.
- It selectively allows essential nutrients, oxygen, and certain molecules such as glucose to enter the brain while blocking the passage of potentially harmful substances like toxins, pathogens, and large molecules.

- **Drug Delivery:** The BBB presents a significant challenge for the delivery of therapeutic agents to the brain.
- Many drugs are unable to cross the BBB due to its selective permeability.
- This limitation complicates the treatment of neurological disorders such as brain tumors, Alzheimer's disease, and Parkinson's disease. Researchers are actively exploring various strategies, such as nanotechnology and drug formulations, to bypass or enhance drug delivery across the BBB.
- **Disease Mechanisms:** Dysfunction of the BBB is implicated in various neurological disorders.
- Increased BBB permeability can occur in conditions such as stroke, traumatic brain injury, multiple sclerosis, and neuroinflammatory diseases.
- This compromised barrier allows inflammatory cells, immune molecules, and toxins to enter the brain, contributing to tissue damage and disease progression.
- **Diagnostic Marker:** Changes in BBB permeability can serve as a diagnostic marker for certain neurological conditions.
- Techniques such as contrast-enhanced MRI can detect abnormalities in BBB integrity, aiding in the diagnosis and monitoring of diseases like brain tumors, neuroinflammation, and neurodegenerative disorders.

### Conclusion:
- The blood-brain barrier is a crucial component of the central nervous system that regulates the passage of molecules between the bloodstream and the brain.
- Understanding its structure and function is essential for developing therapeutic strategies, diagnosing neurological disorders, and protecting the brain from harmful substances.

## 41. Write a note on blood brain barrier in drug distribution and its clinical importance?

- The blood-brain barrier (BBB) plays a critical role in drug distribution within the central nervous system (CNS).
- Its unique structure and function pose significant challenges for the delivery of therapeutic agents to the brain.
- Understanding the BBB's impact on drug distribution is essential for developing effective treatments for neurological disorders.

**BBB in drug distribution and its clinical importance is discussed below:**
- **Barrier to Drug Entry:** The BBB consists of tightly sealed endothelial cells, which limit the

Passive diffusion of most substances, including drugs, from the bloodstream into the brain.

- Lipophilic or small molecules can diffuse across the BBB through passive diffusion, but larger, hydrophilic molecules are typically excluded.
- Efflux transporters, such as P-glycoprotein, actively pump drugs out of the brain endothelial cells back into the bloodstream, further restricting drug entry into the brain.

- **Challenges in Drug Delivery:** The selective permeability of the BBB poses significant challenges for drug delivery to treat neurological disorders.
- Many drugs, including chemotherapy agents and therapeutic proteins, have limited ability to cross the BBB, leading to suboptimal treatment outcomes.
- Strategies to bypass or overcome the BBB, such as invasive methods like intracerebral injections or non-invasive approaches like drug modification or nanotechnology, are being developed to improve drug delivery to the brain.

## Clinical Importance:

- **Neurological Disorders:** Dysfunction of the BBB is implicated in various neurological disorders, including Alzheimer's disease, Parkinson's disease, brain tumors, and multiple sclerosis.
- Understanding the BBB's role in these conditions is crucial for developing targeted therapies.

- **Drug Development:** Knowledge of the BBB's impact on drug distribution is essential in drug development.
- Researchers aim to design drugs that can effectively cross the BBB or develop delivery systems that can bypass its barriers to improve therapeutic outcomes.

- **Personalized Medicine:** Understanding individual variations in BBB permeability can help tailor treatment strategies for patients with neurological disorders.

- Factors such as age, genetics, and disease state can influence BBB function and drug distribution, affecting treatment efficacy and safety.

- **Diagnostic Marker:** Changes in BBB permeability can serve as a diagnostic marker for certain neurological conditions.
- Techniques like contrast-enhanced MRI can detect BBB disruption, aiding in the diagnosis and monitoring of diseases such as brain tumors, neuroinflammation, and neurodegenerative disorders.

## Conclusion:

- The blood-brain barrier significantly influences drug distribution within the CNS, presenting challenges and opportunities for drug delivery in the treatment of neurological disorders.
- Understanding the BBB's role in drug distribution is essential for developing effective therapies and improving patient outcomes.
- Ongoing research aims to better understand the molecular mechanisms of BBB function and dysfunction, as well as develop novel strategies to enhance drug delivery to the brain.
- Advancements in nanotechnology, targeted drug delivery systems, and blood-brain barrier modulation hold promise for improving drug distribution and efficacy in treating neurological disorders.

**42. Write a note on placental barrier in drug distribution and its clinical importance?**

- The placental barrier, also known as the placental membrane, plays a crucial role in drug distribution during pregnancy.

- This barrier separates the maternal bloodstream from the fetal bloodstream and regulates the passage of substances, including drugs, from the mother to the fetus.

- Understanding the placental barrier and its impact on drug distribution is essential for ensuring the safety and efficacy of medications used during pregnancy.

**Placental barrier in drug distribution and its clinical importance is discussed below:**

**Structure of the Placental Barrier:** The placental barrier is composed of several layers, including:

- The placental barrier is selectively permeable, allowing certain substances to pass from the maternal bloodstream to the fetal bloodstream while blocking others.
- Factors influencing the permeability of the placental barrier include the size, charge, lipid solubility, and protein binding of drugs.
- Lipophilic drugs tend to cross the placental barrier more readily, while large molecules and highly protein-bound drugs may be restricted.

**Clinical Importance:**
- **Fetal Drug Exposure:** Drugs taken by pregnant women can cross the placental barrier and reach the fetus, potentially affecting fetal development and health.
- Understanding the placental barrier's permeability to various drugs is crucial for assessing fetal drug exposure and potential risks.

- **Teratogenic Effects:** Some drugs have teratogenic effects, meaning they can cause birth defects or developmental abnormalities in the fetus.
- The placental barrier may mitigate or exacerbate the risk of teratogenicity by regulating drug passage to the fetus.

- **Drug Safety during Pregnancy:** Healthcare providers must consider the placental barrier's permeability and potential fetal risks when prescribing medications to pregnant women.
- Certain drugs may be contraindicated during pregnancy due to their potential to cross the placental barrier and harm the fetus.

- **Pharmacokinetics in Pregnancy:** Pregnancy-induced changes in placental blood flow, hormone levels, and placental barrier function can influence drug pharmacokinetics.
- Monitoring drug levels and adjusting dosage regimens may be necessary to ensure optimal therapeutic outcomes and minimize fetal exposure.

**Research and Clinical Practice:**
- Ongoing research aims to better understand the placental barrier's structure, function, and role in drug distribution during pregnancy.
- Pharmacokinetic studies in pregnant women and animal models provide valuable insights into drug transfer across the placental barrier and its implications for fetal health.
- Clinical guidelines and recommendations for drug use during pregnancy consider the placental barrier's permeability and potential fetal risks, guiding healthcare providers in making informed decisions about medication management during pregnancy.

**Conclusion:**
- Placental barrier plays a critical role in regulating drug distribution from the mother to the fetus during pregnancy.
- Understanding the placental barrier's permeability and its impact on fetal drug exposure is essential for ensuring safe and effective medication use during pregnancy and protecting fetal health.

**43. Write a note on bioavailability of drugs? What are the factors affecting bioavailability? Note on Bioavailability of Drugs:**

- Bioavailability refers to the fraction of an administered dose of a drug that reaches the systemic circulation in its active form, thus determining the extent and rate at which the drug exerts its pharmacological effects.
- It is a critical pharmacokinetic parameter that influences the onset, intensity, and duration of drug action.

- Understanding bioavailability is essential for optimizing drug therapy and ensuring therapeutic efficacy.

**Factors Affecting Bioavailability:**
- **Route of Administration:** The route by which a drug is administered significantly affects its bioavailability.
- Intravenous administration typically provides complete and immediate drug absorption, resulting in high bioavailability.
- Other routes, such as oral, intramuscular, subcutaneous, and transdermal, may exhibit variable bioavailability due to differences in absorption kinetics and first-pass metabolism.

- **Absorption Rate:** The rate at which a drug is absorbed into the systemic circulation affects its bioavailability.
- Factors influencing absorption rate include drug solubility, formulation (e.g., immediate-release vs. sustained-release), particle size, surface area, and presence of food or other drugs that may affect gastrointestinal motility or absorption kinetics.

- **First-Pass Metabolism:** Drugs absorbed through the gastrointestinal tract are subject to first-pass metabolism in the liver before reaching systemic circulation.
- Extensive hepatic metabolism can significantly reduce the bioavailability of orally administered drugs.
- Sublingual and rectal routes bypass first-pass metabolism to varying degrees, leading to higher bioavailability for some drugs.

- **Drug Formulation and Excipients:** The formulation of a drug product, including excipients such as binders, fillers, and coatings, can impact its bioavailability.
- Variations in formulation can affect drug dissolution, absorption, and stability, thereby influencing bioavailability.

- **Drug-Drug Interactions:** Co-administration of drugs can alter the bioavailability of each other through various mechanisms, including competition for absorption sites, induction or inhibition of drug-metabolizing enzymes and transporters, and changes in gastrointestinal pH or motility.
- Drug interactions may result in increased or decreased bioavailability of one or both drugs, affecting therapeutic outcomes and safety.

- **Physiological Factors:** Individual variations in physiological factors, such as gastrointestinal pH, gastrointestinal transit time, gastrointestinal blood flow, intestinal surface area, and intestinal permeability, can influence drug absorption and bioavailability.
- Age, sex, genetics, disease states, and nutritional status may also impact drug absorption and metabolism, leading to variability in bioavailability among patients.

- **Disease States:** Certain disease states affecting gastrointestinal function, liver function, or renal function can alter drug absorption, distribution, metabolism, and elimination, thereby affecting bioavailability.
- Patients with conditions such as malabsorption syndromes, liver cirrhosis, or renal impairment may exhibit altered drug bioavailability and require dosage adjustments.

**Conclusion:**
- Understanding the factors affecting drug bioavailability is crucial for optimizing drug therapy, predicting pharmacokinetic behavior, and ensuring therapeutic efficacy and safety in clinical practice.
- Pharmacokinetic studies and individualized patient assessments help healthcare providers tailor treatment regimens to achieve optimal bioavailability and therapeutic outcomes for patients.

**44. What is bioequivalence? what are the factors affecting bioequivalence?**
- Bioequivalence refers to the similarity in the rate and extent of absorption of two formulations of the same active drug compound administered at the same dose and under similar conditions.
- In other words, if two drug formulations are bioequivalent, they produce comparable levels of the active drug in the bloodstream over time, leading to similar therapeutic effects.

- Bioequivalence is a critical concept in generic drug development and regulatory approval processes, as it ensures that generic versions of brand-name drugs perform similarly in terms of pharmacokinetics and clinical outcomes.

**Factors Affecting Bioequivalence:**
- **Pharmacokinetic Parameters:** Bioequivalence is primarily assessed based on pharmacokinetic parameters such as area under the plasma concentration-time curve (AUC) and peak plasma concentration (Cmax).
- The extent and rate of absorption, as well as the overall exposure to the active drug, should be similar between the test and reference formulations to establish bioequivalence.
- **Formulation Composition:** Differences in the composition of drug formulations, including excipients, binders, fillers, and coatings, can influence drug dissolution, absorption, and bioavailability.
- Formulations with different excipients or manufacturing processes may exhibit variations in bioavailability, affecting bioequivalence.
- **In Vitro Dissolution:** In vitro dissolution testing assesses the rate at which a drug formulation dissolves in simulated gastric and intestinal fluids.
- Similar dissolution profiles between the test and reference formulations are indicative of potential bioequivalence. Variations in dissolution rates may result in differences in drug absorption and bioavailability.
- **Manufacturing Processes:** Variations in manufacturing processes, such as particle size, tablet hardness, compression force, and coating thickness, can affect drug release and dissolution characteristics.
- Consistency in manufacturing processes is essential to ensure bioequivalence between different batches of the same drug formulation.
- **Physicochemical Properties:** Physicochemical properties of the drug compound, such as solubility, stability, and polymorphism, can impact its dissolution and absorption characteristics.
- Differences in the physicochemical properties of the active drug may affect bioequivalence between formulations.

- **Food Effects:** Food intake can influence the absorption and bioavailability of certain drugs.
- Differences in food effects between the test and reference formulations may lead to variations in pharmacokinetic parameters and affect bioequivalence.
- Bioequivalence studies are often conducted under fasting and fed conditions to assess the impact of food on drug absorption.

- **Inter- and Intra-subject Variability:** Variability in drug absorption and pharmacokinetics among individuals, as well as within the same individual over time, can affect the assessment of bioequivalence.
- Large inter- and intra-subject variability may require larger sample sizes or more stringent statistical analyses to establish bioequivalence.
- **Drug-Drug Interactions:** Co-administration of drugs can alter the pharmacokinetics of the active drug and affect its bioavailability.
- Drug-drug interactions may lead to differences in bioequivalence between formulations, particularly if one formulation is more susceptible to interactions than the other.

**Conclusion:**
- Establishing bioequivalence is essential for demonstrating the therapeutic equivalence of generic drug products to their brand-name counterparts.
- Rigorous bioequivalence studies, coupled with comprehensive assessments of formulation composition, manufacturing processes, and physicochemical properties, ensure the safety, efficacy, and quality of generic drugs for patients.

## 45. What is therapeutic equivalence? What are the factors affecting therapeutic equivalence?

- Therapeutic equivalence refers to the similarity in therapeutic effects between two drug products, typically a generic drug and its corresponding brand-name (reference) drug.
- For two drug products to be considered therapeutically equivalent, they must demonstrate comparable efficacy and safety profiles when administered to patients under the same conditions.

- Establishing therapeutic equivalence is crucial for ensuring that generic drugs provide the same clinical benefits as their brand-name counterparts at equivalent doses.

**Factors Affecting Therapeutic Equivalence:**
- **Bioequivalence:** Bioequivalence, as discussed earlier, is a key factor in establishing therapeutic equivalence.
- If two drug products are bioequivalent, it suggests that they produce similar plasma concentration-time profiles and are expected to have comparable therapeutic effects.
- However, bioequivalence alone does not guarantee therapeutic equivalence, as other factors may influence clinical outcomes.
- **Formulation Differences:** Differences in formulation composition, such as excipients, binders, and fillers, can affect drug dissolution, absorption, and bioavailability.
- Variations in formulation may lead to differences in pharmacokinetics and pharmacodynamics, potentially impacting therapeutic equivalence.
- **Manufacturing Processes:** Variations in manufacturing processes, such as particle size, tablet hardness, and coating thickness, can influence drug release, dissolution, and stability.
- Consistency in manufacturing practices is essential to ensure that generic drug products maintain therapeutic equivalence with their brand-name counterparts.
- **Stability:** Stability refers to the ability of a drug product to maintain its physical and chemical properties over time.
- Changes in drug stability, such as degradation or loss of potency, can affect therapeutic equivalence.
- Both generic and brand-name drug products must meet rigorous stability testing requirements to ensure consistent quality and efficacy.
- **Impurities and Degradation Products:** The presence of impurities or degradation products in drug formulations can affect safety and efficacy.
- Differences in impurity profiles between generic and brand-name drugs may influence therapeutic equivalence.

- Regulatory agencies impose strict limits on impurities and require thorough characterization of drug products to ensure patient safety.
- **Drug-Drug Interactions:** Interactions between drugs or with food can alter the pharmacokinetics and pharmacodynamics of a drug product, potentially impacting therapeutic equivalence.
- Drug-drug interactions may occur if one formulation is more susceptible to interactions than the other, leading to differences in clinical outcomes.
- **Patient Variability:** Variability in patient factors, such as age, sex, genetics, disease state, and concomitant medications, can influence drug response and therapeutic outcomes.
- Differences in patient populations enrolled in clinical trials or receiving drug therapy in clinical practice may affect the assessment of therapeutic equivalence.
- **Clinical Endpoints:** Clinical endpoints, such as symptom relief, disease progression, or adverse events, are used to evaluate therapeutic equivalence in clinical trials.
- Differences in clinical endpoints between generic and brand-name drugs may indicate variations in efficacy or safety profiles, affecting therapeutic equivalence.

**Conclusion:**
- Establishing therapeutic equivalence requires comprehensive assessment of multiple factors, including bioequivalence, formulation composition, manufacturing processes, stability, impurities, drug interactions, patient variability, and clinical endpoints.
- Regulatory agencies set stringent standards for demonstrating therapeutic equivalence to ensure the safety, efficacy, and quality of generic drug products for patients.

**46. Describe biotransformation? what is the clinical importance of biotransformation?**
- Biotransformation, also known as drug metabolism, refers to the biochemical processes by which the body alters the chemical structure of drugs and other xenobiotics (foreign compounds) to facilitate their elimination from the body.

- Biotransformation typically involves enzymatic reactions that convert drugs into metabolites that are more hydrophilic (water-soluble) and easier to excrete via urine or bile.
- The liver is the primary organ responsible for drug metabolism, although other tissues such as the kidneys, intestines, lungs, and skin may also contribute to biotransformation.

## Types of Biotransformation Reactions:

- **Phase I Reactions:** Phase I reactions involve the addition of functional groups (e.g., hydroxyl, amino, or carboxyl groups) or the introduction of reactive sites (e.g., oxidation, reduction, hydrolysis) to the drug molecule.
- Cytochrome P450 enzymes, particularly CYP3A4, CYP2D6, and CYP2C9, play a crucial role in phase I metabolism.
- **Phase II Reactions:** Phase II reactions involve the conjugation of the drug or its metabolites with endogenous molecules such as glucuronic acid, sulfate, glycine, or glutathione.
- Conjugation reactions increase the water solubility of the drug metabolites, facilitating their excretion.
- Examples of phase II reactions include glucuronidation, sulfation, acetylation, methylation, and glutathione conjugation.

## Clinical Importance of Biotransformation:

- **Drug Clearance:** Biotransformation is essential for the elimination of drugs and xenobiotics from the body.
- Metabolism transforms lipophilic (fat-soluble) drugs into hydrophilic (water-soluble) metabolites that can be readily excreted via urine or bile.
- Impaired biotransformation can lead to drug accumulation and toxicity.
- **Drug Activation or Inactivation:** Biotransformation can convert inactive prodrugs into active metabolites or inactive metabolites into active drugs.
- Conversely, metabolism may also inactivate active drugs, reducing their pharmacological effects.
- Understanding the metabolic fate of drugs is crucial for optimizing therapeutic efficacy and minimizing adverse effects.

- **Drug-Drug Interactions:** Biotransformation can be affected by drug-drug interactions, where one drug may inhibit or induce the activity of drug-metabolizing enzymes or transporters.
- Drug interactions may alter the metabolism of co-administered drugs, leading to changes in therapeutic efficacy or toxicity.
- Pharmacokinetic studies assess the potential for drug interactions and guide dosing adjustments.
- **Genetic Polymorphisms:** Genetic variations in drug-metabolizing enzymes and transporters can influence drug metabolism and pharmacokinetics among individuals.
- Polymorphisms in genes encoding cytochrome P450 enzymes, UDP-glucuronosyltransferases, and other metabolic enzymes may result in inter-individual differences in drug response and susceptibility to adverse effects.
- Pharmacogenomic testing can help personalize drug therapy and optimize treatment outcomes based on an individual's genetic profile.
- **Toxicity and Adverse Effects:** Biotransformation can lead to the formation of reactive metabolites that may contribute to drug-induced toxicity or adverse effects.
- For example, the metabolism of certain drugs can produce hepatotoxic metabolites that contribute to liver injury.
- Understanding the metabolic pathways and potential toxicities of drugs is essential for drug safety assessment and risk management.

## Conclusion:

- Biotransformation plays a crucial role in drug metabolism, clearance, activation, and detoxification.
- Understanding the clinical importance of biotransformation is essential for optimizing drug therapy, minimizing adverse effects, and ensuring patient safety.
- Pharmacokinetic studies, drug metabolism profiling, and pharmacogenomic testing contribute to personalized medicine approaches that tailor drug therapy to individual patients based on their metabolic characteristics and genetic makeup.

## 47. What are microsomal enzymes in drug metabolism? What is the clinical importance of microsomal enzymes in drug metabolism?

- Microsomal enzymes are a group of enzymes located within the endoplasmic reticulum of cells, particularly in hepatocytes (liver cells).
- These enzymes play a crucial role in drug metabolism, particularly in phase I reactions, which involve the modification of drug molecules to facilitate their elimination from the body.
- The primary microsomal enzymes involved in drug metabolism belong to the cytochrome P450 (CYP) superfamily.
- Cytochrome P450 enzymes catalyze a wide range of oxidative reactions, including hydroxylation, dealkylation, and oxidation, leading to the formation of metabolites with altered pharmacological properties.

### Clinical Importance of Microsomal Enzymes in Drug Metabolism:

- **Drug Clearance:** Microsomal enzymes are responsible for the metabolism of the majority of drugs and xenobiotics in the body.
- They catalyze the biotransformation of lipophilic drugs into more hydrophilic metabolites, which are easier to eliminate via urine or bile.
- Understanding the role of microsomal enzymes in drug metabolism is essential for predicting the clearance and elimination kinetics of drugs.

- **Drug-Drug Interactions:** Microsomal enzymes can be affected by drug-drug interactions, where one drug may inhibit or induce the activity of specific cytochrome P450 enzymes.
- Drug interactions can alter the metabolism of co-administered drugs, leading to changes in drug concentrations, pharmacological effects, and therapeutic outcomes.
- Knowledge of potential drug interactions involving microsomal enzymes is crucial for avoiding adverse effects and optimizing drug therapy.
- **Genetic Polymorphisms:** Genetic variations in genes encoding microsomal enzymes can influence individual differences in drug metabolism and pharmacokinetics.
- Polymorphisms in cytochrome P450 genes may result in altered enzyme activity, leading to inter-individual variability in drug response and susceptibility to adverse effects.
- Pharmacogenomic testing can help identify patients who may require dosage adjustments or alternative medications based on their genetic profile.

- **Toxicity and Adverse Effects:** Some drugs are metabolized by microsomal enzymes to reactive metabolites that may contribute to drug-induced toxicity or adverse effects.
- **Example:** Hepatotoxicity can occur due to the formation of reactive metabolites during the metabolism of certain drugs.
- Understanding the metabolic pathways and potential toxicities of drugs is essential for drug safety assessment and risk management.

- **Therapeutic Drug Monitoring:** Monitoring drug concentrations in plasma or serum is important for optimizing drug therapy and ensuring therapeutic efficacy while minimizing the risk of toxicity.
- Knowledge of the metabolic pathways and enzyme kinetics mediated by microsomal enzymes can help interpret drug concentration data and guide dosing adjustments to achieve target therapeutic levels.

### Conclusion:
- Microsomal enzymes, particularly cytochrome P450 enzymes, play a critical role in drug metabolism, drug-drug interactions, genetic variability in drug response, and drug-induced toxicity.
- Understanding the clinical importance of microsomal enzymes in drug metabolism is essential for optimizing drug therapy, avoiding adverse effects, and ensuring patient safety.

## 48. Name drugs that inhabit metabolism? What is the clinical importance of this?

- Several drugs are known to inhibit drug metabolism, particularly by inhibiting cytochrome P450 (CYP) enzymes, which are responsible for the metabolism of many drugs.

- These drugs can lead to altered pharmacokinetics, increased drug concentrations, and potential drug interactions.

**Following are some examples of drugs that inhibit metabolism and their clinical importance:**

- **Cimetidine:** Cimetidine is a histamine H2 receptor antagonist used to treat peptic ulcers and gastroesophageal reflux disease (GERD).
- It inhibits several CYP enzymes, including CYP1A2, CYP2C9, CYP2D6, and CYP3A4.
- This can lead to increased plasma concentrations of drugs metabolized by these enzymes, potentially resulting in enhanced therapeutic effects or increased risk of adverse effects.
- **Fluoxetine:** Fluoxetine is a selective serotonin reuptake inhibitor (SSRI) used to treat depression, obsessive-compulsive disorder (OCD), and other psychiatric conditions.
- It inhibits CYP2D6 and CYP2C19 enzymes, which may lead to increased plasma concentrations of drugs metabolized by these enzymes, such as tricyclic antidepressants and certain antipsychotics.
- **Fluconazole:** Fluconazole is an antifungal medication used to treat fungal infections.
- It inhibits CYP2C9 and CYP3A4 enzymes, potentially leading to increased plasma concentrations of drugs metabolized by these enzymes, such as warfarin and certain statins.
- This can result in enhanced anticoagulant effects or increased risk of statin-induced myopathy.
- **Ketoconazole:** Ketoconazole is another antifungal medication that inhibits CYP3A4 and other CYP enzymes.
- It is known for its potent inhibition of drug metabolism and is used primarily as a topical treatment for fungal infections.
- Systemic use of ketoconazole can lead to significant drug interactions and increased risk of adverse effects.
- **Erythromycin:** Erythromycin is a macrolide antibiotic used to treat bacterial infections.
- It inhibits CYP3A4 and can increase plasma concentrations of drugs metabolized by this enzyme, such as certain calcium channel blockers and statins.
- Clinicians should monitor for potential drug interactions and adjust dosages accordingly.

**Clinical Importance:**

- Understanding drug interactions involving metabolism inhibitors is crucial for avoiding adverse effects and optimizing therapeutic outcomes.
- Clinicians should be aware of potential interactions when prescribing medications to patients taking metabolism inhibitors, and dosage adjustments may be necessary.
- Monitoring drug concentrations and clinical response is important when patients are receiving drugs that inhibit metabolism to ensure appropriate dosing and minimize the risk of toxicity.
- Pharmacogenomic testing may help identify patients who are at increased risk of drug interactions due to genetic variations in drug-metabolizing enzymes.

**49. Name drugs that induce metabolism? What is the clinical importance of this?**

- Drugs that induce drug metabolism can increase the activity of drug-metabolizing enzymes, particularly cytochrome P450 (CYP) enzymes, leading to accelerated metabolism and decreased plasma concentrations of other drugs metabolized by the same enzymes.
- This can result in reduced efficacy or therapeutic failure of co-administered medications.

**Following are some examples of drugs that induce metabolism and their clinical importance:**

- **Rifampin:** Rifampin is an antibiotic used to treat tuberculosis and certain other bacterial infections. It is a potent inducer of several CYP enzymes, including CYP3A4, CYP2C9, and CYP2C19.
- Rifampin induction can lead to decreased plasma concentrations of drugs metabolized by these enzymes, such as oral contraceptives, anticoagulants, and certain antiepileptic drugs.
- Clinicians should monitor patients receiving rifampin for reduced efficacy of co-administered medications and adjust dosages as needed.
- **Carbamazepine:** Carbamazepine is an antiepileptic drug used to treat seizures and certain mood disorders.
- It induces CYP3A4 and other CYP enzymes, leading to increased metabolism and reduced plasma concentrations of co-administered drugs such as oral contraceptives, antipsychotics, and certain antiretroviral medications.

- Clinicians should monitor patients receiving carbamazepine for reduced efficacy of co-administered medications and consider dosage adjustments or alternative therapies.

- **Phenytoin:** Phenytoin is another antiepileptic drug that induces CYP3A4 and other CYP enzymes. It is used to treat seizures and certain cardiac arrhythmias.
- Phenytoin induction can lead to decreased plasma concentrations of drugs metabolized by these enzymes, such as oral contraceptives, antipsychotics, and certain antiretroviral medications.
- Clinicians should monitor patients receiving phenytoin for reduced efficacy of co-administered medications and consider dosage adjustments as needed.

- **St. John's Wort:** St. John's Wort is a herbal supplement used to treat depression and other mood disorders. It induces several CYP enzymes, including CYP3A4, CYP2C9, and CYP2C19.
- St. John's Wort induction can lead to decreased plasma concentrations of drugs metabolized by these enzymes, such as oral contraceptives, antidepressants, and certain antiretroviral medications.
- Clinicians should advise patients taking St. John's Wort to avoid co-administration with other medications to prevent reduced efficacy.

**Clinical Importance:**
- Understanding drug interactions involving metabolism inducers is crucial for avoiding reduced efficacy of co-administered medications and ensuring optimal therapeutic outcomes.
- Clinicians should be aware of potential interactions when prescribing medications to patients taking metabolism inducers, and dosage adjustments or alternative therapies may be necessary.
- Monitoring drug concentrations and clinical response is important when patients are receiving drugs that induce metabolism to ensure appropriate dosing and therapeutic efficacy.
- Pharmacogenomic testing may help identify patients who are at increased risk of drug interactions due to genetic variations in drug-metabolizing enzymes.

## 50. Name the systemic routes drugs administration? Compare the oral route with parenteral route of drug administration?

- Systemic routes of drug administration involve the delivery of drugs to the bloodstream, allowing distribution to various tissues and organs throughout the body.

**Following are the some common systemic routes of drug administration:**
- **Oral Route:** Drugs administered orally are swallowed and absorbed through the gastrointestinal tract.
- This route is convenient, non-invasive, and suitable for self-administration.
- **Examples:** Oral dosage forms include tablets, capsules, syrups, and solutions.
- Oral administration may result in delayed onset of action due to drug absorption from the gastrointestinal tract and variability in absorption rates among individuals.
- Factors such as gastrointestinal pH, motility, and food intake can influence drug absorption.
- Despite these limitations, the oral route remains one of the most commonly used systemic routes of drug administration due to its ease of use and patient acceptance.
- **Parenteral Routes:** Parenteral routes involve the administration of drugs through routes other than the gastrointestinal tract.
- These routes bypass the gastrointestinal system and deliver drugs directly into the bloodstream or tissues, resulting in rapid onset of action and predictable drug absorption.
- Parenteral routes are commonly used when oral administration is impractical or when immediate drug effects are desired.

**Following are the some of the Examples of parenteral routes of drug administration:**
- **Intravenous (IV) Injection:** Drugs are administered directly into a vein, allowing for rapid and complete drug absorption.
- IV injection is suitable for drugs that require immediate onset of action or precise control of drug concentration.

- **Intramuscular (IM) Injection:** Drugs are injected into the muscle tissue, where they are absorbed into the bloodstream.
- IM injection provides a relatively rapid onset of action and is suitable for drugs that cannot be administered orally or require sustained release.

- **Subcutaneous (SC) Injection:** Drugs are injected into the subcutaneous tissue, where they are absorbed into the bloodstream.
- SC injection provides slower absorption compared to IV or IM injection but may be preferred for certain drugs or patient populations.

## Comparison between Oral and Parenteral Routes:

- **Onset of Action:** Parenteral routes generally provide faster onset of action compared to the oral route, as drugs administered via parenteral routes bypass the gastrointestinal tract and are absorbed directly into the bloodstream or tissues.
- Oral drugs may have delayed onset of action due to variable absorption rates and first-pass metabolism.
- **Bioavailability:** The bioavailability of orally administered drugs may be affected by factors such as gastrointestinal pH, motility, and first-pass metabolism in the liver.
- In contrast, drugs administered via parenteral routes typically exhibit higher bioavailability and more predictable absorption.

- **Convenience and Patient Acceptance:** Oral administration is often preferred by patients due to its convenience, ease of use, and non-invasive nature.
- Parenteral routes may be associated with discomfort, require healthcare professional administration, and may not be suitable for self-administration in all cases.

- **Drug Stability:** Parenteral routes may be preferred for drugs that are unstable in the gastrointestinal tract or undergo extensive first-pass metabolism.
- Oral drugs may require special formulations or coatings to improve stability and enhance absorption.

- **Risk of Infection and Tissue Irritation:** Parenteral routes carry a higher risk of infection and tissue irritation compared to the oral route.
- Proper aseptic technique and site rotation are important for minimizing these risks with parenteral administration.

## Conclusion:

- Both oral and parenteral routes of drug administration offer advantages and limitations, and the choice of route depends on factors such as drug characteristics, patient preferences, and clinical considerations.
- Oral administration is often preferred for its convenience and patient acceptance, while parenteral routes provide rapid onset of action and predictable drug absorption.

## 51. Name the local routes of drugs administration? Compare the local route with systemic route of drug administration?

- Local routes of drug administration involve the delivery of drugs directly to a specific site of action, typically to treat localized conditions or target specific tissues or organs.
- These routes allow for localized drug effects while minimizing systemic exposure and potential side effects.

**Some common local routes of drug administration are discussed below:**

- **Topical Route:** Drugs are applied directly to the skin or mucous membranes for local absorption.
- **Examples:** Topical dosage forms include creams, ointments, gels, lotions, and patches.
- Topical administration is suitable for dermatological conditions, such as eczema, psoriasis, and fungal infections, as well as for localized pain relief and transdermal drug delivery.
- **Ophthalmic Route:** Drugs are administered directly to the eye for the treatment of ocular conditions, such as infections, inflammation, glaucoma, and dry eye syndrome.
- Ophthalmic dosage forms include eye drops, ointments, and inserts.
- Ophthalmic administration allows for targeted drug delivery to the eye while minimizing systemic exposure and potential adverse effects.

- **Otic Route:** Drugs are administered directly to the ear for the treatment of ear infections, inflammation, and other otic conditions.
- Otic dosage forms include ear drops and ear sprays.
- Otic administration allows for localized drug delivery to the ear canal and middle ear, where systemic absorption is minimal.

**Comparison between Local and Systemic Routes:**
- **Site of Action:** Local routes of drug administration target specific tissues or organs at the site of application, providing localized drug effects.
- Systemic routes, on the other hand, deliver drugs to the bloodstream for distribution throughout the body, allowing for systemic drug effects on various tissues and organs.

- **Drug Exposure:** Local routes of administration result in high drug concentrations at the site of application, minimizing systemic exposure and potential side effects.
- Systemic routes may lead to higher systemic drug concentrations and increased risk of systemic adverse effects.

- **Onset of Action:** Local routes of administration may provide rapid onset of action due to direct drug delivery to the target site.
- Systemic routes may have variable onset of action depending on drug absorption and distribution kinetics.

- **Bioavailability:** Local routes of administration typically have lower bioavailability compared to systemic routes, as drugs may be metabolized locally or cleared from the site of application before reaching the systemic circulation.
- Systemic routes allow for higher bioavailability and more predictable drug absorption.

- **Convenience and Patient Acceptance:** Local routes of administration may be preferred for their convenience, ease of use, and minimal systemic side effects.
- Systemic routes may require more invasive procedures (e.g., injections) or patient monitoring, but they provide broader therapeutic effects for systemic conditions.

**Conclusion:**
- Local routes of drug administration provide targeted drug delivery to specific sites of action, minimizing systemic exposure and potential side effects.
- Systemic routes deliver drugs to the bloodstream for distribution throughout the body, allowing for systemic drug effects on various tissues and organs.
- The choice of route depends on factors such as the nature of the condition being treated, drug characteristics, patient preferences, and clinical considerations.

**52. Write a note on transdermal drug administration?**

**Transdermal Drug Administration:**
- Transdermal drug administration involves the delivery of medications through the skin for systemic absorption.
- This route of drug delivery offers several advantages, including non-invasiveness, prolonged drug release, avoidance of first-pass metabolism, and improved patient compliance.
- Transdermal drug delivery systems (TDDS) typically consist of a drug-containing patch or device applied to the skin, allowing for controlled release of the medication over an extended period.

**Details of transdermal drug administration is discussed below:**

**Mechanisms involved in drug penetration:**
- Transdermal drug delivery relies on the ability of drugs to penetrate the skin's outermost layer, the stratum corneum, and reach the systemic circulation.

- Drugs must possess appropriate physicochemical properties, such as low molecular weight, lipophilicity, and appropriate solubility, to permeate the skin barrier and achieve therapeutic concentrations in the bloodstream.

- Transdermal patches contain drug reservoirs or matrices that release the medication gradually, allowing for sustained absorption and prolonged therapeutic effects.

**Advantages of Transdermal Drug Administration:**

- **Non-invasiveness:** Transdermal patches offer a painless and convenient alternative to injections or oral medications, particularly for patients with needle phobia or difficulty in swallowing pills.

- **Prolonged Drug Release:** Transdermal delivery systems provide controlled release of medications over an extended period, maintaining steady plasma concentrations and reducing the need for frequent dosing.

- **Avoidance of First-Pass Metabolism:** Drugs absorbed through the skin bypass hepatic first-pass metabolism, leading to higher bioavailability and more predictable pharmacokinetics compared to oral administration

- **Improved Patient Compliance:** Transdermal patches offer simplicity of use, consistent dosing, and reduced risk of dose-related adverse effects, contributing to improved patient adherence to treatment regimens.

**Applications of Transdermal Drug Delivery:**

- **Pain Management:** Transdermal patches are commonly used for the management of chronic pain conditions, such as arthritis, neuropathic pain, and postoperative pain.

- **Hormone Replacement Therapy:** Transdermal patches deliver hormones, such as estrogen and testosterone, for hormone replacement therapy in menopausal women or individuals with hormonal deficiencies.

- **Smoking Cessation:** Nicotine patches deliver controlled doses of nicotine to help individuals quit smoking by reducing withdrawal symptoms and cravings.

- **Cardiovascular Disorders:** Transdermal patches deliver medications for the treatment of hypertension, angina, and heart failure, providing sustained drug release and improved therapeutic outcomes.

**Considerations for Transdermal Drug Delivery:**

- **Skin Permeation:** Factors influencing drug permeation through the skin include molecular size, lipophilicity, hydration status of the skin, and the presence of permeation enhancers in the formulation.

- **Adhesive Properties:** Transdermal patches should adhere securely to the skin to prevent detachment and ensure consistent drug delivery.
- Skin irritation or allergic reactions to adhesive components should be minimized.

- **Patch Design:** Transdermal patch design influences drug release kinetics, including patch size, drug loading, membrane permeability, and rate-controlling mechanisms.

- **Site of Application:** Transdermal patches should be applied to areas of intact skin with good blood supply, such as the upper arm, back, chest, or abdomen, to facilitate drug absorption.

**Conclusion:**

- Transdermal drug administration offers a convenient, effective, and patient-friendly approach to drug delivery for various therapeutic applications.
- Advances in patch technology and formulation design continue to improve the efficacy, safety, and versatility of transdermal drug delivery systems, making them valuable tools in modern pharmacotherapy.

## 53. Write a note on novel drug delivery systems?

**Note on Novel Drug Delivery Systems:**

- Novel drug delivery systems (NDDS) encompass a diverse range of technologies designed to optimize drug administration, enhance therapeutic efficacy, and improve patient compliance.
- These innovative approaches aim to overcome challenges associated with conventional drug delivery methods, such as poor solubility, limited bioavailability, variable absorption kinetics, and systemic side effects.
- NDDS utilize advanced drug formulations, materials science, nanotechnology, and targeted delivery strategies to achieve precise control over drug release, distribution, and pharmacokinetics.

Following is the overview of importatn novel drug delivery systems:

**Nanotechnology-Based Drug Delivery Systems:**
- **Nanoparticles:** Nanoparticle-based drug delivery systems utilize nanoscale carriers, such as liposomes, polymeric nanoparticles, and dendrimers, to encapsulate and deliver drugs to target tissues or cells.
- Nanoparticles offer advantages such as prolonged circulation time, enhanced drug stability, controlled release, and the ability to bypass biological barriers for targeted delivery.

- **Nanocrystals:** Nanocrystal formulations improve the solubility and bioavailability of poorly water-soluble drugs by reducing particle size to nanoscale dimensions. Nanocrystals increase drug dissolution rates, leading to faster absorption and improved therapeutic outcomes.

**Lipid-Based Drug Delivery Systems:**

- **Liposomes:** Liposomes are spherical vesicles composed of lipid bilayers that encapsulate drugs within their aqueous core or lipid membrane.

- Liposomal formulations enhance drug solubility, stability, and bioavailability while enabling targeted delivery to specific tissues or cells. Liposomes are used in cancer therapy, gene delivery, and vaccine delivery.

- **Solid Lipid Nanoparticles (SLNs) and Nanostructured Lipid Carriers (NLCs):** SLNs and NLCs are lipid-based nanoparticles that offer advantages such as sustained drug release, improved drug loading capacity, and enhanced tissue penetration.
- These formulations are used for oral, topical, and parenteral delivery of drugs.

**Controlled Release Systems:**
- **Implants:** Implantable drug delivery systems consist of biocompatible materials that release drugs over an extended period through diffusion, erosion, or osmosis.
- Implants offer sustained drug release, reduced dosing frequency, and improved patient compliance.
- They are used in hormone replacement therapy, contraception, and pain management.

- **Microparticles and Microspheres:** Microparticulate drug delivery systems are polymeric particles or beads that encapsulate drugs and release them in a controlled manner.
- Microparticles enable targeted delivery to specific sites within the body, such as tumors or inflamed tissues, while minimizing systemic exposure and side effects.

**Targeted Drug Delivery Systems:**
- **Antibody-Drug Conjugates (ADCs):** ADCs are biopharmaceuticals that combine monoclonal antibodies with cytotoxic drugs to selectively target cancer cells expressing specific antigens.
- ADCs deliver potent anticancer agents directly to tumor cells, minimizing damage to healthy tissues and reducing systemic toxicity.

- **Peptide-Based Targeting:** Peptide ligands can be conjugated to drug carriers to facilitate targeted delivery to cells expressing corresponding receptors.

- Peptide-based targeting systems offer specificity, affinity, and versatility for drug delivery applications.

**Smart Drug Delivery Systems:**
- **Responsive Delivery Systems:** Smart drug delivery systems incorporate stimuli-responsive materials that undergo changes in response to environmental cues, such as pH, temperature, enzymes, or light.
- These systems enable triggered drug release at the target site, enhancing therapeutic efficacy and minimizing off-target effects.

- **Magnetic Drug Targeting:** Magnetic drug delivery systems utilize magnetic nanoparticles or carriers that can be guided to specific tissues or organs using external magnetic fields.
- Magnetic targeting enhances drug accumulation at the target site, improving drug efficacy and reducing systemic exposure.

**Conclusion:**
- Novel drug delivery systems represent a rapidly evolving field that holds great promise for revolutionizing drug therapy.
- These innovative technologies offer precise control over drug release, targeting, and pharmacokinetics, leading to improved therapeutic outcomes, reduced side effects, and enhanced patient compliance.
- Continued research and development in NDDS are expected to drive advancements in personalized medicine, precision drug delivery, and the treatment of complex diseases.

**54. What are the oral dosage forms? add note on different types of oral dosage forms?**

- Oral dosage forms are pharmaceutical formulations designed for administration via the oral route, involving ingestion through the mouth and subsequent absorption through the gastrointestinal tract.
- These dosage forms vary in composition, release characteristics, and administration requirements to accommodate diverse patient needs and therapeutic objectives.

**Following are some common types of oral dosage forms along with their characteristics:**

**Tablets:**
- Tablets are solid dosage forms composed of active pharmaceutical ingredients (APIs) and excipients compressed into a flat, disc-shaped form.

- Tablets may be immediate-release, extended-release, or enteric-coated, depending on the desired drug release profile.

- They offer ease of handling, accurate dosing, and stability, making them one of the most widely used oral dosage forms.

**Capsules:**
- Capsules are solid dosage forms consisting of a gelatin or polymer shell filled with powdered, granular, or liquid drug formulations.

- Capsules may be hard (powder-filled) or soft (liquid-filled), offering flexibility in formulation and drug release characteristics.

- They provide improved palatability, easier swallowing, and potential for customized drug combinations or modified-release formulations.

**Powders:**
- Powdered formulations consist of finely divided drug particles mixed with inert excipients or diluents.

- Powders may be dispensed as single-dose packets, sachets, or bulk powders for reconstitution with liquid prior to administration.

- They offer flexibility in dosing, rapid dissolution, and ease of administration, particularly for pediatric or geriatric patients.

**Solutions:**
- Oral solutions are liquid dosage forms containing drug substances dissolved in a suitable solvent or vehicle.

- Solutions offer rapid drug absorption, precise dosing, and ease of administration, particularly for patients with difficulty swallowing or those requiring flexible dosing regimens.

- They may be flavored or sweetened to improve palatability and patient acceptance.

**Suspensions:**
- Oral suspensions are liquid dosage forms containing finely dispersed drug particles suspended in a suitable vehicle.

- Suspensions offer uniform drug distribution, improved stability, and extended shelf-life compared to solutions.

- They require shaking before administration to ensure uniform drug dispersion and accurate dosing.

**Emulsions:**
- Oral emulsions are biphasic liquid dosage forms containing a dispersed phase (oil droplets) and a continuous phase (aqueous medium) stabilized by emulsifying agents.

- Emulsions offer enhanced solubility, stability, and palatability for poorly water-soluble drugs.

- They may provide sustained drug release or targeted drug delivery to specific gastrointestinal sites.

**Lozenges and Troches:**
- Lozenges and troches are solid dosage forms intended to dissolve slowly in the mouth, releasing the drug for local or systemic absorption through the oral mucosa.

- They offer localized drug effects, such as throat soothing or local anesthesia, and are suitable for drugs with poor oral bioavailability or gastrointestinal intolerance.

**Chewable Tablets:**
- Chewable tablets are solid dosage forms designed to be chewed or crushed in the mouth before swallowing.

- They offer improved palatability, ease of administration, and enhanced drug absorption due to increased surface area and prolonged contact time with oral mucosa.

**Conclusion:**
- Oral dosage forms encompass a diverse range of formulations tailored to meet specific patient needs, dosing requirements, and therapeutic objectives.
- Each type of oral dosage form offers unique advantages in terms of drug delivery, administration convenience, patient compliance, and therapeutic outcomes, making them essential components of modern pharmacotherapy.

**55. What are the parenteral dosage forms? add note on different types of parenteral dosage forms?**

- Parenteral dosage forms are pharmaceutical formulations intended for administration via routes other than the digestive tract, typically involving injection or infusion directly into the body tissues or bloodstream.
- These dosage forms allow for rapid drug absorption, precise dosing, and targeted delivery to specific sites within the body.

Following are some common types of parenteral dosage forms along with their characteristics:

**Injections:**
- Injections involve the administration of liquid drug formulations using a syringe and needle into muscles (intramuscular), veins (intravenous), or subcutaneous tissue (subcutaneous).

- Injectable formulations may be solutions, suspensions, or emulsions, depending on the drug's solubility, stability, and intended route of administration.

- Injections offer rapid drug absorption, immediate onset of action, and precise dosing, making them suitable for emergency situations, anesthesia, and critical care settings.

## Infusions:

- Infusions involve the administration of liquid drug formulations intravenously over an extended period using an infusion pump or gravity drip set.

- Infusion solutions may contain drugs, electrolytes, nutrients, or fluids for hydration, electrolyte balance, or parenteral nutrition.

- Infusions provide controlled drug delivery, continuous therapy, and gradual drug titration, making them suitable for long-term treatments, chemotherapy, and intravenous fluid replacement.

## Intradermal Injections:

- Intradermal injections involve the administration of small volumes of liquid drug formulations into the dermal layer of the skin using a shallow angle needle.

- Intradermal injections are used for diagnostic tests (e.g., tuberculin skin test), allergy testing, and local anesthesia.

## Intrathecal and Epidural Injections:

- Intrathecal and epidural injections involve the administration of drugs into the spinal canal (intrathecal) or epidural space (epidural) for regional anesthesia, pain management, or spinal cord drug delivery.

- These injections provide targeted drug delivery to the central nervous system (CNS) or spinal cord, minimizing systemic side effects and enhancing therapeutic efficacy.

## Implants:

- Implantable dosage forms consist of solid or semisolid drug formulations inserted subcutaneously or intramuscularly for sustained drug release over an extended period.

- Implants offer controlled drug delivery, reduced dosing frequency, and prolonged therapeutic effects, making them suitable for hormone replacement therapy, contraception, and pain management.

## Intraocular Injections:

- Intraocular injections involve the administration of drugs directly into the vitreous cavity or anterior chamber of the eye for the treatment of ocular diseases, such as macular degeneration, diabetic retinopathy, or uveitis.

- Intraocular injections provide high drug concentrations at the target site, minimizing systemic exposure and reducing side effects.

## Intra-articular Injections:

- Intra-articular injections involve the administration of drugs directly into the joint space for the treatment of inflammatory joint conditions, such as osteoarthritis or rheumatoid arthritis.

- Intra-articular injections provide localized drug effects, reduce pain and inflammation, and improve joint mobility.

## Conclusion:

- Parenteral dosage forms offer diverse options for drug administration, allowing for rapid drug absorption, precise dosing, and targeted therapy.

- Each type of parenteral dosage form provides unique advantages in terms of drug delivery, administration convenience, patient comfort, and therapeutic outcomes, making them essential components of modern pharmacotherapy, particularly in emergency, critical care, and specialized medical settings.

## 56. What are inhalation dosage forms? What are the advantages and disadvantages of of inhalational route of drug administration?

- Inhalation dosage forms are pharmaceutical formulations designed for administration via inhalation, allowing drugs to be delivered directly to the respiratory tract for systemic or local effects.
- These dosage forms are typically administered as aerosols, vapors, or powders, enabling rapid drug absorption through the lungs.

**Following are some common types of inhalation dosage forms along with their advantages and disadvantages:**

**Types of Inhalation Dosage Forms:**
- **Metered-Dose Inhalers (MDIs):** MDIs deliver a precise dose of medication in aerosol form using a pressurized canister and a propellant.
- They are commonly used for the treatment of asthma, chronic obstructive pulmonary disease (COPD), and other respiratory conditions.

- **Dry Powder Inhalers (DPIs):** DPIs deliver powdered medications directly to the lungs without the need for propellants.
- Patients inhale the medication by generating airflow through the device. DPIs are used for the treatment of asthma, COPD, and cystic fibrosis.

- **Nebulizers:** Nebulizers convert liquid medications into fine aerosol droplets using compressed air or ultrasonic vibrations.
- Patients inhale the aerosol mist through a mask or mouthpiece over an extended period.
- Nebulizers are often used in hospitalized or critically ill patients who have difficulty using MDIs or DPIs.

**Advantages of Inhalational Route:**

- **Rapid Onset of Action:** Inhalation allows for rapid drug absorption directly into the bloodstream through the lungs, leading to fast onset of therapeutic effects.
- This is particularly beneficial for acute conditions requiring immediate relief, such as asthma attacks.

- **Localized Therapy:** Inhalation provides targeted drug delivery to the respiratory tract, allowing for localized treatment of lung diseases with minimal systemic exposure.
- This reduces the risk of systemic side effects and enhances therapeutic efficacy.

- **High Bioavailability:** Inhalational route offers high drug bioavailability due to direct absorption into the pulmonary circulation, bypassing first-pass metabolism in the liver.
- This results in higher drug concentrations at the target site and lower doses required compared to oral administration.

- **Improved Lung Function:** Some inhalational medications, such as bronchodilators and corticosteroids, help improve lung function, reduce airway inflammation, and alleviate respiratory symptoms in patients with asthma, COPD, or cystic fibrosis.

**Disadvantages of Inhalational Route:**

- **Proper Technique of Use of the Device:** Effective use of inhalation devices requires proper technique and coordination between inhalation and device activation.
- Poor inhaler technique can lead to inadequate drug delivery, reduced efficacy, and increased risk of exacerbations.

- **Device Malfunction:** Inhalation devices may malfunction or become clogged, affecting drug delivery and patient adherence to treatment regimens.
- Regular maintenance and device checks are necessary to ensure proper functioning.

- **Limited Drug Compatibility:** Not all drugs are suitable for inhalation due to their physicochemical properties, stability, or potential for respiratory irritation.
- Formulating drugs for inhalation requires specialized expertise and may limit the availability of certain medications.

- **Potential Adverse Effects:** Inhalational medications may cause local adverse effects such as throat irritation, cough, or oral candidiasis (thrush).
- Systemic side effects, such as tachycardia or tremors, may occur with certain bronchodilators or corticosteroids.

### Conclusion:

- Inhalation dosage forms offer several advantages, including rapid onset of action, localized therapy, high bioavailability, and improved lung function.
- However, they require proper technique, device maintenance, and may be limited by drug compatibility and potential adverse effects.
- Clinicians should consider patient preferences, disease characteristics, and therapeutic goals when selecting inhalational therapy for respiratory conditions.

## 57. What are the methods used for delivery of drugs through transmucosal route? what are the advantages and disadvantages of transmucosal route of drug administration?

- Transmucosal drug delivery involves the administration of medications through mucous membranes, allowing for direct absorption into the bloodstream or systemic circulation.
- Several methods are used for delivery of drugs through the transmucosal route, each offering unique advantages and disadvantages:

- **Methods for Delivery of Drugs through Transmucosal Route:**
- **Sublingual Administration:** Sublingual administration involves placing drug formulations under the tongue, where they dissolve or disperse in saliva and are absorbed through the sublingual mucosa into the bloodstream.
- Sublingual tablets, films, or sprays are commonly used for rapid drug absorption and onset of action.

- **Buccal Administration:** Buccal administration involves placing drug formulations against the buccal mucosa (inner lining of the cheek), where they adhere and release drugs for absorption through the buccal mucosa into the systemic circulation.
- Buccal tablets, patches, or gels provide sustained drug delivery and avoid first-pass metabolism.

- **Nasal Administration:** Nasal administration involves delivering drug formulations into the nasal cavity, where they are absorbed through the nasal mucosa into the systemic circulation or reach the central nervous system (CNS) via olfactory nerve pathways.
- Nasal sprays, drops, or powders are used for rapid drug absorption and localized or systemic effects.

- **Vaginal Administration:** Vaginal administration involves inserting drug formulations into the vagina, where they are absorbed through the vaginal mucosa into the systemic circulation or exert local effects on the reproductive tract.
- Vaginal tablets, creams, suppositories, or rings are used for contraception, hormone replacement therapy, or treatment of vaginal infections.

- **Rectal Administration:** Rectal administration involves inserting drug formulations into the rectum, where they are absorbed through the rectal mucosa into the systemic circulation or exert local effects on the gastrointestinal tract.
- Rectal suppositories, enemas, or foams are used for systemic drug delivery, constipation relief, or treatment of inflammatory bowel disease.

**Advantages of Transmucosal Route of Drug Administration:**

- **Rapid Absorption:** Transmucosal drug delivery offers rapid drug absorption into the bloodstream or systemic circulation, bypassing the digestive tract and first-pass metabolism in the liver.

- This results in faster onset of action and higher bioavailability compared to oral administration.

- **Avoidance of Gastric Acid and Enzymes:** Transmucosal drug delivery avoids exposure to gastric acid and digestive enzymes in the gastrointestinal tract, reducing the risk of drug degradation and inactivation.

- **Non-Invasive:** Transmucosal administration is generally non-invasive and well-tolerated by patients, minimizing discomfort and risk of infection associated with parenteral routes of administration.

- **Convenient and Patient-Friendly:** Transmucosal dosage forms are often convenient and easy to use, allowing for self-administration by patients without the need for healthcare professionals or specialized equipment.

## Disadvantages of Transmucosal Route of Drug Administration:

- **Limited Drug Permeability:** Mucosal barriers may limit drug permeability and absorption, leading to variable drug bioavailability and efficacy for certain medications.

- **Local Irritation or Sensitivity:** Some drug formulations may cause local irritation or sensitivity at the site of administration, leading to mucosal inflammation, discomfort, or adverse reactions.

- **Drug Taste or Odor:** Transmucosal dosage forms may have an unpleasant taste or odor, affecting patient acceptability and compliance with treatment regimens.

- **Limited Drug Compatibility:** Not all drugs are suitable for transmucosal administration due to their physicochemical properties, stability, or potential for mucosal irritation or sensitization.

## Conclusion:

- Transmucosal drug delivery offers several advantages, including rapid absorption, avoidance of gastric degradation, non-invasiveness, and patient-friendly administration.

- However, it may be limited by mucosal barriers, local irritation, taste or odor issues, and drug compatibility considerations.
- Clinicians should carefully evaluate the benefits and drawbacks of transmucosal administration when selecting the most appropriate route of drug delivery for individual patients and medications.

## 58. Write a note on structure of cell membrane structure? Method of Transfer of drugs across membrane?

### Structure of Cell Membrane:

- The cell membrane, also known as the plasma membrane, is a vital component of all cells, serving as a selectively permeable barrier that separates the cell's interior from its external environment.
- The structure of the cell membrane is crucial for regulating the movement of substances into and out of the cell.

### The primary components of the cell membrane include:

- **Phospholipid Bilayer:** The basic structural framework of the cell membrane consists of a double layer of phospholipid molecules arranged with their hydrophobic tails facing inward and hydrophilic heads facing outward towards the aqueous environments inside and outside the cell.
- This phospholipid bilayer provides the membrane with its fluidity and flexibility.

- **Proteins:** Integral proteins are embedded within the phospholipid bilayer and span the entire membrane, contributing to its structural integrity and facilitating various cellular functions. Peripheral proteins are located on either side of the membrane and interact with the surface of the phospholipid bilayer or with integral proteins. Proteins play key roles in cell signaling, transport of molecules across the membrane, and cell adhesion.

- **Cholesterol:** Cholesterol molecules are interspersed within the phospholipid bilayer, providing stability and regulating the fluidity of the membrane.
- Cholesterol helps prevent the membrane from becoming too rigid or too fluid, thereby maintaining its integrity and functionality.

- **Glycolipids and Glycoproteins:** Carbohydrate chains attached to lipids (glycolipids) and proteins (glycoproteins) extend from the outer surface of the cell membrane.
- These carbohydrate chains are involved in cell recognition, adhesion, and communication with other cells.

### Methods of Transfer of Drugs across Membrane:

- The transfer of drugs across cell membranes can occur through various mechanisms, depending on the physicochemical properties of the drug and the characteristics of the cell membrane.

### Important methods of drug transfer across membranes include:

- **Passive Diffusion:** Passive diffusion is the movement of drugs across the cell membrane from an area of higher concentration to an area of lower concentration, driven by the concentration gradient.
- Small, hydrophobic molecules, such as lipophilic drugs, can diffuse directly through the lipid bilayer without the need for transporter proteins.

- **Facilitated Diffusion:** Facilitated diffusion involves the movement of drugs across the cell membrane with the assistance of transporter proteins or channels.
- This process is driven by the concentration gradient and does not require energy expenditure.
- Carrier proteins facilitate the transport of specific molecules, while channel proteins form pores that allow for the passive movement of ions or small polar molecules.

- **Active Transport:** Active transport is the movement of drugs across the cell membrane against the concentration gradient, requiring the expenditure of energy in the form of ATP.

- This process is mediated by specific transporter proteins called pumps, which actively transport molecules or ions across the membrane, often maintaining concentration gradients crucial for cellular functions.
- **Endocytosis and Exocytosis:** Endocytosis involves the uptake of large molecules or particles into the cell by the formation of vesicles derived from the cell membrane.
- Exocytosis is the reverse process, where vesicles containing molecules or waste products are transported to the cell surface and released into the extracellular environment.
- These processes are used for the internalization and secretion of macromolecules, such as proteins or lipids.

### Conclusion:

- The structure of the cell membrane, consisting of a phospholipid bilayer embedded with proteins and cholesterol, plays a critical role in regulating the transfer of drugs across the membrane.
- Drugs can cross the membrane through passive diffusion, facilitated diffusion, active transport, or endocytosis/exocytosis, depending on their physicochemical properties and the characteristics of the cell membrane.
- Understanding these mechanisms is essential for predicting and optimizing drug transport and delivery to target cells and tissues.

### 59. What are the Factors affecting absorption of drugs?

- The absorption of drugs refers to the process by which a drug enters the bloodstream from its site of administration.
- Several factors influence the absorption of drugs, impacting the rate and extent of drug absorption.
- Understanding these factors is essential for optimizing drug therapy and predicting drug behavior.

### Following are some key factors affecting the absorption of drugs:

### Physicochemical Properties of the Drug:

- **Molecular Size and Weight:** Smaller molecules generally have higher absorption rates compared to larger molecules.

- **Lipophilicity:** Lipophilic (fat-soluble) drugs tend to penetrate cell membranes more readily and exhibit higher absorption rates compared to hydrophilic (water-soluble) drugs.
- **Ionization State:** The degree of ionization of a drug affects its ability to cross biological membranes. Unionized drugs are typically more lipid-soluble and have higher absorption rates compared to ionized drugs.

## Drug Formulation and Route of Administration:

- The formulation of a drug, including its dosage form (e.g., tablet, capsule, solution) and excipients, can influence its dissolution, solubility, and absorption characteristics.
- The route of administration (e.g., oral, parenteral, transdermal) affects the rate and extent of drug absorption.
- Each route has unique advantages and limitations in terms of absorption kinetics and bioavailability.

## Physiological Factors:

- **Gastrointestinal pH:** The pH of the gastrointestinal tract influences the ionization state and solubility of drugs, thereby affecting their absorption.
- For example, acidic drugs are better absorbed in the acidic environment of the stomach, while basic drugs are better absorbed in the alkaline environment of the small intestine.
- **Gastrointestinal Motility:** Gastric emptying rate and intestinal transit time impact the residence time of drugs in the gastrointestinal tract, affecting absorption kinetics.
- **Surface Area and Blood Flow:** Larger surface area and increased blood flow in absorption sites (e.g., small intestine) enhance drug absorption by facilitating drug dissolution and transport across membranes.

## Biological Factors:

- **Integrity of the Absorptive Surface:** The integrity and condition of the gastrointestinal mucosa or other absorption surfaces (e.g., skin, respiratory epithelium) influence drug absorption.
- Damage or disease of these tissues may impair absorption.
- **Drug Interactions:** Concurrent administration of drugs or food components may affect drug absorption through mechanisms such as altered gastric emptying, chelation, or interference with transporter proteins.

## Patient-related Factors:

- **Age:** Age-related changes in gastrointestinal physiology, such as decreased gastric acidity and decreased gastrointestinal motility, may affect drug absorption in elderly individuals.
- **Genetic Variability:** Genetic polymorphisms in drug transporters, metabolizing enzymes, or membrane receptors can impact drug absorption and disposition, leading to interindividual variability in drug response.
- **Disease States:** Gastrointestinal diseases, malabsorption syndromes, or conditions affecting blood flow (e.g., shock, circulatory disorders) can alter drug absorption kinetics and bioavailability.

## Environmental Factors:

- Environmental factors such as diet, fluid intake, smoking, and physical activity may influence drug absorption indirectly by affecting gastrointestinal motility, pH, or drug metabolism.

## Conclusion:

- Multiple factors influence the absorption of drugs, including the physicochemical properties of the drug, drug formulation and route of administration, physiological factors, biological factors, patient-related factors, and environmental factors.
- Considering these factors is essential for optimizing drug therapy and predicting drug behavior in clinical practice.

**60. What are the factors that affect the absorption from local route of drug absorption with examples?**

- Absorption from local routes of drug administration, such as transmucosal, topical, or inhalational routes, can be influenced by several factors.
- Understanding these factors is crucial for optimizing drug delivery and efficacy.

Following are some of the important factors that affect absorption from local routes:

**Physicochemical Properties of the Drug:**
- **Lipophilicity:** Lipophilic drugs penetrate cell membranes more readily and exhibit higher absorption rates.
- Example: Corticosteroids used topically for skin conditions are often formulated to be lipophilic for better skin penetration and efficacy.
- **Molecular Size:** Smaller molecules generally have higher absorption rates compared to larger molecules.
- Example: Small molecule antibiotics are commonly used in topical preparations for skin infections due to their efficient penetration into the skin layers.

**Drug Formulation and Vehicle:**
- **Formulation Design:** The formulation design, including the type of vehicle (e.g., cream, gel, ointment, solution), affects drug release, solubility, and permeation across biological barriers.
- Example: Hydrophilic drugs may be formulated as aqueous solutions for nasal administration, while lipophilic drugs may be formulated as creams or ointments for topical application to the skin.
- **Enhancers and Penetration Enhancers:** Formulation additives or penetration enhancers can improve drug absorption by enhancing drug solubility, permeability, or diffusion across biological membranes.
- Example: Surfactants or fatty acids may be added to topical formulations to enhance skin penetration of drugs.

**Biological Factors:**
- **Condition of the Absorptive Surface:** The condition of the local tissue or mucosal surface affects drug absorption.
- Healthy, intact mucosa or skin allows for efficient drug absorption, while damaged or inflamed tissues may impair drug absorption.
- Example: Inflamed nasal mucosa in allergic rhinitis may reduce drug absorption from intranasal corticosteroid sprays.
- **Blood Flow:** Adequate blood flow to the absorption site is essential for drug absorption.
- Increased blood flow enhances drug delivery and distribution to target tissues.
- Example: Vasodilation induced by heat or massage may increase skin permeability and enhance drug absorption from topical preparations.

**Drug Concentration and Dose:**
- **Drug Concentration:** Higher drug concentrations may enhance drug absorption by increasing the driving force for diffusion across biological barriers.
- However, excessively high concentrations may lead to tissue irritation or toxicity.
- Example: High-concentration topical corticosteroids are used for severe inflammatory skin conditions to achieve optimal therapeutic effects.
- **Dose Volume:** The volume of drug applied or administered affects drug distribution and absorption.
- Small volumes may facilitate drug penetration into tissues, while large volumes may lead to dilution and reduced absorption.
- Example: Intranasal sprays deliver small volumes of drug solution to the nasal mucosa for local or systemic effects.

**Physiological Factors:**
- **pH and Ionization:** The pH of the local environment influences drug ionization and solubility, thereby affecting drug absorption.
- Example: Acidic drugs may be better absorbed in acidic environments, such as the stomach for oral medications or the vaginal mucosa for intravaginal formulations.

- **Temperature:** Temperature can influence drug absorption by altering blood flow, membrane permeability, or drug dissolution rates.
- Example: Heat applied to the skin may enhance drug absorption from topical preparations by increasing skin blood flow and permeability.

## Conclusion:

- Several factors influence drug absorption from local routes of administration, including the physicochemical properties of the drug, drug formulation and vehicle, biological factors such as tissue condition and blood flow, drug concentration and dose, and physiological factors such as pH and temperature.
- Considering these factors is essential for optimizing local drug delivery and achieving desired therapeutic outcomes.

## 61. What are the factors that affect the absorption from systemic route of drug absorption with examples?

- Absorption from the systemic route of drug administration, such as oral, parenteral, or transdermal routes, can be influenced by various factors.
- These factors affect the rate and extent of drug absorption into the bloodstream, ultimately impacting drug bioavailability and therapeutic efficacy.

**Following are some important factors that affect absorption from the systemic route:**

### Physicochemical Properties of the Drug:

- **Lipophilicity:** Lipophilic drugs tend to be absorbed more readily than hydrophilic drugs. For example, diazepam, a lipophilic benzodiazepine, is well absorbed after oral administration.

- **Molecular Size:** Smaller molecules typically have higher absorption rates compared to larger molecules.
- Example: Aspirin, with its small molecular size, is rapidly absorbed after oral administration.

### Drug Formulation and Route of Administration:

- **Oral Formulation:** The formulation of oral medications (e.g., tablets, capsules, solutions) affects drug dissolution, solubility, and absorption kinetics.
- Example: Enteric-coated tablets are designed to bypass the acidic environment of the stomach, improving absorption in the small intestine.
- **Parenteral Administration:** Parenteral formulations (e.g., injections, infusions) provide direct access to the bloodstream, bypassing gastrointestinal barriers.
- Example: Insulin is administered via subcutaneous injection for rapid systemic absorption.

### Physiological Factors:

- **Gastrointestinal pH:** The pH of the gastrointestinal tract affects drug ionization and solubility, impacting absorption.
- Example: Proton pump inhibitors are best absorbed in the acidic environment of the stomach.
- **Gastrointestinal Motility:** Gastric emptying rate and intestinal transit time influence drug absorption by affecting residence time in the gastrointestinal tract.
- Example: Delayed gastric emptying prolongs absorption of some drugs.

### Biological Factors:

- **Integrity of Absorptive Surfaces:** The condition of absorptive surfaces (e.g., gastrointestinal mucosa) affects drug absorption.
- Example: Inflammation in Crohn's disease may reduce absorption of oral medications.
- **Blood Flow:** Adequate blood flow to absorption sites enhances drug absorption.
- Example: Subcutaneous injections rely on good blood flow for absorption.

### Metabolic Factors:

- **First-Pass Metabolism:** Drugs undergo metabolism in the liver before reaching systemic circulation.

- For example, oral morphine undergoes extensive first-pass metabolism, resulting in reduced bioavailability.
- **Metabolic Enzymes:** Variability in enzyme activity affects drug absorption.
- Example: Genetic polymorphisms in CYP2D6 enzyme impact the metabolism of codeine to morphine, affecting its absorption and efficacy.

### Patient-related Factors:

- **Age:** Age-related changes in gastrointestinal physiology can affect absorption.
- Example: Decreased gastric acidity in older adults may alter drug absorption.
- **Disease States:** Gastrointestinal diseases or liver dysfunction can impair absorption.
- Example: Liver cirrhosis can lead to reduced first-pass metabolism, affecting drug absorption.

### Conclusion:

- Factors influencing drug absorption from the systemic route include the physicochemical properties of the drug, drug formulation and route of administration, physiological factors, biological factors, metabolic factors, and patient-related factors.
- Understanding these factors is crucial for optimizing drug therapy and achieving desired therapeutic outcomes.

## 62. Define distribution of drugs and factors affecting distribution of drugs with examples?

- Drug distribution refers to the process by which a drug is transported throughout the body after absorption into the bloodstream.
- Once in the systemic circulation, drugs are distributed to various tissues and organs, where they exert their pharmacological effects or undergo metabolism and elimination.
- Drug distribution involves the movement of drugs across biological barriers, such as cell membranes, and their distribution within the extracellular and intracellular compartments of tissues.

- **Following are the factors that influence the drug distribution:**

### Physicochemical Properties of the Drug:

- **Lipophilicity:** Lipophilic drugs tend to distribute more readily into tissues with high lipid content, such as the brain, adipose tissue, and skin. Hydrophilic drugs, on the other hand, may have limited distribution to lipid-rich tissues.
- Example: Benzodiazepines like diazepam, which are highly lipophilic, readily penetrate the blood-brain barrier and distribute into the central nervous system, exerting their sedative effects.
- **Ionization State:** The ionization state of a drug affects its distribution due to differences in lipid solubility.
- Unionized forms of weak acids or weak bases tend to penetrate cell membranes more readily than ionized forms.
- Example: Aspirin, a weak acid, can readily cross cell membranes in its non-ionized form, allowing it to distribute widely throughout the body and exert its anti-inflammatory and analgesic effects.

### Tissue Permeability and Blood Flow:

- **Tissue Perfusion:** Blood flow to tissues plays a crucial role in drug distribution.
- Highly perfused tissues, such as the liver, kidneys, heart, and brain, receive a larger fraction of cardiac output and therefore have higher drug concentrations.
- Example: Drugs administered intravenously distribute rapidly to highly perfused tissues, leading to rapid onset of action.
- **Capillary Permeability:** Capillary permeability varies among tissues and influences drug distribution.
- Tissues with fenestrated capillaries, such as the liver and spleen, allow for more rapid drug distribution compared to tissues with tight junctions, such as the brain.
- Example: Antibiotics like penicillin distribute well into tissues with fenestrated capillaries, allowing them to effectively treat infections in these tissues.

**Plasma Protein Binding:**

- **Protein Binding:** Drugs may bind to plasma proteins, such as albumin and alpha-1-acid glycoprotein, which affects their distribution.
- Only unbound (free) drug is pharmacologically active and able to distribute into tissues.
- Drugs with high protein binding may have a reduced distribution into tissues.
- Example: Warfarin, a highly protein-bound anticoagulant, has limited distribution into tissues due to its extensive plasma protein binding.

**Tissue Binding and Accumulation:**

- **Tissue Binding:** Some drugs may bind to specific tissue components, such as receptors, enzymes, or intracellular structures, leading to drug accumulation in certain tissues.
- Example: Tetracycline antibiotics bind to calcium ions in bones and teeth, resulting in tissue accumulation and potential toxicity.
- **Tissue Retention:** Drugs may be retained within tissues for varying durations, depending on factors such as tissue blood flow, protein binding, and tissue binding.
- This can prolong the duration of drug action or lead to tissue toxicity.
- Example: Drugs like amiodarone may accumulate in adipose tissue and have a long half-life due to slow release from this tissue reservoir.

**Drug Metabolism and Elimination:**

- **Metabolism:** Metabolism of drugs, primarily in the liver, can lead to the formation of metabolites that may exhibit different distribution patterns compared to the parent drug.
- Some metabolites may be more or less potent than the parent compound and may accumulate in specific tissues.
- For example, morphine is metabolized to morphine-6-glucuronide, a highly active metabolite that may accumulate in renal tissue and contribute to renal toxicity.
- **Elimination:** Drugs and their metabolites are eliminated from the body via renal excretion, hepatic metabolism, or other routes.
- Drugs and metabolites may undergo redistribution from tissues back into the bloodstream during elimination processes.

- For example, during dialysis, drugs bound to tissue proteins may be released into the bloodstream and subsequently eliminated from the body.

**Physiological Factors:**

- **Age:** Age-related changes in tissue composition, blood flow, and organ function can influence drug distribution.
- Example: Decreased muscle mass and blood flow in elderly individuals may affect drug distribution.
- **Disease States:** Gastrointestinal diseases or liver dysfunction can impair absorption.
- Example: Liver cirrhosis can lead to reduced first-pass metabolism, affecting drug distribution.

**Conclusion:**

- Drug distribution is a complex process influenced by multiple factors, including the physicochemical properties of the drug, tissue permeability and blood flow, plasma protein binding, tissue binding and accumulation, drug metabolism and elimination, and physiological factors such as age and disease states.
- Understanding these factors is crucial for predicting drug distribution patterns, optimizing drug therapy, and minimizing the risk of adverse effects.

**63. What are the factors that affect the penetration of drug into CSF with examples?**

- The penetration of drugs into the cerebrospinal fluid (CSF) and the central nervous system (CNS) is a complex process influenced by various factors.
- CSF serves as a protective fluid surrounding the brain and spinal cord, and drugs must overcome several barriers to reach therapeutic concentrations in this compartment.

**Following are the some of the factors that affect the penetration of drugs into CSF:**

- **Lipophilicity and Molecular Size:** Lipophilic drugs with low molecular weight tend to penetrate the blood-brain barrier (BBB) more readily than hydrophilic or larger molecules.

- Example: Benzodiazepines like diazepam and lorazepam are highly lipophilic and effectively penetrate the BBB to exert their sedative effects.

- **Protein Binding:** Drugs that are highly protein-bound in plasma may have limited penetration into CSF because only unbound (free) drug can cross the BBB.
- Example: Warfarin, a highly protein-bound anticoagulant, has limited penetration into the CNS due to its extensive plasma protein binding.

- **Ionization State:** The degree of ionization of a drug affects its ability to penetrate lipid-rich membranes.
- Unionized forms of weak acids or weak bases can passively diffuse across the BBB more readily than ionized forms.
- Example: The non-ionized form of aspirin can penetrate the BBB more effectively than the ionized form.

- **Active Transport Systems:** Specific transporter systems at the BBB facilitate the transport of certain drugs into the CNS.
- Example: Some opioid analgesics, such as morphine and fentanyl, are substrates for transporters like P-glycoprotein (P-gp), which actively transports these drugs into the brain.

- **Blood-Brain Barrier Integrity:** Pathological conditions or disruptions in the BBB integrity, such as inflammation or injury, can enhance the penetration of drugs into the CNS.
- Example: In cases of meningitis or brain tumors, the compromised BBB allows for increased penetration of antibiotics or chemotherapeutic agents into the CSF.

- **CSF Flow Dynamics:** The flow dynamics of CSF can affect the distribution of drugs within the CNS.
- Example: Drugs administered intrathecally or intraventricularly bypass the BBB and directly enter the CSF, leading to higher drug concentrations in the CNS compared to systemic administration.

- **Drug Metabolism and Efflux Transporters:** Metabolism of drugs within the CNS and the presence of efflux transporters, such as P-gp and multidrug resistance-associated proteins (MRPs), can limit drug concentrations in CSF.
- Example: Antiepileptic drugs like phenytoin and carbamazepine are substrates for efflux transporters, reducing their CNS penetration.

- **Lumbar Puncture and Intrathecal Administration:** Direct administration of drugs into the CSF via lumbar puncture or intrathecal injection bypasses the BBB and allows for immediate access to the CNS.
- Example: Intrathecal administration of opioids like morphine is used for pain management in certain clinical settings.

**Conclusion:**
- The penetration of drugs into the CSF is influenced by factors such as lipophilicity, protein binding, ionization state, active transport systems, BBB integrity, CSF flow dynamics, drug metabolism, and route of administration.
- Understanding these factors is crucial for optimizing drug therapy for CNS disorders and achieving therapeutic concentrations in the CSF.

**64. What are the factors that affect the passage across placenta with examples?**
- The passage of drugs across the placenta, from the maternal circulation to the fetal circulation, is influenced by several factors.
- The placenta serves as a barrier between the maternal and fetal circulations, and drug transfer across this barrier can impact fetal development and health.

Following are the factors that affect the passage of drugs across the placenta:

**Physicochemical Properties of the Drug:**
- **Lipophilicity:** Lipophilic drugs tend to cross the placenta more readily than hydrophilic drugs.
- Example: Lipid-soluble drugs such as opioids, benzodiazepines, and certain antibiotics can easily pass through the placental membrane and reach the fetal circulation.

- **Molecular Size:** Small molecules can diffuse more easily across the placenta than larger molecules.
- Drugs with low molecular weight, such as ethanol and caffeine, can readily cross the placental barrier and reach the fetal compartment.
- **Placental Permeability:** The placental barrier consists of several layers, including the syncytiotrophoblast, fetal capillary endothelium, and connective tissue.
- Placental permeability varies depending on gestational age and specific placental regions.
- Example: During early pregnancy, the placenta is more permeable due to a thinner syncytiotrophoblast layer, allowing for increased drug transfer.
- **Placental Blood Flow:** Blood flow through the placenta influences the rate of drug transfer to the fetus. Higher maternal blood flow to the placenta facilitates greater drug delivery to the fetal circulation. For example, vasoactive drugs that alter maternal blood flow, such as angiotensin-converting enzyme (ACE) inhibitors, can affect placental perfusion and drug transfer to the fetus.
- **Protein Binding:** Drugs that are highly protein-bound in maternal plasma may have limited transfer across the placenta because only unbound (free) drug can diffuse through the placental membrane.
- Example: Drugs such as warfarin and phenytoin, which are highly protein-bound, have reduced placental transfer compared to drugs with lower protein binding.
- **Drug Metabolism and Elimination:** Some drugs undergo metabolism and elimination by placental enzymes, reducing their concentration in the fetal circulation.
- Example: Drugs like nicotine and caffeine can be metabolized by placental enzymes, leading to decreased fetal exposure.

- **Gestational Age:** The stage of pregnancy can affect placental permeability and drug transfer.
- During early pregnancy, the placenta may be more permeable due to incomplete development of the placental barrier.
- However, as pregnancy progresses, the placental barrier becomes thicker and more selective, reducing drug transfer.

- **pH Gradient:** Variations in pH between the maternal and fetal compartments can influence drug ionization and placental transfer.
- Unionized forms of weak acids or weak bases can diffuse more readily across the placenta.
- Example: Acidic drugs like salicylates and antibiotics may accumulate in the fetal compartment due to ion trapping.

- **Fetal Physiology:** Fetal metabolism and elimination mechanisms can affect the disposition of drugs in the fetal circulation.
- Example: Some drugs may be metabolized by fetal hepatic enzymes or excreted by fetal renal mechanisms, reducing fetal exposure.

**Conclusion:**
- The passage of drugs across the placenta is influenced by various factors, including the physicochemical properties of the drug, placental permeability, placental blood flow, protein binding, drug metabolism and elimination, gestational age, pH gradient, and fetal physiology.
- Understanding these factors is crucial for assessing the potential risks associated with drug exposure during pregnancy and optimizing maternal and fetal health outcomes.

**65. What is first pass metabolism? What is the clinical importance of first pass metabolism? Explain with examples?**
- First-pass metabolism refers to the biotransformation of a drug that occurs before it reaches systemic circulation, typically in the liver.
- When a drug is administered orally, it is absorbed from the gastrointestinal tract and transported to the liver via the portal vein before entering the general circulation.
- During this initial passage through the liver, some drugs undergo extensive metabolism by hepatic enzymes, leading to a significant reduction in the bioavailability of the drug that reaches systemic circulation.

- The clinical importance of first-pass metabolism lies in its potential to affect the therapeutic efficacy and pharmacokinetic profile of orally administered drugs.
- By metabolizing drugs before they enter systemic circulation, first-pass metabolism can significantly reduce the amount of active drug available to exert pharmacological effects.
- This can necessitate higher oral doses of drugs to achieve therapeutic concentrations in the bloodstream.

**Following are the examples of drugs that undergo significant first-pass metabolism:**

- **Propranolol:** Propranolol, a beta-blocker used to treat hypertension and other cardiovascular conditions, undergoes extensive first-pass metabolism in the liver, resulting in low oral bioavailability (approximately 25-30%).
- As a result, higher oral doses are often required to achieve therapeutic effects.

- **Morphine:** Morphine, a potent opioid analgesic, undergoes substantial first-pass metabolism in the liver, primarily via glucuronidation, resulting in low oral bioavailability (approximately 25-30%).
- To bypass first-pass metabolism, alternative routes of administration, such as intravenous or transdermal, may be preferred for more predictable drug absorption and efficacy.

- **Nitroglycerin:** Nitroglycerin, a vasodilator used to treat angina pectoris, undergoes rapid metabolism by hepatic enzymes, leading to low oral bioavailability.
- To avoid first-pass metabolism and achieve rapid onset of action, nitroglycerin is often administered sublingually or via transdermal patches.

- **Lidocaine:** Lidocaine, a local anesthetic, undergoes extensive first-pass metabolism in the liver, resulting in low oral bioavailability.
- For this reason, lidocaine is primarily administered via topical application or parenteral routes (e.g., intravenous, intramuscular) for local or regional anesthesia.

**Conclusion:**
- First-pass metabolism plays a crucial role in determining the bioavailability and pharmacokinetic profile of orally administered drugs.
- Understanding the extent of first-pass metabolism for specific drugs is essential for optimizing drug dosing regimens and ensuring therapeutic efficacy in clinical practice.

## 66. What is the clinical importance of plasma protein binding. Explain with examples?

- Plasma protein binding refers to the reversible binding of drugs to proteins present in the bloodstream, primarily albumin and alpha-1-acid glycoprotein.
- Only unbound (free) drug molecules are pharmacologically active and able to distribute into tissues and exert therapeutic effects.
- The clinical importance of plasma protein binding lies in its influence on drug distribution, pharmacokinetics, and pharmacodynamics.

**Following are some examples that illustrate the clinical significance of plasma protein binding:**

- **Drug Distribution and Volume of Distribution:** Plasma protein binding affects the distribution of drugs within the body.
- Drugs that are highly protein-bound have a limited distribution into tissues because only the unbound fraction can cross biological barriers such as cell membranes.
- As a result, the apparent volume of distribution (Vd) of highly protein-bound drugs is typically lower than that of drugs with lower protein binding.
- Example: Warfarin, an anticoagulant, is highly protein-bound (more than 99%) and has a relatively small Vd, leading to limited distribution into tissues.
- Diazepam, a benzodiazepine used for anxiety and seizures, is also highly protein-bound but has a larger Vd compared to warfarin due to its greater lipid solubility, allowing it to penetrate the blood-brain barrier and exert sedative effects.

- **Pharmacokinetic Properties:** Plasma protein binding influences the pharmacokinetic profile of drugs, including their distribution, metabolism, and elimination.
- Highly protein-bound drugs may exhibit altered pharmacokinetics due to competition for binding sites and displacement interactions with other drugs.
- Example: Displacement interactions can occur when one drug displaces another from plasma protein binding sites, leading to an increase in the free fraction of the displaced drug and potentially higher pharmacological effects or toxicity.
- For instance, nonsteroidal anti-inflammatory drugs (NSAIDs) like ibuprofen or naproxen may displace warfarin from protein binding sites, increasing the risk of bleeding.
- Drugs that are extensively protein-bound may exhibit prolonged half-lives and slower clearance rates due to reduced renal or hepatic elimination.
- For example, phenytoin, an antiepileptic drug, is highly protein-bound and has nonlinear pharmacokinetics, with saturation of protein binding sites leading to dose-dependent changes in clearance.

- **Drug Interactions:** Plasma protein binding interactions can occur when two or more drugs compete for binding to the same plasma proteins.
- These interactions can lead to changes in the free fraction and pharmacological effects of one or both drugs.
- Example: Concurrent administration of two highly protein-bound drugs may lead to displacement interactions and increased free fractions of both drugs, potentially enhancing their pharmacological effects or toxicity.
- Conversely, co-administration of a highly protein-bound drug with a low protein-bound drug may result in decreased free fractions of the low protein-bound drug, reducing its efficacy.
- Example: Valproic acid, a highly protein-bound antiepileptic drug, may decrease the free fraction of phenytoin, potentially reducing its antiepileptic effects.

**Conclusion:**
- Plasma protein binding plays a crucial role in determining the pharmacokinetic and pharmacodynamic properties of drugs.
- Understanding the extent and implications of plasma protein binding is essential for predicting drug distribution, evaluating drug interactions, and optimizing drug therapy in clinical practice.

## 67. What is biotransformation of drugs? Explain the importance of microsomal enzymes in biotranformation of drugs with examples?

- Biotransformation of drugs, also known as drug metabolism, refers to the chemical modification of drugs within the body to facilitate their elimination.
- Drug metabolism typically occurs in the liver, although other organs such as the kidneys, lungs, and intestines may also contribute.
- The primary purpose of biotransformation is to convert drugs into more water-soluble metabolites that can be easily excreted from the body, primarily via the kidneys or bile.
- Microsomal enzymes, particularly those found in the endoplasmic reticulum of hepatocytes, play a crucial role in drug metabolism.
- These enzymes are collectively referred to as cytochrome P450 (CYP) enzymes, and they catalyze the oxidative metabolism of a wide range of drugs and xenobiotics.

**The importance of microsomal enzymes in drug biotransformation is explained below:**
- **Phase I Metabolism:** Cytochrome P450 enzymes catalyze phase I reactions, which involve the introduction or unmasking of functional groups (e.g., hydroxyl, amino, or carboxyl groups) on the drug molecule.
- Phase I reactions typically increase the polarity of the drug, making it more amenable to conjugation reactions in phase II metabolism.
- Examples of phase I reactions include hydroxylation, oxidation, dealkylation, and deamination.
- Example: The metabolism of acetaminophen (paracetamol) involves hydroxylation by CYP

enzymes to form a reactive intermediate, which is further metabolized by phase II enzymes to produce a non-toxic, water-soluble metabolite that is readily excreted.

- **Phase II Metabolism:** Phase II metabolism involves conjugation reactions, where the drug or its phase I metabolites are conjugated with endogenous molecules such as glucuronic acid, sulfate, glutathione, or amino acids.
- Conjugation reactions further increase the water solubility of drugs and facilitate their elimination.
- Microsomal enzymes may indirectly influence phase II metabolism by generating reactive intermediates that serve as substrates for conjugation reactions.
- Example: Morphine undergoes glucuronidation by UDP-glucuronosyltransferase (UGT) enzymes to form morphine-3-glucuronide (M3G) and morphine-6-glucuronide (M6G), which are less active metabolites and readily excreted in the urine.

- **Drug-Drug Interactions:** Microsomal enzymes can be inhibited or induced by various drugs, leading to altered metabolism and potential drug-drug interactions.
- Enzyme inhibition can result in decreased metabolism and increased plasma concentrations of drugs that are substrates for the inhibited enzyme.
- Conversely, enzyme induction can lead to increased metabolism and decreased plasma concentrations of drugs that are substrates for the induced enzyme.
- Example: Rifampin, an antibiotic used to treat tuberculosis, is a potent inducer of CYP enzymes.
- Co-administration of rifampin with oral contraceptives can lead to decreased plasma concentrations of the contraceptive drugs due to enhanced metabolism by induced CYP enzymes, potentially reducing contraceptive efficacy.

## Conclusion:

- Microsomal enzymes, particularly cytochrome

- P450 enzymes, are essential for drug metabolism, facilitating the conversion of drugs into more water-soluble metabolites that can be readily eliminated from the body.
- Understanding the role of microsomal enzymes in drug metabolism is crucial for predicting drug interactions, optimizing drug therapy, and minimizing the risk of adverse effects in clinical practice.

## 68. What are routes of drug excretion? Explain with examples?

- Drug excretion refers to the removal of drugs and their metabolites from the body.
- Excretion is a vital process in drug elimination, as it helps maintain drug concentrations within therapeutic ranges and prevents accumulation of potentially toxic substances.
- Several routes of drug excretion exist, each with its mechanism and significance.

**The main routes of drug excretion include:**

- **Renal Excretion:** Renal excretion involves the elimination of drugs and metabolites via the kidneys into the urine.
- This process relies on glomerular filtration, tubular secretion, and tubular reabsorption.
- Example: Many drugs are excreted renally, either unchanged or as metabolites.
- For instance, antibiotics like penicillin and cephalosporins are primarily eliminated via renal excretion.
- Similarly, diuretics such as furosemide and thiazides enhance renal excretion of water and electrolytes.
- **Biliary Excretion:** Biliary excretion involves the elimination of drugs and metabolites into bile, which is then excreted into the gastrointestinal tract.
- From there, drugs may be eliminated in feces or undergo enterohepatic recirculation.
- Example: Some drugs, such as statins (e.g., atorvastatin) and opioids (e.g., morphine), undergo significant biliary excretion.
- In the case of statins, biliary excretion may contribute to their hepatobiliary effects, while in opioids, it may contribute to the prolongation of their effects through enterohepatic recirculation.

- **Pulmonary Excretion:** Pulmonary excretion involves the elimination of volatile drugs and gases via exhalation.
- This route is significant for drugs that are volatile or highly lipophilic and readily cross the alveolar-capillary membrane.
- Example: Anesthetic gases such as nitrous oxide and volatile anesthetics (e.g., isoflurane) are eliminated primarily via pulmonary excretion.
- Similarly, volatile solvents like ethanol can also be eliminated through exhalation.

- **Sweat and Salivary Excretion:** Sweat and salivary glands can excrete drugs and their metabolites through sweat and saliva, respectively.
- However, this route of excretion is generally minor compared to renal and biliary excretion.
- Example: Drugs like ethanol and certain heavy metals (e.g., lead, mercury) can be excreted in sweat.
- Additionally, drugs administered topically, such as transdermal patches containing fentanyl, may lead to localized drug excretion through sweat glands.

- **Mammary Excretion:** Mammary excretion involves the secretion of drugs and metabolites into breast milk during lactation.
- This route can lead to drug exposure in nursing infants and is an important consideration for breastfeeding mothers.
- Example: Many drugs can be excreted in breast milk, including antibiotics (e.g., penicillins, cephalosporins), analgesics (e.g., opioids, NSAIDs), and antihypertensives (e.g., beta-blockers, calcium channel blockers).
- It is essential for healthcare providers to assess the potential risks and benefits of drug use during breastfeeding.

## Conclusion:

- Drugs can be eliminated from the body through various routes, including renal excretion, biliary excretion, pulmonary excretion, sweat and salivary excretion, and mammary excretion.
- Understanding the mechanisms and significance of each route of excretion is essential for optimizing drug therapy and minimizing the risk of adverse effects.

## 69. How to prolong the action of the drug? Explain with examples?

- Prolongation of a drug's action can be achieved by altering its pharmacokinetics (PK) and pharmacodynamics (PD).
- Pharmacokinetics refers to what the body does to the drug, including absorption, distribution, metabolism, and excretion (ADME).
- Pharmacodynamics, on the other hand, refers to what the drug does to the body, including its effects and mechanisms of action.

**Altering Pharmacokinetics (PK):**

- **Slow-release formulations**: These formulations are designed to release the drug slowly over time, resulting in a prolonged duration of action.
- This can be achieved through various mechanisms such as matrix systems, osmotic pumps, and coated pellets.
- Example: Extended-release formulations of drugs like metformin for diabetes or morphine for pain management.
- **Prodrug conversion**: Converting a drug into its prodrug form can alter its PK parameters, such as absorption or metabolism, leading to a longer duration of action.
- Example: Lisdexamfetamine, a prodrug of dextroamphetamine, has a longer duration of action compared to immediate-release amphetamine formulations for ADHD treatment.
- **Inhibition of metabolism or elimination**: Inhibiting drug-metabolizing enzymes or renal excretion can prolong the drug's presence in the body, thereby extending its action.
- Example: Cimetidine, an H2 receptor antagonist, inhibits the metabolism of drugs like theophylline, prolonging their action.
- **Formulation with excipients**: Excipients can be used to modify drug release characteristics, such as viscosity enhancers or absorption enhancers, to prolong the drug's action.
- Example: Using hydrogels or mucoadhesive polymers in drug formulations to prolong their residence time at the site of action.
- **Encapsulation in nanoparticles**: Method: Drugs encapsulated in nanoparticles exhibit prolonged release kinetics due to controlled dissolution or degradation.

- **Example**: Paclitaxel-loaded nanoparticles for cancer therapy provide sustained drug release and prolonged antitumor effects.
- **Modification of drug delivery route**: Changing the drug delivery route alters its absorption kinetics and prolongs its action.
- **Example**: Transdermal patches for nicotine delivery provide a continuous release over several hours, aiding in smoking cessation.
- **Combination therapy with enzyme inhibitors**: Combining the drug with enzyme inhibitors inhibits its metabolism, extending its duration of action.
- **Example**: Ritonavir, an HIV protease inhibitor, used in combination therapy with other antiretroviral drugs to prolong their half-life.
- **Development of depot formulations**: Depot formulations release the drug slowly from an implanted or injectable depot, prolonging its action.
- **Example**: Depot medroxyprogesterone acetate (DMPA) injections for contraception provide contraceptive effects for several months per dose.
- **Targeted drug delivery systems**: Directing the drug to specific tissues or cells prolongs its action at the target site.
- **Example**: Antibody-drug conjugates (ADCs) deliver cytotoxic drugs selectively to tumor cells, prolonging their action while minimizing systemic toxicity.
- **Design of sustained-release implants**: Implants release the drug continuously over an extended period, maintaining therapeutic levels.
- **Example**: Subcutaneous implants of buprenorphine provide continuous opioid agonist effects for opioid dependence treatment over several months.

**Altering Pharmacodynamics (PD)**:
- **Receptor modifications**: Modifying drug receptors or their downstream signaling pathways can alter the drug's pharmacodynamic effects, potentially prolonging its action.
- Example: Long-acting beta-agonists (LABAs) like salmeterol have a longer duration of action compared to short-acting beta-agonists (SABAs) like albuterol due to their higher affinity for beta-2 adrenergic receptors and slower dissociation rate.
- **Target tissue alterations**: Changes in the target tissue's responsiveness or sensitivity to the drug can prolong its pharmacological effects.
- Example: Sensitizing insulin target tissues (e.g., muscle and adipose tissue) to insulin action can prolong the glucose-lowering effect of insulin in diabetic patients.

- **Downregulation of drug transporters or efflux pumps**: Inhibiting drug efflux pumps or enhancing drug uptake can prolong the drug's action by increasing its concentration at the target site.
- Example: P-glycoprotein inhibitors like verapamil can increase the intracellular concentration of anti-cancer drugs such as vincristine, leading to prolonged cytotoxic effects.

**Conclusion:**
- By strategically altering either pharmacokinetic or pharmacodynamic properties, drug developers can extend the duration of action of medications, improving patient compliance and therapeutic outcomes.

## 70. How to prolong the drug excretion? Explain with examples?

- Prolonging drug excretion involves delaying the elimination of a drug from the body, which can be desirable in certain situations to maintain therapeutic levels or reduce the risk of toxicity.
- However, prolonging drug excretion is less common than strategies to prolong drug action.

**Some of the approaches used to slow down drug elimination are discussed below:**

- **Altering Urinary pH:** The rate of renal excretion of drugs can be influenced by urinary pH.
- Adjusting urinary pH can affect the ionization of drugs and alter their reabsorption or excretion in the kidneys.
- Example: Acidification of urine (lowering urinary pH) can enhance the excretion of weak bases like amphetamine or methamphetamine, which are more ionized and thus more readily excreted in acidic urine.
- Conversely, alkalinization of urine (increasing urinary pH) can increase the elimination of weak acids like salicylates or barbiturates.

- **Fluid Administration:** Increasing fluid intake can increase urine output and enhance renal excretion of drugs by promoting glomerular filtration and urine flow rate.

- Example: Intravenous hydration with isotonic fluids is commonly used to increase urine output and enhance the excretion of drugs in cases of drug overdose or poisoning.

- **Urinary Alkalinization:** Alkalinization of urine can enhance the excretion of weak acids by increasing their ionization and reducing their reabsorption in the renal tubules.
- Example: Sodium bicarbonate administration is used to alkalinize urine and enhance the elimination of salicylates in cases of salicylate overdose.

- **Inhibition of Renal Tubular Transporters:** Drugs that inhibit renal tubular transporters involved in drug reabsorption can increase renal excretion of certain drugs.
- Example: Probenecid inhibits the organic anion transporter (OAT) in the renal tubules, reducing the reabsorption of penicillin and other beta-lactam antibiotics and increasing their excretion.

- **Hemodialysis or Hemoperfusion:** Hemodialysis and hemoperfusion are extracorporeal techniques used to remove drugs from the bloodstream in cases of severe drug toxicity or overdose.
- Example: Hemodialysis is effective for removing small, water-soluble molecules like ethanol, methanol, or lithium from the bloodstream, providing rapid elimination in cases of acute poisoning.

- **Chelation Therapy:** Chelation therapy involves the administration of chelating agents to enhance the excretion of heavy metals or toxic metals by forming stable complexes that are more readily excreted in the urine or bile.

- Example: Dimercaprol (BAL) and EDTA (ethylenediaminetetraacetic acid) are chelating agents used for the treatment of heavy metal poisoning, such as lead or mercury toxicity.

**Conclusion:**
- Prolonging drug excretion involves various strategies to delay the elimination of drugs from the body.
- These approaches may be employed in clinical settings to enhance the elimination of drugs in cases of overdose or toxicity or to manage drug interactions or accumulation in patients with impaired renal or hepatic function.

## 71. What is half life of a drug? what is first order kinetics? what is zero order kinetics? explain each with example?

- The half-life of a drug is a pharmacokinetic parameter that represents the time it takes for the concentration of a drug in the bloodstream (or plasma concentration) to decrease by half.
- It is a measure of the rate of elimination of the drug from the body.

**First-Order Kinetics:**
- First-order kinetics describes the elimination of most drugs from the body, where the rate of elimination is directly proportional to the concentration of the drug in the body.
- In other words, a constant fraction of the drug is eliminated per unit of time.
- Example: Let's consider a drug with a half-life of 4 hours. In first-order kinetics, after 4 hours, approximately half of the drug concentration will be eliminated, leaving half of the original concentration in the body.
- After another 4 hours (total of 8 hours), half of the remaining concentration will be eliminated, and so on. The concentration decreases exponentially over time.

**Zero-Order Kinetics:**
- Zero-order kinetics describes drug elimination when the rate of elimination is constant over time, regardless of the drug concentration in the body.
- In other words, a constant amount of the drug is eliminated per unit of time.
- Example: Ethanol metabolism follows zero-order kinetics at higher concentrations.

- Example: if a person consumes a large amount of alcohol (e.g., binge drinking), the rate of ethanol elimination remains constant, typically around 10-15 mg/dL per hour, irrespective of the blood alcohol concentration (BAC).
- This is because alcohol dehydrogenase, the enzyme responsible for ethanol metabolism, becomes saturated at higher concentrations, leading to zero-order kinetics.

**Conclusion:**
- The half-life of a drug represents the time required for the concentration of the drug in the bloodstream to decrease by half and is influenced by the drug's elimination kinetics.
- In first-order kinetics, the rate of elimination is proportional to the drug concentration, leading to an exponential decrease in concentration over time.
- In contrast, zero-order kinetics involve constant drug elimination rates, resulting in a linear decrease in concentration over time.

**72. What is half life of a drug? what are different kind of kinetics of drug? explain each with example?**
- The half-life of a drug is a pharmacokinetic parameter that describes the time it takes for the concentration of the drug in the bloodstream (or plasma concentration) to decrease by half.
- It is a fundamental measure of the rate of elimination of a drug from the body.
- Different types of drug kinetics describe how drugs are eliminated from the body, and they include first-order kinetics, zero-order kinetics, and mixed-order kinetics.

- **First-Order Kinetics:** First-order kinetics describe drug elimination when the rate of elimination is proportional to the concentration of the drug in the body.
- In other words, a constant fraction of the drug is eliminated per unit of time.
- This leads to an exponential decrease in drug concentration over time.

- Example: Let's consider a drug with a half-life of 4 hours. In first-order kinetics, after 4 hours, approximately half of the drug concentration will be eliminated, leaving half of the original concentration in the body.
- After another 4 hours (total of 8 hours), half of the remaining concentration will be eliminated, and so on.
- The concentration decreases exponentially over time.

- **Zero-Order Kinetics:** Zero-order kinetics describe drug elimination when the rate of elimination is constant over time, regardless of the drug concentration in the body.
- In other words, a constant amount of the drug is eliminated per unit of time.
- This leads to a linear decrease in drug concentration over time.
- Example: Ethanol metabolism follows zero-order kinetics at higher concentrations.
- For example, if a person consumes a large amount of alcohol (e.g., binge drinking), the rate of ethanol elimination remains constant, typically around 10-15 mg/dL per hour, irrespective of the blood alcohol concentration (BAC).
- This is because alcohol dehydrogenase, the enzyme responsible for ethanol metabolism, becomes saturated at higher concentrations, leading to zero-order kinetics.

- **Mixed-Order Kinetics:** Mixed-order kinetics describe drug elimination when the rate of elimination changes over time or with changes in drug concentration.
- Mixed-order kinetics can occur when multiple elimination pathways are involved or when saturation of elimination processes occurs.
- Example: Phenytoin, an antiepileptic drug, exhibits mixed-order kinetics at therapeutic doses.
- At low concentrations, phenytoin follows first-order kinetics, but at higher concentrations, it switches to zero-order kinetics due to saturation of the enzymes responsible for its metabolism.
- As a result, the elimination rate becomes independent of the drug concentration.

**Conclusion:**

- The half-life of a drug represents the time required for the concentration of the drug in the bloodstream to decrease by half.

- Different types of drug kinetics, including first-order kinetics, zero-order kinetics, and mixed-order kinetics, describe how drugs are eliminated from the body and influence drug dosing regimens and therapeutic outcomes.

## 73. What is loading dose? How to calculate loading dose? explain with examples?

- A loading dose is an initial higher dose of a medication that is administered to rapidly achieve therapeutic levels in the bloodstream.

- Loading doses are commonly used for drugs with a long half-life or a delayed onset of action to reach therapeutic concentrations more quickly.

- Once the loading dose is administered, subsequent maintenance doses are given to maintain the desired therapeutic levels.

- The calculation of a loading dose involves consideration of the drug's volume of distribution (Vd) and the desired plasma concentration (C) that needs to be achieved.

- The formula to calculate the loading dose is:

- Loading Dose = Desired Plasma Concentration (C) × Volume of Distribution (Vd)

- However, it's important to note that in clinical practice, loading doses are often rounded to practical and safe values, and they may be adjusted based on factors such as patient age, weight, renal function, and pharmacokinetic parameters.

- Example: Let's consider a hypothetical drug with a volume of distribution (Vd) of 40 liters and a desired plasma concentration (C) of 10 mg/L. To calculate the loading dose:

- Loading Dose = Desired Plasma Concentration (C) × Volume of Distribution (Vd)

- Loading Dose = 10 mg/L × 40 liters Loading Dose = 400 mg

- In this example, the loading dose required to achieve a plasma concentration of 10 mg/L for the hypothetical drug would be 400 mg.

- After administering the loading dose, subsequent maintenance doses would be given at regular intervals to maintain the desired therapeutic levels.

## 74. What is maintenance dose? How to calculate maintenance dose? explain with examples?

- A maintenance dose is a regular and ongoing dose of a medication administered after the loading dose to maintain therapeutic drug levels in the bloodstream.

- Maintenance doses are typically administered at regular intervals to sustain the desired therapeutic effect over time.

- The calculation of a maintenance dose involves consideration of the drug's clearance (Cl) and the desired steady-state plasma concentration (Css).

- The formula to calculate the maintenance dose is:

- Maintenance Dose = Steady-State Plasma Concentration (Css) × Clearance (Cl) × Dosage Interval

- Where: Steady-State Plasma Concentration (Css) is the target concentration of the drug in the bloodstream at steady state.

- Clearance (Cl) is the rate at which the drug is removed from the body (usually expressed in volume per unit time, such as liters per hour).

- Dosage Interval is the time between each maintenance dose administration (e.g., every 8 hours, every 24 hours).

- It's important to note that in clinical practice, maintenance doses are often rounded to practical and safe values, and they may be adjusted based on factors such as patient age, weight, renal function, and pharmacokinetic parameters.

- Example: Let's consider a hypothetical drug with
  - a clearance (Cl) of 50 liters per hour and
  - a desired steady-state plasma concentration (Css) of 10 mg/L.
  - The drug is administered every 8 hours.

- Maintenance Dose = Steady-State Plasma Concentration (Css) × Clearance (Cl) × Dosage Interval
- Maintenance Dose = 10 mg/L × 50 L/hour × 8 hours
- Maintenance Dose = 4000 mg

- In this example, the maintenance dose required to maintain a steady-state plasma concentration of 10 mg/L for the hypothetical drug would be 4000 mg administered every 8 hours.
- This maintenance dose would be administered regularly to sustain therapeutic drug levels in the bloodstream.

## 75. What is elimination of drug? How to calculate rate of elimination? Explain with an example?

- Elimination of a drug refers to the process by which the drug is removed from the body, primarily through metabolism and excretion.
- Drug elimination involves various physiological mechanisms, including hepatic metabolism, renal excretion, biliary excretion, pulmonary excretion, and others, depending on the specific drug and its properties.
- The rate of drug elimination describes how quickly a drug is removed from the body and is typically expressed as the amount of drug eliminated per unit of time.
- The rate of elimination can be calculated using pharmacokinetic principles, specifically using the concept of clearance.
- Clearance (Cl) is a pharmacokinetic parameter that represents the volume of plasma from which the drug is completely removed per unit of time.
- It is often expressed in terms of volume per unit time (e.g., liters per hour).
- The rate of elimination (E) can be calculated using the formula:
- Rate of Elimination (E) = Clearance (Cl) × Concentration of the Drug (C )

Where:
- Clearance (Cl) is the rate at which the drug is removed from the body.

- Concentration of the Drug (C) is the plasma concentration of the drug at a given time point.
- It is important to note that the rate of elimination may vary over time and may be influenced by factors such as drug metabolism, renal function, hepatic function, and drug interactions.

- Example: Let's consider a hypothetical drug with a clearance (Cl) of 50 liters per hour and a plasma concentration (C) of 20 mg/L.
- Rate of Elimination (E) = Clearance (Cl) × Concentration of the Drug (C)
- Rate of Elimination (E) = 50 L/hour × 20 mg/L
- Rate of Elimination (E) = 1000 mg/hour

- In this example, the rate of elimination of the hypothetical drug is 1000 mg per hour.
- This means that 1000 milligrams of the drug are being removed from the body every hour through various elimination pathways, such as metabolism and excretion.

## 76. What is therapeutic drug monitoring? what are the methods available for therapeutic drug monitoring? Explain with an examples?

- Therapeutic drug monitoring (TDM) is a clinical practice that involves measuring drug concentrations in a patient's bloodstream to optimize drug therapy and ensure therapeutic efficacy while minimizing the risk of adverse effects.
- TDM is particularly useful for drugs with narrow therapeutic windows, variable pharmacokinetics, or significant inter-individual variability in drug response.
- By monitoring drug concentrations over time, healthcare providers can adjust dosage regimens to maintain drug levels within the therapeutic range for each individual patient.

- Several methods are available for therapeutic drug monitoring, each with its advantages, limitations, and applicability to different drugs.

Some common methods include:

- **Immunoassays:** Immunoassays are biochemical tests that use antibodies to detect and quantify the concentration of a drug in biological samples, such as blood or urine.
- Immunoassays are widely used for TDM due to their simplicity, rapidity, and cost-effectiveness.
- Example: Enzyme-linked immunosorbent assays (ELISA) are commonly used immunoassays for TDM.
- For instance, ELISA kits are available for monitoring serum concentrations of drugs like digoxin, cyclosporine, and therapeutic monoclonal antibodies.
- **Chromatographic Techniques:** Chromatographic techniques, such as high-performance liquid chromatography (HPLC) and gas chromatography (GC), separate and quantify drug compounds based on their physical and chemical properties.
- Chromatography offers high sensitivity, specificity, and accuracy, making it suitable for TDM of various drugs.
- Example: HPLC is widely used for TDM of drugs like anticonvulsants (e.g., phenytoin, carbamazepine), antibiotics (e.g., vancomycin, aminoglycosides), and immunosuppressants (e.g., tacrolimus, sirolimus).
- **Mass Spectrometry (MS):** Mass spectrometry is a highly sensitive and specific analytical technique used to identify and quantify drugs and their metabolites based on their mass-to-charge ratio.
- Mass spectrometry offers excellent selectivity and can detect multiple analytes simultaneously. Example: Liquid chromatography-tandem mass spectrometry (LC-MS/MS) is commonly used for TDM of drugs like antiretrovirals (e.g., protease inhibitors, integrase inhibitors), antidepressants (e.g., selective serotonin reuptake inhibitors), and antipsychotics (e.g., clozapine).
- **Therapeutic Drug Monitoring Programs:** Some drugs have established therapeutic drug monitoring programs that provide guidelines and recommendations for monitoring drug concentrations, interpreting results, and adjusting dosage regimens based on patient-specific factors.
- Example: Warfarin, an oral anticoagulant, has well-established therapeutic drug monitoring programs that recommend regular monitoring of international normalized ratio (INR) to optimize anticoagulant therapy and reduce the risk of bleeding or thrombosis.

**Conclusion:**

- Therapeutic drug monitoring plays a crucial role in optimizing drug therapy and ensuring therapeutic efficacy while minimizing the risk of adverse effects.
- Various methods, including immunoassays, chromatographic techniques, mass spectrometry, and therapeutic drug monitoring programs, are available for monitoring drug concentrations in clinical practice, allowing healthcare providers to personalize treatment regimens for individual patients.

**77. What is good clinical practice? Explain the 13 principles of good clinical practice with examples?**

- Good Clinical Practice (GCP) is a set of internationally recognized ethical and scientific quality standards that govern the design, conduct, recording, and reporting of clinical trials involving human subjects. These standards ensure that the rights, safety, and well-being of trial participants are protected and that the data generated from clinical trials are reliable and credible.

**The 13 principles of Good Clinical Practice, as outlined by the International Council for Harmonisation of Technical Requirements for Pharmaceuticals for Human Use (ICH), include:**

- **Ethical Conduct**: Clinical trials should be conducted in accordance with ethical principles that prioritize the rights, safety, and well-being of human subjects.
- Example: Researchers must obtain informed consent from participants before enrolling them in a clinical trial, providing comprehensive information about the study's purpose, procedures, potential risks and benefits, and participants' rights.

- **Scientifically Sound Design**: Clinical trials should be designed scientifically soundly, with clear objectives, methodologies, and data analysis plans.
- Example: A clinical trial testing the efficacy of a new drug should be designed using appropriate study designs, such as randomized controlled trials, and include suitable control groups for comparison.
- **Compliance with Regulatory Requirements**: Clinical trials should be conducted in compliance with applicable regulatory requirements and standards.
- Example: Researchers must adhere to regulations set forth by government agencies such as the Food and Drug Administration (FDA) in the United States or the European Medicines Agency (EMA) in the European Union.
- **Protocol Compliance**: Clinical trials should be conducted in compliance with the protocol agreed upon by the investigator, sponsor, and regulatory authorities.
- Example: Investigators must strictly adhere to the study protocol regarding participant eligibility criteria, treatment interventions, and data collection procedures.
- **Informed Consent**: Participants should provide informed consent voluntarily and based on a clear understanding of the study's purpose, procedures, risks, and benefits.
- Example: Participants must sign an informed consent form after receiving detailed information about the clinical trial and having the opportunity to ask questions.
- **Data Quality and Integrity**: Data collected during clinical trials should be accurate, reliable, and verifiable.
- Example: Researchers should use standardized data collection methods and ensure that data are recorded promptly and accurately on case report forms (CRFs).
- **Confidentiality Protection**: Participant confidentiality should be protected through secure data handling and storage practices.
- Example: Personal information collected from participants should be de-identified and stored securely to prevent unauthorized access.
- **Safety Monitoring and Reporting**: Adverse events and safety concerns should be monitored throughout the trial, and appropriate measures should be taken to ensure participant safety.

- Example: Researchers should promptly report any adverse events or serious adverse events (SAEs) to regulatory authorities and ethics committees and take necessary actions to mitigate risks to participants.
- **Investigator Responsibilities**: Investigators should have the qualifications, training, and resources necessary to conduct the clinical trial properly.
- Example: Investigators should undergo training in GCP principles and have access to adequate facilities and personnel to conduct the trial.
- **Record Keeping**: Comprehensive and accurate records should be maintained for all aspects of the clinical trial.
- Example: Records should include documentation of protocol amendments, informed consent forms, participant eligibility criteria, and adverse event reports.
- **Drug Accountability**: Investigational drugs should be used, handled, and stored in accordance with applicable regulations and sponsor instructions.
- Example: Investigators should maintain accurate records of drug receipt, dispensing, and return, and ensure that investigational drugs are stored securely and administered correctly.
- **Monitoring and Audit**: Clinical trials should be monitored regularly to ensure compliance with GCP standards and regulatory requirements.
- Example: Independent monitors may conduct site visits to review study documents, data, and procedures, while regulatory authorities may conduct audits to assess overall trial compliance.
- **Clinical Study Report**: A final clinical study report should be prepared that accurately summarizes the trial's results and conclusions.
- Example: The clinical study report should include detailed descriptions of the study design, participant characteristics, treatment interventions, efficacy and safety outcomes, statistical analyses, and interpretations of the findings.

**Conclusion:**
- By adhering to these 13 principles of Good Clinical Practice, researchers and sponsors can ensure the ethical conduct, scientific integrity, and regulatory compliance of clinical trials, thereby protecting participant rights and producing reliable data to advance medical knowledge and patient care.

## 78. Explain the principles of drugs action? explain with examples?

- The principles of drug action refer to the mechanisms by which drugs exert their effects on the body.
- Drugs can interact with specific molecular targets within the body, leading to physiological responses that produce therapeutic effects or adverse reactions.
- Understanding the principles of drug action is essential for rational drug design, optimization of therapy, and management of drug-related complications.

**Following are some key principles of drug action, along with examples:**

**Receptor Binding:**
- Many drugs exert their effects by binding to specific receptors on cell surfaces or within cells.
- Receptor binding can activate or inhibit cellular signaling pathways, leading to physiological responses.
- **Example:** Beta-blockers such as propranolol bind to beta-adrenergic receptors on cardiac muscle cells, blocking the action of adrenaline and reducing heart rate and blood pressure in patients with hypertension or cardiac arrhythmias.

**Enzyme Inhibition:**
- Some drugs act by inhibiting specific enzymes involved in biochemical pathways, thereby modulating physiological processes.
- **Example:** Statins such as atorvastatin inhibit the enzyme HMG-CoA reductase, which is involved in cholesterol synthesis.
- By inhibiting this enzyme, statins reduce cholesterol production in the liver, leading to decreased levels of LDL cholesterol and reduced risk of cardiovascular events.

**Ion Channel Modulation:**
- Drugs can interact with ion channels in cell membranes, altering the flow of ions across the membrane and affecting cellular excitability and function.
- **Example:** Calcium channel blockers like verapamil block calcium channels in cardiac and smooth muscle cells, leading to vasodilation and decreased cardiac contractility, which is beneficial in the treatment of hypertension and angina.

**Transporter Modulation:**
- Certain drugs act by modulating the activity of membrane transporters responsible for the uptake or efflux of specific substances across cell membranes.
- **Example:** Selective serotonin reuptake inhibitors (SSRIs) such as fluoxetine block the serotonin transporter (SERT), thereby increasing extracellular levels of serotonin in the brain.
- This increase in serotonin levels contributes to the antidepressant effects of SSRIs.

**Altered Gene Expression:**
- Some drugs exert their effects by modulating gene expression, either by activating or inhibiting specific transcription factors or signaling pathways.
- **Example:** Glucocorticoids such as prednisone bind to cytoplasmic glucocorticoid receptors, which then translocate to the nucleus and modulate gene expression by interacting with specific DNA sequences.
- This results in anti-inflammatory and immunosuppressive effects, which are beneficial in the treatment of inflammatory conditions.

**Physical Interactions:**
- Some drugs exert their effects through physical interactions rather than binding to specific receptors or enzymes.
- **Example:** Osmotic agents like mannitol increase osmotic pressure in the renal tubules, leading to increased urine output and reduced intracranial pressure in patients with cerebral edema.

**Conclusion:**
- Drugs exert their effects through various mechanisms, including receptor binding, enzyme inhibition, ion channel modulation, transporter modulation, altered gene expression, and physical interactions.
- Understanding these principles of drug action is crucial for optimizing drug therapy and managing drug-related complications in clinical practice.

## 79. Explain different mechanism of actions of drugs with examples?

- Drugs can act through various mechanisms to produce their effects on the body.

Following are the common mechanisms of drug action along with examples:

## Receptor Agonism:

- Drugs can bind to specific receptors on cell surfaces and activate them, mimicking the action of endogenous ligands and producing a physiological response.
- **Example:** Morphine binds to opioid receptors in the central nervous system, activating them and producing analgesia (pain relief) by inhibiting neurotransmitter release.

## Receptor Antagonism:

- Drugs can bind to specific receptors and block their activation by endogenous ligands, preventing the physiological response.
- **Example:** Propranolol binds to beta-adrenergic receptors in the heart and blocks the action of adrenaline, resulting in decreased heart rate and blood pressure.

## Enzyme Inhibition:

- Drugs can inhibit specific enzymes involved in biochemical pathways, altering cellular function.
- **Example:** Acetylcholinesterase inhibitors like donepezil inhibit the enzyme acetylcholinesterase, increasing the concentration of acetylcholine at synapses and improving cognitive function in patients with Alzheimer's disease.

## Ion Channel Modulation:

- Drugs can interact with ion channels in cell membranes, altering the flow of ions and affecting cellular excitability.
- **Example:** Calcium channel blockers such as verapamil block calcium channels in cardiac muscle cells, leading to vasodilation and decreased cardiac contractility, which is beneficial in the treatment of hypertension and angina.

## Transporter Modulation:

- Drugs can modulate the activity of membrane transporters responsible for the uptake or efflux of specific substances across cell membranes.
- **Example:** Selective serotonin reuptake inhibitors (SSRIs) like fluoxetine block the serotonin transporter (SERT), leading to increased extracellular levels of serotonin in the brain and relieving symptoms of depression.

## Altered Gene Expression:

- Drugs can modulate gene expression by activating or inhibiting specific transcription factors or signaling pathways.
- **Example:** Glucocorticoids such as prednisone bind to cytoplasmic glucocorticoid receptors, which then translocate to the nucleus and modulate gene expression, resulting in anti-inflammatory and immunosuppressive effects.

## Physical Interactions:

- Some drugs exert their effects through physical interactions rather than binding to specific receptors or enzymes.
- **Example:** Osmotic diuretics like mannitol increase osmotic pressure in the renal tubules, leading to increased urine output and reduced intracranial pressure in patients with cerebral edema.
- These are just a few examples of the diverse mechanisms by which drugs can act in the body to produce their therapeutic effects.
- Understanding these mechanisms is essential for rational drug design, optimization of therapy, and management of drug-related complications in clinical practice.

## 80. What are receptors? Explain different types of receptors with examples?

- Receptors are specialized proteins located on the surface of cells or within cells that bind to specific molecules (ligands) and initiate cellular responses.
- Receptors play a crucial role in mediating the effects of neurotransmitters, hormones, drugs, and other signaling molecules in the body.
- There are several types of receptors, categorized based on their structure, mechanism of action, and location.

Following are the some common types of receptors, along with examples:

### Ion Channel Receptors (Ligand-Gated Ion Channels):

- Ion channel receptors are integral membrane proteins that form ion channels across cell membranes.
- Binding of a ligand to the receptor causes conformational changes that open or close the ion channel, allowing ions to flow across the membrane.
- **Example:** Nicotinic acetylcholine receptors in the neuromuscular junction open in response to acetylcholine binding, allowing the influx of sodium ions and depolarizing the muscle cell membrane, leading to muscle contraction.

### G Protein-Coupled Receptors (GPCRs):

- GPCRs are a large family of cell surface receptors that interact with heterotrimeric G proteins.
- Ligand binding to GPCRs induces conformational changes that activate intracellular signaling pathways mediated by G proteins.
- **Example:** Beta-adrenergic receptors bind to adrenaline (epinephrine) and activate G proteins, leading to the stimulation of adenylyl cyclase and the production of cyclic AMP (cAMP), which mediates various physiological responses such as increased heart rate and bronchodilation.

### Enzyme-Linked Receptors:

Enzyme-linked receptors are cell surface receptors that possess enzymatic activity or are associated with intracellular enzymes.

- Ligand binding to these receptors activates the enzymatic domain, leading to intracellular signaling.
- **Example:** Insulin receptors are tyrosine kinase receptors that autophosphorylate upon insulin binding.
- Phosphorylation of intracellular substrates mediates various metabolic responses, including glucose uptake and glycogen synthesis.

### Nuclear Receptors:

- Nuclear receptors are intracellular receptors that regulate gene expression in response to ligand binding.
- Ligand-bound nuclear receptors act as transcription factors that bind to specific DNA sequences and modulate gene transcription.
- **Example:** The glucocorticoid receptor is a nuclear receptor that binds cortisol. Upon ligand binding, the glucocorticoid receptor translocates to the nucleus, where it regulates the expression of genes involved in metabolism, inflammation, and stress response.

### Tyrosine Kinase Receptors:

- Tyrosine kinase receptors are cell surface receptors with intrinsic kinase activity.
- Ligand binding to these receptors activates their kinase domain, leading to autophosphorylation and activation of downstream signaling pathways.
- **Example:** Epidermal growth factor receptor (EGFR) binds to epidermal growth factor (EGF) and activates intracellular tyrosine kinase activity.
- Activation of EGFR signaling pathways regulates cell proliferation, survival, and differentiation.

### Conclusion:

- These are some of the major types of receptors found in the body, each with specific roles in mediating cellular responses to various signaling molecules.
- Understanding receptor function and signaling pathways is crucial for drug development and therapeutic interventions targeting specific receptors.

## 81. What is an agonist? Explain with examples?

- An agonist is a type of ligand that binds to a receptor and activates it, thereby producing a physiological response.
- Agonists mimic the action of endogenous ligands by binding to the receptor and initiating the same downstream signaling pathways.
- The magnitude of the response elicited by an agonist depends on factors such as the affinity of the agonist for the receptor and the efficacy of the agonist in activating the receptor.

Examples of agonists include:

### Drug Agonists:

- Morphine is an opioid agonist that binds to opioid receptors in the central nervous system, producing analgesia and other effects similar to endogenous opioids.
- Albuterol is a beta-2 adrenergic agonist used as a bronchodilator in the treatment of asthma. It binds to beta-2 adrenergic receptors in the airway smooth muscle, leading to relaxation and bronchodilation.

### Endogenous Agonists:

- Acetylcholine is an endogenous neurotransmitter that acts as an agonist at muscarinic and nicotinic acetylcholine receptors. It mediates various physiological responses, including muscle contraction, heart rate modulation, and neurotransmission.
- Epinephrine (adrenaline) is a hormone released by the adrenal glands in response to stress. It acts as an agonist at alpha and beta-adrenergic receptors, producing effects such as vasoconstriction, increased heart rate, and bronchodilation.

### Partial Agonists:

- Partial agonists bind to a receptor and activate it but produce a submaximal response compared to full agonists. They have lower intrinsic efficacy.
- Buprenorphine is a partial agonist at opioid receptors used in the treatment of opioid dependence and pain management. It produces less respiratory depression and euphoria compared to full opioid agonists like morphine.

Conclusion:

- Agonists are ligands that bind to receptors and activate them, resulting in a physiological response.
- They can be exogenous drugs or endogenous molecules and play important roles in modulating cellular signaling pathways and physiological functions.

## 82. What is antagonist? explain with examples?

- An antagonist is a type of ligand that binds to a receptor but does not activate it.
- In addition, antagonists block the activation of the receptor by endogenous agonists or other ligands, thereby inhibiting or reducing the physiological response mediated by the receptor.
- Antagonists compete with agonists for binding to the receptor but do not produce a response themselves.

Examples of antagonists include:

### Competitive Antagonists:

- Competitive antagonists bind to the same site on the receptor as the agonist and compete with the agonist for binding. They do not activate the receptor but prevent the agonist from binding and eliciting a response.
- **Example:** Propranolol is a competitive antagonist at beta-adrenergic receptors. It competes with adrenaline (epinephrine) for binding to beta-adrenergic receptors, blocking their activation and reducing heart rate and blood pressure.

### Noncompetitive Antagonists:

- Noncompetitive antagonists bind to a site on the receptor distinct from the agonist-binding site.
- Their binding to the receptor induces conformational changes that inhibit the activation of the receptor by the agonist.

- Example: Phenoxybenzamine is a noncompetitive antagonist at alpha-adrenergic receptors. It irreversibly binds to the receptors, blocking their activation by endogenous catecholamines and producing vasodilation.

### Inverse Agonists:
- Inverse agonists bind to the same site as the agonist but induce an opposite response compared to the agonist. They stabilize the inactive conformation of the receptor and reduce its basal activity.
- **Example:** Rimonabant is an inverse agonist at cannabinoid CB1 receptors. It binds to CB1 receptors and reduces their basal activity, leading to appetite suppression and weight loss.

### Partial Agonists/Antagonists (Mixed Agonist/ Antagonists):
- Partial agonists/antagonists bind to the receptor and can produce either agonistic or antagonistic effects, depending on the presence of endogenous agonists.
- **Example:** Naloxone is a partial agonist/ antagonist at opioid receptors. It acts as a competitive antagonist at mu-opioid receptors, reversing the effects of opioid agonists such as morphine and providing rapid reversal of opioid overdose.

### Conclusion:
- Antagonists are ligands that bind to receptors without activating them, thereby inhibiting the activation of the receptor by endogenous agonists or other ligands.
- They play important roles in pharmacotherapy by modulating cellular signaling pathways and physiological responses.

### 83. Explain the transducer mechanisms involved in drugs action with examples?
- In pharmacology, transducer mechanisms refer to the processes by which the interaction of a drug with its molecular target (receptor) leads to a cellular response.
- These mechanisms involve the conversion of the initial drug-receptor interaction into a series of intracellular events that ultimately produce the observed physiological or pharmacological effect.

Following are the some common transducer mechanisms involved in drug action, along with examples:

### Second Messenger Systems:
- Many drugs act through second messenger systems, where the initial drug-receptor interaction leads to the activation or inhibition of intracellular signaling pathways mediated by second messengers such as cyclic AMP (cAMP), cyclic GMP (cGMP), or calcium ions (Ca2+).
- **Example:** Beta-adrenergic receptors, upon activation by adrenaline (epinephrine), stimulate adenylyl cyclase to produce cAMP, which activates protein kinase A (PKA) and phosphorylates target proteins, leading to various physiological responses such as increased heart rate and bronchodilation.

### Ion Channel Modulation:
- Some drugs act by modulating ion channels in cell membranes, altering the flow of ions across the membrane and affecting cellular excitability and function.
- **Example:** Sodium channel blockers such as lidocaine bind to voltage-gated sodium channels in neurons, blocking the influx of sodium ions and inhibiting action potential propagation, thereby producing local anesthesia.

### Enzyme Activation or Inhibition:
- Drugs can modulate the activity of intracellular enzymes, either by activating or inhibiting them, leading to alterations in biochemical pathways and cellular function.
- **Example:** Acetylcholinesterase inhibitors like neostigmine inhibit the enzyme acetylcholinesterase, which hydrolyzes the neurotransmitter acetylcholine.

- By inhibiting acetylcholinesterase, neostigmine increases the concentration of acetylcholine at synapses, leading to enhanced cholinergic neurotransmission.

**Gene Expression Regulation:**

- Some drugs act by modulating gene expression, either by activating or inhibiting specific transcription factors or signaling pathways, leading to changes in protein synthesis and cellular responses.
- **Example:** Glucocorticoids such as prednisone bind to cytoplasmic glucocorticoid receptors, which then translocate to the nucleus and regulate gene transcription. Activation of glucocorticoid receptors leads to the expression of anti-inflammatory proteins and suppression of immune responses.

**Protein-Protein Interactions:**

- Drugs can interact with intracellular proteins, either by binding to them directly or by modulating protein-protein interactions, leading to alterations in protein function and cellular responses.
- **Example:** Kinase inhibitors such as imatinib bind to the active site of tyrosine kinases involved in cancer cell signaling pathways, blocking their activity and inhibiting cell proliferation and survival.

**Conclusion:**

- These transducer mechanisms represent various ways in which drugs can elicit cellular responses upon binding to their molecular targets, ultimately producing the observed pharmacological effects.
- Understanding these mechanisms is crucial for rational drug design and optimization of therapeutic interventions.

## 84. Explain G protein coupled receptors with examples?

- G protein-coupled receptors (GPCRs), also known as seven-transmembrane domain receptors or serpentine receptors, are a large family of cell surface receptors that play crucial roles in mediating cellular responses to a wide variety of extracellular signals, including hormones, neurotransmitters, and sensory stimuli.
- GPCRs are involved in regulating diverse physiological processes such as neurotransmission, hormone signaling, sensory perception, and immune responses.

Following is an explanation of GPCRs along with examples:

**Structure and Function:**

- GPCRs are characterized by their structure, which consists of seven transmembrane alpha helices connected by intra- and extracellular loops. The N-terminus of the receptor is located extracellularly, while the C-terminus is located intracellularly.
- Upon ligand binding to the extracellular domain of the receptor, conformational changes are induced, leading to the activation of intracellular signaling pathways mediated by G proteins.

**G Protein Signaling:**

- G proteins are heterotrimeric proteins composed of three subunits: alpha ($\alpha$), beta ($\beta$), and gamma ($\gamma$). In the inactive state, the $\alpha$ subunit is bound to GDP (guanosine diphosphate). Upon activation by ligand-bound GPCRs, the GDP is exchanged for GTP (guanosine triphosphate), leading to dissociation of the $\alpha$ subunit from the $\beta\gamma$ dimer.
- Both the $\alpha$ subunit and the $\beta\gamma$ dimer can interact with and regulate downstream effector proteins, such as adenylyl cyclase, phospholipase C (PLC), and ion channels, leading to the generation of intracellular second messengers and modulation of cellular responses.

**Examples of GPCRs:**

- Beta-Adrenergic Receptors: Beta-adrenergic receptors are activated by adrenaline (epinephrine) and noradrenaline (norepinephrine). They are involved in mediating the fight-or-flight response and regulate processes such as heart rate, smooth muscle relaxation, and glycogenolysis. Examples include $\beta1$-adrenergic receptors in the heart and $\beta2$-adrenergic receptors in bronchial smooth muscle.

**Muscarinic Acetylcholine Receptors:**

- Muscarinic acetylcholine receptors are activated by the neurotransmitter acetylcholine. They are found in various tissues, including smooth muscle, cardiac muscle, and glands, and mediate parasympathetic nervous system responses. Examples include M1, M2, and M3 subtypes of muscarinic receptors.

**Dopamine Receptors:**

- Dopamine receptors are activated by the neurotransmitter dopamine and play roles in regulating mood, reward, and movement. They are implicated in various neurological and psychiatric disorders, including schizophrenia and Parkinson's disease. Examples include D1-like receptors (D1 and D5) and D2-like receptors (D2, D3, and D4).

**Opioid Receptors:**

- Opioid receptors are activated by endogenous opioid peptides such as enkephalins, endorphins, and dynorphins, as well as exogenous opioid drugs such as morphine and fentanyl. They mediate analgesia, euphoria, and other effects of opioids. Examples include mu ($\mu$), delta ($\delta$), and kappa ($\kappa$) opioid receptors.
- These examples illustrate the diverse roles of GPCRs in mediating cellular responses to extracellular signals and highlight their importance as targets for drug development in various therapeutic areas.

**85. Explain ion channel receptors with examples?**

- Ion channel receptors, also known as ligand-gated ion channels, are membrane proteins that form channels in the cell membrane, allowing the passage of ions in response to the binding of specific ligands.
- These receptors play critical roles in mediating fast synaptic transmission in the nervous system and in regulating electrical excitability in various cell types.

Following is an explanation of ion channel receptors along with examples:

**Structure and Function:**

- Ion channel receptors typically consist of multiple subunits arranged around a central pore through which ions can pass. The binding of a specific ligand to the extracellular domain of the receptor induces conformational changes that open or close the ion channel, allowing ions to flow across the cell membrane.
- The movement of ions through ion channel receptors can lead to changes in membrane potential, electrical excitability, and synaptic transmission.

**Examples of Ion Channel Receptors:**

**Nicotinic Acetylcholine Receptors (nAChRs):**

- Nicotinic acetylcholine receptors are ion channel receptors activated by the neurotransmitter acetylcholine. They are found at neuromuscular junctions and in the central and peripheral nervous systems. Activation of nAChRs leads to the influx of sodium ions (Na+) and efflux of potassium ions (K+), resulting in depolarization of the cell membrane and muscle contraction or synaptic transmission.

**GABA-A Receptors:**

- Gamma-aminobutyric acid (GABA) receptors are ion channel receptors activated by the neurotransmitter GABA. GABA-A receptors are chloride ion (Cl-) channels that mediate inhibitory neurotransmission in the central nervous system. Binding of GABA to GABA-A receptors leads to the influx of chloride ions, hyperpolarizing the cell membrane and inhibiting neuronal excitability.

**NMDA Receptors:**

- N-methyl-D-aspartate (NMDA) receptors are ion channel receptors activated by the neurotransmitter glutamate. They are permeable to calcium ions (Ca2+), sodium ions (Na+), and potassium ions (K+). NMDA receptors play critical roles in synaptic plasticity, learning, and memory. Activation of NMDA receptors requires both glutamate binding and depolarization of the cell membrane, making them important for synaptic integration and long-term potentiation.

**Voltage-Gated Ion Channels:**

- While not strictly ligand-gated, voltage-gated ion channels are membrane proteins that open or close in response to changes in membrane potential.
- They play essential roles in generating action potentials and electrical signaling in excitable cells such as neurons and muscle cells.
- **Examples** include voltage-gated sodium channels, voltage-gated potassium channels, and voltage-gated calcium channels.

**Conclusion:**

- These examples illustrate the diverse roles of ion channel receptors in mediating cellular responses to neurotransmitters and other signaling molecules, as well as in regulating electrical excitability and synaptic transmission in the nervous system.
- Dysfunction of ion channel receptors can lead to neurological disorders, making them important targets for drug development and therapeutic intervention.

## 86. Explain transmembrane linked enzyme receptors with examples?

- Transmembrane-linked enzyme receptors are cell surface receptors that possess enzymatic activity in their cytoplasmic domains.
- These receptors typically consist of an extracellular ligand-binding domain, a single transmembrane domain, and an intracellular domain with enzymatic activity.
- Upon ligand binding, these receptors undergo conformational changes that activate their enzymatic domains, leading to the initiation of intracellular signaling pathways.
- 

**Following is an explanation of transmembrane-linked enzyme receptors along with examples:**

**Structure and Function:**

- Transmembrane-linked enzyme receptors are integral membrane proteins that span the cell membrane.
- The extracellular domain of the receptor binds to specific ligands, such as growth factors or hormones, while the intracellular domain possesses enzymatic activity.
- Ligand binding induces dimerization or oligomerization of the receptor, bringing the cytoplasmic domains into close proximity and activating their enzymatic functions. The enzymatic activity of these receptors typically involves phosphorylation or dephosphorylation of target proteins, leading to the activation of intracellular signaling cascades.

**Examples of Transmembrane-linked Enzyme Receptors:**

**Receptor Tyrosine Kinases (RTKs):**

- Receptor tyrosine kinases are transmembrane receptors with intrinsic tyrosine kinase activity in their cytoplasmic domains. Ligand binding to the extracellular domain of RTKs induces receptor dimerization and autophosphorylation of tyrosine residues in the cytoplasmic domain. Phosphorylated tyrosine residues then serve as docking sites for intracellular signaling proteins, initiating signaling cascades involved in cell growth, differentiation, and survival.
- **Examples** of RTKs include the epidermal growth factor receptor (EGFR), insulin receptor, and platelet-derived growth factor receptor (PDGFR).

**Receptor Serine/Threonine Kinases:**

- Receptor serine/threonine kinases are transmembrane receptors that phosphorylate serine or threonine residues in their cytoplasmic domains upon ligand binding. They play critical roles in various cellular processes, including development, immune response, and cell cycle regulation.
- **Examples** include the transforming growth factor-beta (TGF-β) receptors and bone morphogenetic protein (BMP) receptors.

**Guanylyl Cyclase Receptors:**

- Guanylyl cyclase receptors are transmembrane receptors that possess guanylyl cyclase activity in their cytoplasmic domains.

- Ligand binding to the extracellular domain of guanylyl cyclase receptors stimulates the production of cyclic guanosine monophosphate (cGMP) from guanosine triphosphate (GTP). cGMP acts as a second messenger that regulates various physiological processes, including smooth muscle relaxation, vasodilation, and phototransduction.
- **Examples** include the atrial natriuretic peptide receptor and the nitric oxide receptor (soluble guanylyl cyclase).

## Conclusion:

- These examples illustrate the diverse roles of transmembrane-linked enzyme receptors in mediating cellular responses to extracellular signals and regulating various physiological processes.
- Dysregulation of these receptors can contribute to the pathogenesis of various diseases, making them important targets for drug development and therapeutic intervention.

## 87. Explain transmembrane JAK STAT receptors with examples?

- Transmembrane JAK-STAT receptors are a type of cell surface receptor that plays a crucial role in mediating signaling by certain cytokines and growth factors. JAK-STAT signaling is involved in various cellular processes, including immune response, hematopoiesis, and inflammation.

**Following is an explanation of transmembrane JAK-STAT receptors along with examples:**

**Structure and Function:**

- Transmembrane JAK-STAT receptors consist of an extracellular ligand-binding domain, a single transmembrane domain, and an intracellular domain that interacts with Janus kinases (JAKs) and signal transducer and activator of transcription (STAT) proteins.
- Ligand binding to the extracellular domain of the receptor induces receptor dimerization or oligomerization, bringing the cytoplasmic domains of the receptor into close proximity.
- JAK proteins are non-receptor tyrosine kinases associated with the intracellular domain of the receptor. Upon receptor activation, JAKs phosphorylate tyrosine residues on the receptor itself and on specific tyrosine residues on the intracellular domain of the receptor, creating docking sites for STAT proteins.
- Once recruited to the receptor, STAT proteins are phosphorylated by JAKs and form homo- or heterodimers. These STAT dimers translocate to the nucleus, where they regulate gene expression by binding to specific DNA sequences and activating or repressing transcription of target genes.

**Examples of Transmembrane JAK-STAT Receptors:**

**Interferon Receptors:**

- Interferons are cytokines involved in antiviral, antitumor, and immunomodulatory responses. Interferon receptors are transmembrane receptors that bind to interferons and activate JAK-STAT signaling pathways.
- **Examples** include the interferon-alpha receptor, interferon-beta receptor, and interferon-gamma receptor.

**Cytokine Receptors:**

- Various cytokines, such as interleukins and growth factors, signal through JAK-STAT pathways via transmembrane receptors.
- **Example:** The receptors for interleukin-2 (IL-2), interleukin-6 (IL-6), granulocyte colony-stimulating factor (G-CSF), and erythropoietin (EPO) utilize JAK-STAT signaling to regulate immune cell proliferation, differentiation, and survival.

**Hormone Receptors:**

- Certain hormones also utilize JAK-STAT signaling pathways via transmembrane receptors.
- **Example:** The growth hormone receptor and the prolactin receptor signal through JAK-STAT pathways to regulate growth, metabolism, and lactation.

## Conclusion:

- These examples demonstrate the importance of transmembrane JAK-STAT receptors in mediating cellular responses to cytokines, growth factors, and hormones.
- Dysregulation of JAK-STAT signaling pathways can contribute to the pathogenesis of various diseases, including cancer, autoimmune disorders, and inflammatory conditions, making them important targets for drug development and therapeutic intervention.

## 88. Explain Nuclear receptors with examples?

- Nuclear receptors are a class of transcription factors that regulate gene expression in response to ligand binding.
- These receptors are located in the cell nucleus and play critical roles in mediating cellular responses to hormones, vitamins, and other signaling molecules.
- Nuclear receptors regulate the expression of target genes by binding to specific DNA sequences called hormone response elements (HREs) in the promoter regions of target genes, thereby modulating their transcription.

**Following is an explanation of nuclear receptors along with examples:**

**Structure and Function:**

- Nuclear receptors typically consist of several functional domains, including a ligand-binding domain (LBD), a DNA-binding domain (DBD), and transcriptional activation or repression domains.
- In the absence of ligand binding, nuclear receptors are often found in complexes with corepressor proteins, which inhibit transcriptional activity. Upon ligand binding, conformational changes occur in the receptor, leading to the dissociation of corepressor complexes and recruitment of coactivator proteins.
- Ligand-bound nuclear receptors then bind to specific DNA sequences in the promoter regions of target genes, resulting in the activation or repression of gene transcription.

- **Examples of Nuclear Receptors:**

**Steroid Hormone Receptors:**

**Estrogen Receptor (ER):**

- ERs are nuclear receptors that bind to the hormone estrogen. Estrogen signaling through ERs regulates gene expression involved in cell proliferation, differentiation, and reproductive function.

**Androgen Receptor (AR):**

- AR is a nuclear receptor that binds to the hormone testosterone. Androgen signaling through AR regulates gene expression involved in male sexual development, muscle growth, and other physiological processes.

**Glucocorticoid Receptor (GR):**

- GR is a nuclear receptor that binds to glucocorticoid hormones such as cortisol. Glucocorticoid signaling through GR regulates gene expression involved in metabolism, immune response, and stress adaptation.

**Thyroid Hormone Receptors (TRs):**

- Thyroid Hormone Receptor (TR): TR is a nuclear receptor that binds to thyroid hormones such as triiodothyronine (T3) and thyroxine (T4). Thyroid hormone signaling through TR regulates gene expression involved in metabolism, growth, and development.

**Vitamin D Receptor (VDR):**

- VDR is a nuclear receptor that binds to the active form of vitamin D, calcitriol. Vitamin D signaling through VDR regulates gene expression involved in calcium homeostasis, bone metabolism, and immune function.

**Retinoic Acid Receptors (RARs) and Retinoid X Receptors (RXRs):**

- RARs and RXRs are nuclear receptors that bind to retinoic acid, the active form of vitamin A. Retinoic acid signaling through RARs and RXRs regulates gene expression involved in cell growth, differentiation, and development.

## Conclusion:

- These examples illustrate the diverse roles of nuclear receptors in mediating cellular responses to hormones, vitamins, and other signaling molecules, and highlight their importance in regulating gene expression and physiological processes.

Dysregulation of nuclear receptor signaling pathways can contribute to the pathogenesis of various diseases, making them important targets for drug development and therapeutic intervention.

## 89. Explain method of expression of receptors with examples?

- The expression of receptors refers to the process by which cells produce and present receptors on their surface or within their cytoplasm.
- The expression levels of receptors can vary depending on factors such as cell type, developmental stage, and physiological conditions.

**Following is an explanation of the methods of receptor expression, along with examples:**

### Transcriptional Regulation:

- Cells regulate the expression of receptors at the transcriptional level by controlling the rate of mRNA synthesis from the corresponding genes.
- Transcription factors bind to specific regulatory sequences in the promoter regions of receptor genes, either enhancing or repressing transcription.
- **Example:** The expression of estrogen receptor alpha (ERα) in breast cancer cells is regulated by estrogen-responsive elements (EREs) in the promoter region of the ESR1 gene. Estrogen binding to ERα activates transcription, leading to increased receptor expression.

### Post-Transcriptional Regulation:

- Cells can regulate receptor expression through post-transcriptional mechanisms such as mRNA stability, alternative splicing, and microRNA-mediated degradation.
- Regulatory proteins and non-coding RNAs can bind to mRNA transcripts, influencing their stability and translation efficiency.
- **Example:** The expression of the serotonin 5-HT2A receptor can be regulated by microRNAs (miRNAs) that target the mRNA transcript for degradation, thereby reducing receptor levels.

### Translation and Protein Folding:

- Following mRNA transcription, ribosomes translate mRNA into protein, and newly synthesized receptors undergo folding and post-translational modifications in the endoplasmic reticulum (ER) and Golgi apparatus.
- Chaperone proteins assist in the proper folding and assembly of receptors, ensuring their correct conformation and function.
- **Example:** The proper expression of G protein-coupled receptors (GPCRs) on the cell surface requires interactions with chaperone proteins such as calnexin and calreticulin in the ER to facilitate protein folding and trafficking.

### Transport and Trafficking:

- Once synthesized, receptors are transported from the endoplasmic reticulum (ER) to the Golgi apparatus and then to the cell surface or other subcellular compartments through vesicular trafficking pathways.
- Transport proteins and vesicle coat proteins mediate receptor trafficking and sorting to specific destinations within the cell.
- **Example:** The transport of neurotransmitter receptors such as glutamate receptors from the ER to the synaptic membrane is facilitated by trafficking proteins such as the GTPase ARF1 and the adaptor protein AP-1.

### Regulation by Signaling Pathways:

- Cellular signaling pathways can regulate receptor expression in response to extracellular stimuli or intracellular signaling molecules.

- Activation of signaling pathways can lead to changes in transcriptional activity, mRNA stability, protein synthesis, and receptor trafficking.
- **Example:** Activation of the PI3K-Akt pathway by growth factors such as insulin can stimulate the expression of glucose transporter proteins (GLUTs) in target cells, leading to increased glucose uptake.

## Conclusion:

- These methods of receptor expression illustrate the complex regulatory mechanisms involved in controlling the levels and localization of receptors in cells, ensuring appropriate cellular responses to environmental stimuli and physiological cues.
- Dysregulation of receptor expression can contribute to various diseases and disorders, highlighting the importance of understanding these mechanisms for therapeutic intervention.

## 90. Explain up regulation and down regulation of receptors with examples?

- Upregulation and downregulation of receptors refer to the processes by which cells adjust the expression levels of receptors in response to changes in their environment or cellular signaling.
- These regulatory mechanisms play crucial roles in modulating cellular responsiveness to extracellular signals and maintaining homeostasis.

**Following is an explanation of upregulation and downregulation of receptors with examples:**

**Upregulation:**

- Upregulation refers to an increase in the expression of receptors on the cell surface or within the cell. This can occur in response to low concentrations of ligands or in situations where cells require enhanced sensitivity to a particular signal.
- Upregulation can occur through increased transcription and translation of receptor genes, as well as enhanced transport and trafficking of receptors to the cell surface.

- **Example:** Chronic exposure to low levels of insulin can lead to upregulation of insulin receptors on target cells, such as adipocytes and skeletal muscle cells. This increases the cell's sensitivity to insulin and enhances glucose uptake, helping to maintain glucose homeostasis in the body.

**Downregulation:**

- Downregulation refers to a decrease in the expression of receptors on the cell surface or within the cell. This can occur in response to high concentrations of ligands or prolonged stimulation of receptors, leading to desensitization or adaptation of the cell.
- Downregulation can occur through decreased transcription and translation of receptor genes, increased receptor internalization and degradation, or altered receptor trafficking.
- **Example:** Prolonged exposure to high levels of cortisol, such as during chronic stress, can lead to downregulation of glucocorticoid receptors in target tissues, such as the hippocampus. This reduces the cell's sensitivity to cortisol and helps prevent excessive stress responses that could be detrimental to the organism.

**Physiological and Pathological Implications:**

- Upregulation and downregulation of receptors are important regulatory mechanisms that allow cells to adapt to changes in their environment and maintain appropriate responsiveness to extracellular signals.
- Dysregulation of receptor expression, such as persistent upregulation or downregulation, can contribute to the pathogenesis of various diseases and disorders, including diabetes, cancer, and neurological disorders.
- Therapeutic interventions that modulate receptor expression, such as receptor agonists, antagonists, or targeted gene therapies, can be used to restore normal cellular responsiveness and treat disease.

**Conclusion:**
- Upregulation and downregulation of receptors are dynamic processes that allow cells to adjust their sensitivity to extracellular signals and maintain homeostasis.
- These regulatory mechanisms play crucial roles in cellular physiology and have important implications for disease pathogenesis and therapeutic interventions.

## 91. Explain potency and efficacy with examples?
- Potency and efficacy are two important pharmacological concepts used to describe the characteristics of drugs and their effects on biological systems. While related, they represent distinct aspects of drug action.

**Following is an explanation of potency and efficacy, along with examples:**

**Potency:**
- Potency refers to the concentration or dose of a drug required to produce a specific effect of a given magnitude. It reflects the relative strength or activity of a drug in producing its pharmacological effect.
- A drug with higher potency requires a lower concentration or dose to achieve a certain level of response compared to a drug with lower potency.
- Potency is often expressed quantitatively as the concentration or dose of the drug required to produce a defined effect, such as half-maximal response (EC50) or inhibition (IC50).
- **Example:** Drug A has an EC50 of 10 mg/mL, while Drug B has an EC50 of 50 mg/mL for inhibiting the growth of bacteria. In this case, Drug A is more potent than Drug B because it achieves the same level of bacterial growth inhibition at a lower concentration.

**Efficacy:**
- Efficacy refers to the maximum effect or intrinsic activity that a drug can produce, regardless of its potency. It represents the extent to which a drug can elicit a response when all available receptors are occupied.
- A drug with higher efficacy produces a greater maximal effect, while a drug with lower efficacy produces a smaller maximal effect, even if it is more potent.
- Efficacy is often determined by comparing the maximal response of a drug to that of a full agonist or reference compound.

- **Example:** Drug X and Drug Y both bind to the same receptor and produce a similar maximal response of 80% of the maximum possible effect. However, Drug X achieves this maximal effect at a lower concentration compared to Drug Y. In this case, both drugs have similar efficacy, but Drug X is more potent.

**Comparison:**
- Potency and efficacy are independent pharmacological properties that describe different aspects of drug action.
- A drug can be more potent but less efficacious than another drug, or it can be less potent but more efficacious.
- Potency primarily reflects the concentration or dose-response relationship of a drug, while efficacy reflects the magnitude of the pharmacological effect produced by the drug.
- In drug development, optimizing both potency and efficacy is important to achieve therapeutic effects with minimal side effects and toxicity.

**Conclusion:**
- Potency and efficacy are fundamental concepts in pharmacology that help characterize the pharmacodynamic properties of drugs.
- Understanding the differences between potency and efficacy is crucial for selecting appropriate drugs for clinical use and optimizing therapeutic outcomes.

## 92. Explain dose response curve and its importance with example?
- A dose-response curve is a graphical representation of the relationship between the dose or concentration of a drug and its pharmacological effect.

- It illustrates how the magnitude of the drug's effect changes as the dose or concentration of the drug is varied.
- Dose-response curves are fundamental tools in pharmacology and toxicology for assessing the potency, efficacy, and safety of drugs.

**Following is an explanation of dose-response curves and their importance, along with an example:**

### Construction of Dose-Response Curve:
- Dose-response curves are typically plotted with the dose or concentration of the drug on the x-axis (in logarithmic scale) and the magnitude of the pharmacological effect on the y-axis.
- Each point on the curve represents the mean response observed at a specific dose or concentration of the drug, often derived from experimental data obtained from in vitro or in vivo studies.
- The shape of the dose-response curve can vary depending on factors such as the nature of the drug, the receptor-ligand interaction, and the presence of physiological or pathological conditions.

### Key Parameters:

### EC50 (Effective Concentration 50):
- The EC50 represents the concentration or dose of the drug required to produce 50% of the maximal effect. It is a measure of the drug's potency and is often used to compare the relative efficacy of different drugs.

### Emax (Maximal Response):
- The Emax represents the maximum effect produced by the drug when all available receptors are occupied. It is a measure of the drug's efficacy and reflects its intrinsic activity.

### Hill Slope:
- The Hill slope describes the steepness of the dose-response curve and provides information about the cooperativity or interaction between drug molecules and receptors.

### Importance of Dose-Response Curves:

### Assessment of Potency and Efficacy:
- Dose-response curves allow researchers to quantitatively assess the potency and efficacy of drugs by determining their EC50 and Emax values.

### Characterization of Drug Action:
- Dose-response curves provide insights into the mechanism of action of drugs and the nature of the receptor-ligand interaction. They can help differentiate between agonists, antagonists, and partial agonists based on their effects on receptor activation.

### Optimization of Drug Therapy:
- Dose-response curves assist in selecting appropriate drug doses for therapeutic use and optimizing treatment regimens to achieve desired pharmacological effects while minimizing adverse effects and toxicity.

### Evaluation of Safety and Toxicity:
- Dose-response curves are used to assess the safety profile of drugs by determining the therapeutic index (TI), which is the ratio of the lethal dose (LD50) to the effective dose (ED50). A wider therapeutic index indicates a safer drug with a lower risk of toxicity.

- **Example:** Consider a dose-response curve for a pain-relieving medication, where the x-axis represents increasing doses of the drug (e.g., in milligrams) and the y-axis represents the degree of pain relief (e.g., on a numerical scale). The curve shows that as the dose of the medication increases, the degree of pain relief also increases, reaching a plateau at higher doses.

- The EC50 represents the dose of the medication that produces 50% pain relief, while the Emax represents the maximum achievable pain relief with the medication.

**Conclusion:**
- The dose-response curves provide valuable information about the potency, efficacy, mechanism of action, and safety profile of drugs.
- They are essential tools in drug development, pharmacology research, and clinical practice for optimizing drug therapy and evaluating the therapeutic and toxicological effects of drugs.

## 93. What is therapeutic index? explain with an example? explain with examples of drugs with higher and lower therapeutic index?

- The therapeutic index (TI) is a pharmacological concept that quantifies the relative safety of a drug by comparing its effective dose (ED50) with its toxic dose (TD50) in a population.
- It provides a measure of the margin of safety of a drug and indicates how wide or narrow the gap is between the dose that produces therapeutic effects and the dose that produces toxic effects.

- The therapeutic index is calculated using the formula:

$$\text{Therapeutic Index (TI)} = TD50/ED50$$

- A higher therapeutic index indicates a safer drug with a wider margin of safety, as the effective dose is much lower than the toxic dose.
- Conversely, a lower therapeutic index suggests a higher risk of toxicity, as the effective dose is closer to the toxic dose.

**Following is an explanation of therapeutic index with examples of drugs with higher and lower therapeutic indices:**

**Drugs with Higher Therapeutic Index:**
- **Example: Acetaminophen (paracetamol)**
- Acetaminophen is a commonly used analgesic and antipyretic medication.

- The effective dose (ED50) of acetaminophen for pain relief and fever reduction is relatively low.

- The toxic dose (TD50) of acetaminophen is much higher and is associated with hepatotoxicity, especially in cases of overdose.

- Calculating the therapeutic index of acetaminophen:

$$\text{Therapeutic Index (TI)} = TD50/ED50$$

- Since the toxic dose is much higher than the effective dose, acetaminophen has a higher therapeutic index, indicating a relatively safe medication when used within recommended doses.

**Drugs with Lower Therapeutic Index:**
- **Example: Warfarin**
- Warfarin is an anticoagulant medication used to prevent blood clotting and reduce the risk of thromboembolic events.

- The effective dose (ED50) of warfarin for anticoagulation is relatively close to its toxic dose (TD50) for bleeding complications.

- The therapeutic index of warfarin is lower compared to acetaminophen, indicating a narrower margin of safety.

- Due to its narrow therapeutic index, warfarin requires careful monitoring of blood clotting parameters (e.g., INR) to avoid hemorrhagic complications while maintaining anticoagulant efficacy.

**Conclusion:**

- In summary, the therapeutic index provides valuable information about the safety profile of a drug by comparing its effective dose with its toxic dose.
- Drugs with higher therapeutic indices are considered safer, while drugs with lower therapeutic indices require more careful dosing and monitoring to minimize the risk of toxicity.

## 94. Explain risk benefit ratio of drugs with examples?

- The risk-benefit ratio of a drug refers to the balance between the potential risks associated with its use and the potential benefits it offers in treating a specific condition.
- This concept is fundamental in clinical decision-making and drug development, as it helps healthcare providers and regulatory agencies evaluate the overall utility of a medication in comparison to its potential adverse effects.
- The goal is to ensure that the benefits of using a drug outweigh the risks, thereby maximizing therapeutic efficacy while minimizing harm.

**Following is an explanation of the risk-benefit ratio of drugs with examples:**

**Evaluation of Risks:**

- Risks associated with drug therapy can include adverse effects, drug interactions, potential for dependence or abuse, and other safety concerns.
- Adverse effects may range from mild and transient side effects to more severe and potentially life-threatening reactions.
- Risks can vary depending on factors such as patient characteristics (e.g., age, comorbidities), drug properties (e.g., pharmacokinetics, mechanism of action), and dosing regimens.

**Assessment of Benefits:**

- Benefits of drug therapy encompass the desired therapeutic effects and improvements in patient outcomes, such as symptom relief, disease management, prevention of complications, and improved quality of life.
- Benefits may also include secondary or indirect effects, such as reduced healthcare utilization, decreased morbidity and mortality, and cost-effectiveness compared to alternative treatments.

**Evaluation of Risk-Benefit Ratio:**

- The risk-benefit ratio of a drug is determined by weighing the potential risks against the potential benefits, considering both the magnitude and likelihood of each.
- A favorable risk-benefit ratio indicates that the benefits of using the drug outweigh the risks, making it an appropriate choice for treatment.
- Conversely, an unfavorable risk-benefit ratio suggests that the risks associated with the drug may outweigh the potential benefits, necessitating careful consideration of alternative treatments or risk mitigation strategies.

- **Example:** Consider the use of nonsteroidal anti-inflammatory drugs (NSAIDs) for pain relief in patients with osteoarthritis:

**Risks:**

- NSAIDs are associated with gastrointestinal (GI) side effects such as gastric ulcers, bleeding, and perforation. They can also increase the risk of cardiovascular events, renal dysfunction, and fluid retention.

**Benefits:**

- NSAIDs provide effective pain relief and improve joint function, allowing patients to maintain mobility and perform daily activities with less discomfort.

**Risk-Benefit Ratio:**

- The risk-benefit ratio of NSAIDs in osteoarthritis treatment depends on factors such as the patient's age, comorbidities, and concurrent medications.
- In some cases, the benefits of pain relief may outweigh the risks of GI and cardiovascular complications, especially when NSAIDs are used at lower doses and for short-term symptomatic relief.

## Conclusion:

- Evaluating the risk-benefit ratio of drugs involves careful consideration of the potential risks and benefits associated with their use in specific patient populations and clinical scenarios.
- Healthcare providers must weigh these factors to make informed decisions about drug therapy, optimize patient outcomes, and minimize harm.
- Regulatory agencies also consider the risk-benefit profile of drugs when assessing their safety and efficacy for approval and marketing authorization.

## 95. Explain therapeutic window with examples?

- The therapeutic window, also known as the therapeutic range or therapeutic index, refers to the range of drug concentrations in the body that produces the desired therapeutic effect without causing significant toxicity or adverse effects.
- It represents the optimal dosing range within which the drug achieves its intended therapeutic benefits while minimizing the risk of harm. The therapeutic window is determined by the balance between the drug's efficacy and its toxicity profile.

### Following is an explanation of the therapeutic window with examples

### Definition and Importance:

- The therapeutic window is a critical concept in pharmacotherapy as it helps guide dosing regimens and treatment decisions.
- Drugs with a narrow therapeutic window require careful monitoring of serum concentrations to avoid subtherapeutic or toxic effects.
- In contrast, drugs with a wider therapeutic window offer greater flexibility in dosing and are less likely to cause dose-dependent toxicity.

### Components of the Therapeutic Window:

### Minimum Effective Concentration (MEC):

- The lowest concentration of the drug in the body that produces the desired therapeutic effect.

### Maximum Tolerated Concentration (MTC):

- The highest concentration of the drug that can be achieved without causing significant toxicity or adverse effects.

### Example: Digoxin

- Digoxin is a medication commonly used to treat heart failure and certain arrhythmias.

### Therapeutic Window:

- The therapeutic window of digoxin is relatively narrow due to its narrow margin of safety.

### Minimum Effective Concentration (MEC):

- The MEC of digoxin is typically in the range of 0.5 to 2 ng/mL, at which it provides therapeutic benefits in heart failure and arrhythmia control.

### Maximum Tolerated Concentration (MTC):

- The MTC of digoxin is generally considered to be greater than 2 ng/mL, beyond which there is an increased risk of toxicity, including cardiac arrhythmias, nausea, vomiting, and visual disturbances.

### Therapeutic Monitoring:

- Due to its narrow therapeutic window, serum digoxin levels are routinely monitored to ensure that concentrations remain within the therapeutic range and to adjust dosing as needed to minimize toxicity.

### Example: Acetaminophen (Paracetamol)

- Acetaminophen is a widely used analgesic and antipyretic medication.

### Therapeutic Window:

- Acetaminophen has a relatively wide therapeutic window, making it a safe and effective choice for pain relief and fever reduction when used at recommended doses.

## Minimum Effective Concentration (MEC):
- The MEC of acetaminophen for pain relief and antipyresis is generally considered to be lower than 10 µg/mL.

## Maximum Tolerated Concentration (MTC):
- The MTC of acetaminophen is higher, typically above 200 µg/mL, beyond which there is an increased risk of hepatotoxicity, especially in cases of overdose or excessive use.

## Therapeutic Use:
- Acetaminophen is commonly used for the treatment of mild to moderate pain and fever in both adults and children, with few adverse effects when used as directed.

## Conclusion:
- The therapeutic window represents the range of drug concentrations that produce therapeutic effects while minimizing the risk of toxicity.
- Understanding the therapeutic window of a drug is essential for safe and effective medication management, guiding dosing decisions, and preventing adverse drug reactions.

## 96. Explain Tmax with an example?
- Tmax, or time to maximum concentration, is a pharmacokinetic parameter that represents the time it takes for a drug to reach its maximum concentration (Cmax) in the bloodstream after administration.
- Tmax is an important aspect of drug absorption and is used to characterize the rate and extent of drug absorption from its dosage form. It provides insights into the onset of drug action and helps optimize dosing regimens for therapeutic effectiveness.

**Following is an explanation of Tmax with an example:**
- **Example:** Consider the administration of a commonly prescribed oral antibiotic, amoxicillin, to treat a bacterial infection.

## Administration of Amoxicillin:
- A patient takes a 500 mg tablet of amoxicillin orally with a glass of water as prescribed by their healthcare provider.

## Absorption of Amoxicillin:
- After oral administration, the amoxicillin tablet dissolves in the gastrointestinal tract, and the drug is absorbed into the bloodstream through the intestinal mucosa.
- The absorption of amoxicillin begins shortly after ingestion and continues as the drug is transported through the bloodstream to its target tissues.

## Measurement of Blood Concentrations:
- Blood samples are collected from the patient at regular intervals following administration of amoxicillin.
- The concentration of amoxicillin in each blood sample is determined using analytical techniques such as chromatography or immunoassays.

## Determination of Tmax:
- By analyzing the blood concentration-time profile of amoxicillin, the time at which the drug reaches its maximum concentration (Cmax) is identified.

- **Tmax is defined as the time elapsed from drug administration to the occurrence of Cmax.**

## Interpretation:
- For amoxicillin, Tmax typically occurs within 1 to 2 hours after oral administration in adults when taken with food. Without food, Tmax may occur slightly earlier.

- This means that it takes approximately 1 to 2 hours for amoxicillin to reach its maximum concentration in the bloodstream after oral ingestion.

- The rapid absorption of amoxicillin allows for relatively quick onset of action against susceptible bacteria, contributing to its efficacy in treating bacterial infections.

**Clinical Implications:**
- Understanding the Tmax of amoxicillin helps healthcare providers optimize dosing regimens to ensure timely and effective treatment of bacterial infections.
- Knowing when the drug reaches its peak concentration allows for better coordination of dosing schedules and ensures that therapeutic levels are maintained throughout the course of treatment.

**Conclusion:**
- Tmax represents the time it takes for a drug to reach its maximum concentration in the bloodstream after administration.
- It is an important pharmacokinetic parameter used to assess the rate of drug absorption and optimize dosing regimens for therapeutic effectiveness.

## 97. Explain Cmax with example? what is the clinical importance of Cmax?

- Cmax, or maximum concentration, is a pharmacokinetic parameter that represents the peak concentration of a drug in the bloodstream after administration. It indicates the highest level of drug exposure achieved in the body and provides valuable information about the rate and extent of drug absorption, distribution, and elimination.
- Cmax is an essential parameter used in pharmacokinetic studies to characterize the pharmacokinetic profile of drugs and optimize dosing regimens.

**Following is an explanation of Cmax with an example and its clinical importance:**
- **Example:** Consider the administration of a commonly prescribed pain reliever, ibuprofen, to a patient for the treatment of acute pain.

**Administration of Ibuprofen:**
- The patient takes a 400 mg tablet of ibuprofen orally as directed by their healthcare provider to alleviate pain.

**Absorption of Ibuprofen:**
- After oral administration, the ibuprofen tablet dissolves in the gastrointestinal tract, and the drug is absorbed into the bloodstream through the intestinal mucosa.
- The absorption of ibuprofen begins rapidly, and the drug is transported through the bloodstream to reach its target sites of action, such as inflamed tissues.

**Measurement of Blood Concentrations:**
- Blood samples are collected from the patient at various time points following administration of ibuprofen.
- The concentration of ibuprofen in each blood sample is determined using analytical techniques such as chromatography or immunoassays.

**Determination of Cmax:**
- By analyzing the blood concentration-time profile of ibuprofen, the peak concentration of the drug (Cmax) is identified.
- Cmax is defined as the maximum concentration of ibuprofen achieved in the bloodstream after oral administration.

**Interpretation:**
- For ibuprofen, Cmax typically occurs within 1 to 2 hours after oral administration in adults when taken with food. Without food, Cmax may occur slightly earlier.
- The Cmax value represents the peak level of ibuprofen in the bloodstream, indicating the maximum exposure of the body to the drug.

**Clinical Importance of Cmax:**
- Cmax is an important pharmacokinetic parameter used to assess the rate and extent of drug absorption and to characterize the pharmacokinetic profile of drugs.

- The magnitude of Cmax is influenced by various factors, including the drug's formulation, route of administration, dosing regimen, and patient-specific factors (e.g., age, renal function).
- Clinically, Cmax is used to determine the optimal dosing regimen to achieve therapeutic efficacy while minimizing the risk of adverse effects.
- Drugs with higher Cmax values may have a faster onset of action and provide more rapid symptom relief, whereas drugs with lower Cmax values may have a slower onset of action but longer duration of effect.
- Monitoring Cmax levels and adjusting dosing regimens accordingly can help optimize therapeutic outcomes and prevent under- or overdosing of medications.

### Conclusion:
- Cmax is the peak concentration of a drug in the bloodstream after administration and plays a crucial role in assessing drug absorption, distribution, and dosing regimens.
- Understanding Cmax values helps healthcare providers optimize drug therapy and achieve desired therapeutic outcomes while minimizing the risk of adverse effects.

## 98. Explain steady state concentration with example? Explain its clinical importance?

- Steady-state concentration refers to the condition in pharmacokinetics where the rate of drug administration (input) equals the rate of drug elimination (output), resulting in a constant and stable concentration of the drug in the body over time.
- This equilibrium state occurs when the amount of drug absorbed and distributed equals the amount eliminated, typically achieved after approximately four to five half-lives of the drug.
- Steady-state concentration is an important concept in pharmacokinetics and is used to guide dosing regimens to maintain therapeutic drug levels.

- **Following is an explanation of steady-state concentration with an example and its clinical importance:**

- **Example:** Consider the administration of a medication, such as amlodipine, used to treat hypertension.

### Administration of Amlodipine:
- A patient is prescribed a 5 mg tablet of amlodipine once daily to control blood pressure.

### Absorption and Distribution of Amlodipine:
- After oral administration, the amlodipine tablet is absorbed from the gastrointestinal tract into the bloodstream and distributed to target tissues, including blood vessels and the heart.
- The drug undergoes metabolism in the liver and is eliminated primarily via renal excretion.

### Achievement of Steady State:
- Following regular daily dosing of amlodipine, the drug gradually accumulates in the body over several days due to its relatively long elimination half-life.
- After approximately five days (about five half-lives) of continuous dosing, steady-state concentration is reached, where the rate of drug intake from daily dosing equals the rate of drug elimination.

### Steady-State Concentration:
- At steady state, the concentration of amlodipine in the bloodstream remains relatively constant and stable over time.
- The steady-state concentration of amlodipine is determined by factors such as the dose administered, dosing interval, absorption rate, distribution volume, and elimination half-life of the drug.

### Clinical Importance of Steady State:
- Steady-state concentration is crucial for achieving and maintaining therapeutic drug levels necessary to optimize treatment outcomes.

- Clinically, steady-state concentration guides dosing regimens to ensure that therapeutic drug levels are maintained while minimizing the risk of under- or overdosing.

- For drugs with a narrow therapeutic window or concentration-dependent efficacy, maintaining steady-state concentration is particularly important to avoid fluctuations in drug levels that may lead to suboptimal efficacy or increased risk of adverse effects.

- Healthcare providers may adjust dosing regimens or monitor drug levels in patients to ensure that steady-state concentration is reached and maintained, especially in situations where rapid onset of action or precise dosing is required.

## Conclusion:
- Steady-state concentration is the state in pharmacokinetics where the rate of drug intake equals the rate of drug elimination, resulting in a constant and stable concentration of the drug in the body.
- Achieving and maintaining steady-state concentration is essential for optimizing therapeutic outcomes and guiding dosing regimens in clinical practice.

## 99. Explain therapeutic range with example? explain its clinical importance?

- The therapeutic range, also known as the therapeutic window, refers to the range of drug concentrations in the bloodstream that is associated with optimal therapeutic efficacy while minimizing the risk of adverse effects.
- It represents the concentration range within which a drug is most likely to produce its desired therapeutic effects without causing significant toxicity.
- The therapeutic range is determined based on pharmacokinetic and pharmacodynamic considerations and is used to guide dosing regimens and monitor drug therapy in clinical practice.

- **Following is an explanation of the therapeutic range with an example and its clinical importance:**
- **Example:** Consider the administration of a commonly prescribed anticoagulant medication, warfarin, used to prevent blood clot formation.

## Administration of Warfarin:
- A patient is prescribed warfarin to reduce the risk of thromboembolic events, such as stroke or pulmonary embolism.

- Warfarin is typically administered orally in tablet form, and the dose is individualized based on factors such as the patient's age, weight, medical history, and target international normalized ratio (INR).

## Monitoring Warfarin Therapy:
- Due to the narrow therapeutic window of warfarin and its potential for significant variability in response among patients, routine monitoring of coagulation parameters, such as the INR, is necessary to ensure therapeutic efficacy and safety.
- The INR reflects the patient's coagulation status and provides an indirect measure of the anticoagulant effect of warfarin. The target INR varies depending on the indication for therapy, such as atrial fibrillation, deep vein thrombosis, or mechanical heart valve replacement.

## Therapeutic Range of Warfarin:
- The therapeutic range of warfarin is typically defined by a target INR range, such as 2.0 to 3.0 for most indications.

- INR values below the lower limit of the therapeutic range (<2.0) indicate subtherapeutic anticoagulation, increasing the risk of thromboembolic events, while INR values above the upper limit of the therapeutic range (>3.0) indicate supratherapeutic anticoagulation, increasing the risk of bleeding complications.

**Clinical Importance of Therapeutic Range:**

- The therapeutic range of warfarin serves as a guide for dosing adjustments to achieve and maintain optimal anticoagulation while minimizing the risk of bleeding or thrombosis.
- Regular monitoring of INR levels allows healthcare providers to assess the patient's response to warfarin therapy and make appropriate dose adjustments to keep INR values within the target therapeutic range.
- Inadequate anticoagulation due to subtherapeutic INR levels increases the risk of thromboembolic events, such as stroke or venous thromboembolism, while excessive anticoagulation due to supratherapeutic INR levels increases the risk of bleeding complications, such as gastrointestinal bleeding or intracranial hemorrhage.
- By maintaining INR values within the target therapeutic range, healthcare providers can optimize the efficacy and safety of warfarin therapy, reducing the risk of adverse outcomes and improving patient outcomes.

**Conclusion:**

- The therapeutic range represents the optimal concentration range of a drug associated with therapeutic efficacy and safety.
- For warfarin and other drugs with a narrow therapeutic window, maintaining drug levels within the target therapeutic range is essential for achieving optimal therapeutic outcomes while minimizing the risk of adverse effects.
- Regular monitoring of drug concentrations or surrogate markers allows healthcare providers to adjust dosing regimens and optimize drug therapy in individual patients.

**100. What is drug drug interaction? explain its clinical importance with example?**

- A drug-drug interaction (DDI) occurs when the effects of one drug are altered by the presence of another drug, leading to changes in pharmacokinetic or pharmacodynamic properties of either or both drugs.

- Drug interactions can occur when two or more drugs are administered concurrently, resulting in either enhanced or diminished therapeutic effects or an increased risk of adverse effects.
- Understanding and managing drug interactions is crucial in clinical practice to ensure safe and effective pharmacotherapy.

**Following is an explanation of drug-drug interactions with an example and its clinical importance:**

- **Example:** Consider a patient who is prescribed warfarin, an anticoagulant, for the prevention of blood clots, and is also taking amiodarone, an antiarrhythmic medication, for the treatment of atrial fibrillation.

**Warfarin and Amiodarone Interaction:**

- Warfarin is metabolized in the liver by the cytochrome P450 (CYP) enzyme system, particularly CYP2C9 and CYP3A4 enzymes.
- Amiodarone is known to inhibit CYP2C9 and CYP3A4 enzymes, which are responsible for the metabolism of warfarin.
- As a result, concurrent use of amiodarone with warfarin can lead to decreased metabolism and clearance of warfarin, resulting in increased plasma concentrations and a higher risk of bleeding complications.

**Clinical Importance of Drug-Drug Interactions:**

**Efficacy and Safety:**

- Drug interactions can affect the efficacy and safety of pharmacotherapy by altering drug concentrations and pharmacological effects. For example, in the case of warfarin and amiodarone interaction, increased warfarin levels can potentiate anticoagulant effects, leading to an increased risk of bleeding, which can be life-threatening.

**Therapeutic Failure:**

- Drug interactions may result in therapeutic failure if the desired therapeutic effects are diminished or nullified.

- For instance, if an antibiotic reduces the efficacy of an oral contraceptive pill by altering its metabolism, it can lead to contraceptive failure and unintended pregnancy.

**Adverse Effects:**

- Drug interactions can increase the risk of adverse effects or toxicity by enhancing the pharmacological effects of drugs. For example, combining two medications that have sedative effects, such as opioids and benzodiazepines, can lead to excessive sedation, respiratory depression, and coma.

**Treatment Complexity:**

- Managing drug interactions adds complexity to medication regimens, especially in patients with multiple comorbidities and polypharmacy. Healthcare providers must consider potential interactions when prescribing medications and adjust doses or select alternative therapies to minimize the risk of adverse outcomes.

**Monitoring and Surveillance:**

- Routine monitoring of drug levels, laboratory parameters, and clinical symptoms is essential for detecting and managing drug interactions in clinical practice. Timely identification of interactions allows for appropriate interventions, such as dose adjustments, drug substitutions, or discontinuation of medications to mitigate adverse effects and optimize therapeutic outcomes.

**Conclusion:**

- Drug-drug interactions occur when the effects of one drug are altered by the presence of another drug, leading to changes in pharmacokinetic or pharmacodynamic properties.
- Understanding the mechanisms, clinical significance, and management of drug interactions is essential for safe and effective pharmacotherapy, particularly in patients with complex medical conditions or polypharmacy.
- Healthcare providers must be vigilant in identifying and managing drug interactions to optimize treatment outcomes and minimize the risk of adverse effects.

## 101. What is synergism? Explain its clinical importance with example?

- Synergism, in the context of pharmacology, refers to a phenomenon where the combined effect of two or more drugs or substances is greater than the sum of their individual effects when used alone.
- In other words, synergism occurs when the drugs interact in such a way that their combined effect is amplified, resulting in enhanced therapeutic efficacy or potency.
- Synergistic interactions can occur at various levels, including pharmacokinetic and pharmacodynamic mechanisms. Understanding synergism is important in clinical practice as it can lead to more effective treatment outcomes or allow for dose reduction, minimizing the risk of adverse effects.

**Following is an explanation of synergism with an example and its clinical importance:**

- **Example:** Consider the treatment of bacterial infections with a combination of two antibiotics, penicillin and clavulanic acid.

**Mechanism of Synergism:**

- Penicillin is an antibiotic that inhibits bacterial cell wall synthesis, leading to bacterial cell death.
- Clavulanic acid is a β-lactamase inhibitor that prevents bacterial enzymes (β-lactamases) from deactivating penicillin, thereby enhancing its activity against β-lactamase-producing bacteria.
- When penicillin and clavulanic acid are used together, they exert a synergistic effect against bacterial infections by inhibiting cell wall synthesis and preventing β-lactamase-mediated resistance simultaneously.

**Clinical Importance of Synergism:**

- **Enhanced Efficacy:**
- Synergistic interactions can result in enhanced therapeutic efficacy, allowing for more effective treatment of infections. In the case of penicillin and clavulanic acid, the combination therapy provides broader coverage against a wider range

of bacteria, including those resistant to penicillin alone, leading to improved clinical outcomes.

## Reduced Resistance:

- Combining drugs with synergistic activity can help reduce the development of antibiotic resistance by targeting multiple pathways or mechanisms of bacterial growth and survival. By inhibiting β-lactamases, clavulanic acid enhances the activity of penicillin, making it more effective against resistant bacteria.

## Dose Reduction:

- Synergistic interactions may allow for dose reduction of individual drugs while achieving the desired therapeutic effect. Lowering the doses of individual drugs can help minimize the risk of adverse effects or toxicity associated with higher drug concentrations, improving patient safety and tolerability.

## Therapeutic Options:

- Synergistic drug combinations expand the therapeutic options available for treating infections, especially in cases of multidrug-resistant organisms or complicated infections. Healthcare providers can select combination therapies based on the susceptibility profile of the infecting organism and the clinical presentation of the patient, optimizing treatment outcomes.

## Drug Development:

- Understanding synergistic interactions between drugs can guide drug development strategies, leading to the design of novel combination therapies with enhanced efficacy and improved safety profiles. Synergistic drug combinations may also provide opportunities for repurposing existing drugs or developing new treatment regimens for challenging medical conditions.

## Conclusion:

- Synergism occurs when the combined effect of two or more drugs is greater than the sum of their individual effects, leading to enhanced therapeutic efficacy or potency.

- Recognizing synergistic interactions is important in clinical practice as it can lead to more effective treatment outcomes, reduced resistance, dose optimization, and expanded therapeutic options for patients.
- Healthcare providers should consider synergism when selecting drug therapies, especially in the management of infections or other complex medical conditions.

## 102. Explain additive effect with example? explain its clinical importance?

- An additive effect in pharmacology refers to a phenomenon where the combined effect of two or more drugs or substances is equal to the sum of their individual effects when used alone. In other words, when drugs exhibit an additive effect, their combined effect is merely additive, with no amplification or diminution of therapeutic efficacy or potency.
- Additive interactions can occur at various levels, including pharmacokinetic and pharmacodynamic mechanisms.
- Understanding additive effects is important in clinical practice as they can help predict treatment outcomes, guide dosing regimens, and minimize the risk of adverse effects.

**Following is an explanation of additive effect with an example and its clinical importance:**

- **Example:** Consider the treatment of pain using a combination of two analgesic medications, acetaminophen and ibuprofen.

**Mechanism of Additive Effect:**

- Acetaminophen and ibuprofen are both analgesic medications that relieve pain by inhibiting the synthesis of prostaglandins, substances that mediate pain and inflammation in the body.
- When acetaminophen and ibuprofen are used together, they exert an additive effect on pain relief by targeting different pathways involved in pain perception and inflammation. However, their combined effect is merely additive, with no synergistic or antagonistic interactions.

## Clinical Importance of Additive Effect:

### Predictable Treatment Outcomes:
- Additive interactions between drugs result in predictable treatment outcomes, allowing healthcare providers to anticipate the combined effect of medications and adjust dosing regimens accordingly. In the case of acetaminophen and ibuprofen, the additive effect on pain relief provides consistent and reliable analgesia for patients with mild to moderate pain.

### Dose Optimization:
- Additive interactions may allow for dose optimization of individual drugs while achieving the desired therapeutic effect. Lowering the doses of individual drugs can help minimize the risk of adverse effects or toxicity associated with higher drug concentrations, improving patient safety and tolerability.

### Combination Therapy:
- Additive effects between drugs enable the use of combination therapies to enhance therapeutic efficacy without increasing the risk of adverse effects. Healthcare providers may prescribe combination therapies to achieve additive effects when single-agent therapy is inadequate or when synergistic interactions are not feasible or desired.

### Clinical Versatility:
- Additive interactions provide clinical versatility in drug selection and treatment planning, allowing healthcare providers to tailor therapy to individual patient needs and preferences. Additive drug combinations offer flexibility in managing various medical conditions, providing multiple options for achieving therapeutic goals.

### Risk Management:
- Understanding additive effects helps healthcare providers minimize the risk of adverse drug reactions or drug interactions by selecting appropriate drug combinations and monitoring patients for signs of toxicity or therapeutic failure.

- By considering additive interactions, healthcare providers can optimize treatment outcomes and improve patient care.

### Conclusion:
- Additive effect occurs when the combined effect of two or more drugs is equal to the sum of their individual effects, resulting in predictable treatment outcomes and dose optimization.
- Recognizing additive interactions is important in clinical practice as they guide treatment decisions, facilitate combination therapy, and enhance therapeutic efficacy while minimizing the risk of adverse effects.
- Healthcare providers should consider additive effects when selecting drug therapies, especially in the management of pain and other common medical conditions.

## 103. What is supra-additive effect with example? explain its clinical significance?

- A supra-additive effect, also known as a synergistic effect, occurs when the combined effect of two or more drugs or substances is greater than the sum of their individual effects when used alone. In other words, when drugs exhibit a supra-additive effect, their combined effect is amplified, resulting in enhanced therapeutic efficacy or potency beyond what would be expected based on the effects of each drug individually.
- Supra-additive interactions can occur at various levels, including pharmacokinetic and pharmacodynamic mechanisms. Understanding supra-additive effects is important in clinical practice as they can lead to more effective treatment outcomes, dose optimization, and expanded therapeutic options for patients.

### Following is an explanation of supra-additive effect with an example and its clinical significance:
- **Example:** Consider the treatment of bacterial infections with a combination of two antibiotics, amoxicillin and clavulanic acid.

**Mechanism of Supra-Additive Effect:**
- Amoxicillin is a broad-spectrum antibiotic that inhibits bacterial cell wall synthesis, leading to bacterial cell death.
- Clavulanic acid is a β-lactamase inhibitor that prevents bacterial enzymes (β-lactamases) from deactivating amoxicillin, thereby enhancing its activity against β-lactamase-producing bacteria.
- When amoxicillin and clavulanic acid are used together, they exert a supra-additive effect against bacterial infections by inhibiting cell wall synthesis and preventing β-lactamase-mediated resistance simultaneously.

**Clinical Significance of Supra-Additive Effect:**

**Enhanced Efficacy:**
- Supra-additive interactions result in enhanced therapeutic efficacy, allowing for more effective treatment of infections than either drug alone.
- In the case of amoxicillin and clavulanic acid, the combination therapy provides broader coverage against a wider range of bacteria, including those resistant to amoxicillin alone, leading to improved clinical outcomes.

**Reduced Resistance:**
- Combining drugs with supra-additive activity can help reduce the development of antibiotic resistance by targeting multiple pathways or mechanisms of bacterial growth and survival.
- By inhibiting β-lactamases, clavulanic acid enhances the activity of amoxicillin, making it more effective against resistant bacteria.

**Dose Optimization:**
- Supra-additive interactions may allow for dose optimization of individual drugs while achieving the desired therapeutic effect.
- Lowering the doses of individual drugs can help minimize the risk of adverse effects or toxicity associated with higher drug concentrations, improving patient safety and tolerability.

**Expanded Therapeutic Options:**
- Supra-additive drug combinations provide expanded therapeutic options for treating infections, especially in cases of multidrug-resistant organisms or complicated infections.
- Healthcare providers can select combination therapies based on the susceptibility profile of the infecting organism and the clinical presentation of the patient, optimizing treatment outcomes.

**Drug Development:**
- Understanding supra-additive interactions between drugs can guide drug development strategies, leading to the design of novel combination therapies with enhanced efficacy and improved safety profiles.
- Supra-additive drug combinations may also provide opportunities for repurposing existing drugs or developing new treatment regimens for challenging medical conditions.

**Conclusion:**
- Supra-additive effect occurs when the combined effect of two or more drugs is greater than the sum of their individual effects, resulting in enhanced therapeutic efficacy or potency.
- Recognizing supra-additive interactions is important in clinical practice as they can lead to more effective treatment outcomes, reduced resistance, dose optimization, and expanded therapeutic options for patients.
- Healthcare providers should consider supra-additive effects when selecting drug therapies, especially in the management of infections or other complex medical conditions.

## 104. Explain drug antagonism with example? explain its clinical significance?
- Drug antagonism occurs when the effect of one drug is inhibited or diminished by the presence of another drug, resulting in a reduction in therapeutic efficacy or potency.
- Antagonistic interactions can occur at various levels, including pharmacokinetic and pharmacodynamic mechanisms. Understanding drug antagonism is important in clinical practice as it can lead to treatment failure, therapeutic

inefficacy, or the need for dose adjustments to achieve desired outcomes. Here's an explanation of drug antagonism with an example and its clinical significance:

- **Example:** Consider the treatment of hypertension using two antihypertensive medications, a beta-blocker (e.g., propranolol) and a sympathomimetic agent (e.g., epinephrine).

## Mechanism of Drug Antagonism:

- Propranolol is a beta-blocker that inhibits the effects of catecholamines, such as epinephrine, by blocking beta-adrenergic receptors in the heart and blood vessels.
- Epinephrine is a sympathomimetic agent that stimulates beta-adrenergic receptors, leading to increased heart rate and blood pressure.

## Clinical Scenario:

- A patient with hypertension is prescribed propranolol to reduce heart rate and blood pressure.
- However, during an emergency situation, the patient receives epinephrine (e.g., for anaphylaxis or cardiac arrest) to increase blood pressure and restore cardiac function.

## Antagonistic Interaction:

- When epinephrine is administered concurrently with propranolol, its effects on beta-adrenergic receptors are blocked by propranolol, resulting in a diminished beta adrenergic response to epinephrine.
- As a result, the intended increase in cardiac output produced by epinephrine is attenuated, leading to a reduced therapeutic effect of epinephrine.

## Clinical Significance of Drug Antagonism:

## Treatment Failure:

- Drug antagonism can result in treatment failure or therapeutic inefficacy by blocking the intended pharmacological effects of a drug.

- In the case of propranolol and epinephrine, the antagonistic interaction may compromise the effectiveness of epinephrine in managing emergency situations, potentially leading to adverse outcomes for the patient.

## Dose Adjustment:

- Healthcare providers may need to adjust the doses or timing of medications to minimize the effects of drug antagonism and achieve desired therapeutic outcomes.
- **For example,** in the scenario described, alternative treatments may be required to overcome the antagonistic effects of propranolol.

## Risk of Adverse Events:

- Drug antagonism can increase the risk of adverse events or complications by interfering with the pharmacological actions of medications.
- In some cases, the attenuated response to a drug due to antagonistic interactions may necessitate additional interventions or alternative therapies to achieve the desired clinical effect.

## Monitoring and Management:

- Healthcare providers should be vigilant in monitoring patients receiving potentially antagonistic drug combinations and be prepared to intervene promptly if treatment failure or adverse events occur.
- Awareness of potential drug interactions and their clinical implications is essential for optimizing patient care and minimizing the risk of therapeutic failure or harm.

## Conclusion:

- Drug antagonism occurs when the effect of one drug is inhibited or diminished by the presence of another drug, leading to reduced therapeutic efficacy or potency.
- Recognizing drug antagonism is important in clinical practice as it can lead to treatment failure, therapeutic inefficacy, or adverse outcomes. Healthcare providers should consider potential drug interactions and antagonistic effects

when selecting and managing medication regimens to optimize therapeutic outcomes and ensure patient safety.

## 105. What are the different types of drug antagonism? explain with examples?

- Drug antagonism refers to the inhibition or diminution of the effect of one drug by another drug or substance.
- There are several types of drug antagonism, each characterized by different mechanisms.

**Following are the main types of drug antagonism explained with examples:**

### Competitive Antagonism:

- Competitive antagonism occurs when a drug competes with another drug for binding to the same receptor site, thereby blocking or reducing the effect of the agonist.
- **Example:** Naloxone, a competitive antagonist, blocks the effects of opioids such as morphine by competing for binding to opioid receptors. In cases of opioid overdose, naloxone can reverse the respiratory depression and sedation caused by opioids by displacing them from their receptors.

### Non-competitive Antagonism:

- Non-competitive antagonism occurs when a drug binds to a different site on the receptor or alters the receptor's conformation, thereby reducing the receptor's ability to respond to the agonist.
- **Example:** Phenoxybenzamine, a non-competitive antagonist, irreversibly blocks alpha-adrenergic receptors, inhibiting the vasoconstrictor effects of catecholamines such as norepinephrine. It is used in the management of conditions like pheochromocytoma and Raynaud's disease.

### Physiological Antagonism:

- Physiological antagonism occurs when two drugs produce opposite effects through different mechanisms, counteracting each other's effects without directly interacting at the same receptor site.
- **Example:** Histamine and adrenaline have opposing effects on smooth muscle contraction. Histamine causes bronchoconstriction, while adrenaline causes bronchodilation.
- Administering adrenaline can counteract the bronchoconstriction induced by histamine through physiological antagonism.

### Chemical Antagonism:

- Chemical antagonism occurs when one drug neutralizes the effects of another drug through chemical reaction or inactivation.
- **Example:** Protamine sulfate is used as a chemical antagonist for heparin. Protamine sulfate binds to heparin molecules, forming a stable complex that prevents heparin from exerting its anticoagulant effects, thereby reversing the anticoagulant activity of heparin.

### Functional Antagonism:

- Functional antagonism occurs when two drugs produce opposing effects on the same physiological process, resulting in an overall reduction in the effect of one or both drugs.
- **Example:** Histamine, which causes vasodilation and increased vascular permeability, can counteract the vasoconstrictive effects of norepinephrine in certain vascular beds. This functional antagonism leads to a reduction in the net effect of either drug on vascular tone.

### Conclusion:

- Understanding the different types of drug antagonism is essential in clinical practice as it helps healthcare providers predict potential interactions between drugs, optimize therapeutic regimens, and minimize the risk of adverse effects or therapeutic failure.
- It also guides the selection of appropriate interventions to manage drug interactions effectively.

## 106. Compare competitive and non competitive antagonism with examples?

- Competitive and non-competitive antagonism are two distinct types of drug interactions that occur when one drug inhibits or diminishes the effects of another drug.

**Following is the comparison between competitive and non-competitive antagonism, along with examples:**

**Competitive Antagonism:**
- Mechanism: In competitive antagonism, the antagonist competes with the agonist for binding to the same receptor site.
- Both the agonist and antagonist can bind to the receptor, but the antagonist has lower intrinsic activity and does not activate the receptor. As a result, the antagonist blocks or reduces the effect of the agonist.
- **Effect on Agonist:** Competitive antagonism reduces the affinity of the agonist for the receptor, requiring a higher concentration of the agonist to produce a response.
- **Reversibility:** Competitive antagonists can be displaced from the receptor by increasing the concentration of the agonist, making the antagonism reversible.
- **Example:** Naloxone is a competitive antagonist that blocks the effects of opioids such as morphine by competing for binding to opioid receptors. In cases of opioid overdose, naloxone can reverse respiratory depression and sedation by displacing opioids from their receptors.

**Non-competitive Antagonism:**
- **Mechanism:** In non-competitive antagonism, the antagonist binds to a different site on the receptor or alters the receptor's conformation, thereby reducing the receptor's ability to respond to the agonist.
- The antagonist does not compete with the agonist for binding to the receptor.
- **Effect on Agonist:** Non-competitive antagonism reduces the maximal response of the agonist, without affecting its affinity for the receptor.
- **Reversibility:** Non-competitive antagonists bind irreversibly or with high affinity to the receptor, making the antagonism generally irreversible.
- **Example:** Phenoxybenzamine is a non-competitive antagonist that irreversibly blocks alpha-adrenergic receptors, inhibiting the vasoconstrictor effects of catecholamines such as norepinephrine.
- It is used in the management of conditions like pheochromocytoma and Raynaud's disease.

**Comparison:**
- **Binding Site:** Competitive antagonists bind to the same site as the agonist on the receptor, while non-competitive antagonists bind to a different site.
- **Affinity vs. Maximal Response:** Competitive antagonism affects the affinity of the agonist for the receptor, while non-competitive antagonism affects the maximal response of the agonist.
- **Reversibility:** Competitive antagonism is generally reversible, while non-competitive antagonism is often irreversible or difficult to reverse.

**Conclusion:**
- Understanding the differences between competitive and non-competitive antagonism is essential for predicting and managing drug interactions in clinical practice.
- Depending on the type of antagonism involved, different strategies may be required to overcome or mitigate the effects of antagonists and optimize therapeutic outcomes.

## 107. What are fixed dose combinations (FDC)? explain the advantages and disadvantages of FDCs?

- Fixed-dose combinations (FDCs) refer to pharmaceutical preparations that contain two or more active ingredients combined in a single dosage form, with fixed proportions of each component in every dose.

- These combinations are formulated to treat a specific medical condition or achieve therapeutic goals more effectively than individual drugs administered separately. Here are the advantages and disadvantages of fixed-dose combinations:

**Advantages of Fixed-Dose Combinations (FDCs):**

- **Improved Treatment Adherence:** FDCs simplify medication regimens by reducing the number of pills or doses that patients need to take each day. This can improve treatment adherence, particularly in patients who may find it challenging to manage multiple medications.

- **Enhanced Efficacy:** Combining two or more active ingredients with complementary mechanisms of action in a fixed-dose formulation can enhance therapeutic efficacy by targeting multiple pathways involved in disease pathogenesis. This may lead to better control of symptoms and improved clinical outcomes compared to monotherapy.

- **Reduced Risk of Treatment Failure:** FDCs minimize the risk of treatment failure due to incomplete or inadequate treatment by ensuring that patients receive all necessary medications in the correct proportions with each dose. This can be particularly beneficial in conditions where inadequate treatment can lead to disease progression or complications.

- **Synergistic Effects:** Some FDCs may exhibit synergistic interactions between the active ingredients, resulting in enhanced therapeutic effects compared to individual drugs administered separately. This can provide additional benefits in terms of symptom relief and disease management.

- **Simplified Prescribing and Dispensing:** FDCs streamline the prescribing and dispensing process for healthcare providers, as they only need to prescribe and dispense one medication instead of multiple individual drugs. This can save time and reduce the potential for medication errors.

**Disadvantages of Fixed-Dose Combinations (FDCs):**

- **Limited Dosing Flexibility:** FDCs have fixed proportions of each active ingredient in every dose, which may limit dosing flexibility for individual patients. Patients who require dose adjustments or titration of specific components may not have the option to do so with FDCs.

- **Increased Risk of Side Effects:** Combining multiple active ingredients in a single dosage form increases the risk of adverse drug reactions or side effects compared to monotherapy. Patients may experience side effects related to one or more components of the FDC, which can be challenging to manage.

- **Difficulty in Identifying Causative Agent:** When patients experience adverse effects or drug interactions with an FDC, it can be challenging to determine which specific component is responsible. This may complicate the process of identifying and managing adverse reactions or switching to alternative treatments.

- **Cost Considerations:** FDCs may be more expensive than individual drugs administered separately, particularly if they contain patented or brand-name ingredients. This can pose a financial burden for patients, healthcare systems, or payers, especially if generic alternatives are available for individual components.

- **Regulatory Challenges:** Developing and obtaining regulatory approval for FDCs can be complex, requiring evidence of safety, efficacy, and quality for each component as well as for the combination product. This may result in delays in availability or limited access to FDCs for certain patient populations.

**Conclusion:**

- In summary, fixed-dose combinations offer several advantages, including improved treatment adherence, enhanced efficacy, and simplified prescribing. However, they also have disadvantages such as limited dosing flexibility, increased risk of side effects, and cost considerations. Healthcare providers should carefully weigh the potential benefits and drawbacks of FDCs when considering treatment options for their patients, taking into account individual patient characteristics, preferences, and treatment goals.

## 108. Mention 15 factors modifying drug action? Explain them with examples?

- Various factors can modify the action of drugs, influencing their pharmacokinetics and pharmacodynamics.

**Following are 15 factors that can modify drug action, along with explanations and examples for each:**

### Age:

- **Explanation:** Age-related changes in physiology, metabolism, and organ function can affect drug absorption, distribution, metabolism, and excretion (ADME), as well as drug response.
- **Example:** Pediatric patients may have differences in drug metabolism due to immature hepatic enzymes, while elderly patients may experience altered drug kinetics due to decreased renal function.

### Gender:

- **Explanation:** Biological differences between males and females, such as body composition, hormonal levels, and enzyme activity, can influence drug pharmacokinetics and pharmacodynamics.
- **Example:** Women may require different dosing regimens for certain drugs due to hormonal fluctuations affecting drug metabolism and clearance rates.

### Genetics:

- **Explanation:** Genetic variations in drug-metabolizing enzymes, transporters, and drug targets can lead to interindividual differences in drug response and susceptibility to adverse effects.
- **Example:** Genetic polymorphisms in the CYP2D6 gene can affect the metabolism of drugs such as codeine, leading to variability in analgesic efficacy and risk of toxicity.

### Disease States:

- **Explanation:** The presence of underlying medical conditions can alter drug absorption, distribution, metabolism, and excretion, as well as drug response.
- **Example:** Liver disease can impair drug metabolism, leading to increased drug concentrations and potential toxicity, while renal impairment can decrease drug clearance, necessitating dosage adjustments.

### Concurrent Medications:

- **Explanation:** Drug-drug interactions can occur when two or more drugs interact pharmacokinetically or pharmacodynamically, affecting their efficacy, safety, or both.
- **Example:** Concurrent administration of warfarin (an anticoagulant) and aspirin (an antiplatelet agent) may increase the risk of bleeding due to additive effects on blood clotting.

### Diet:

- **Explanation:** Dietary factors can influence drug absorption, metabolism, and excretion, affecting drug bioavailability and efficacy.
- **Example:** Grapefruit juice inhibits intestinal CYP3A4 enzymes, leading to increased systemic exposure to certain drugs like statins and calcium channel blockers.

### Smoking:

- **Explanation:** Smoking can alter drug metabolism and clearance rates through induction of hepatic enzymes and changes in drug distribution.
- Example: Smoking can decrease the efficacy of certain medications, such as oral contraceptives, due to increased metabolism and clearance rates.

### Alcohol Consumption:

- **Explanation:** Alcohol can interact with drugs pharmacokinetically and pharmacodynamically, affecting drug metabolism, absorption, distribution, and drug response.

- **Example:** Alcohol can potentiate the sedative effects of benzodiazepines and opioids, leading to increased risk of respiratory depression and central nervous system depression.

## Body Weight and Composition:
- **Explanation:** Variations in body weight, fat distribution, and muscle mass can affect drug distribution and clearance rates, influencing drug efficacy and toxicity.
- **Example:** Obese individuals may require higher doses of lipophilic drugs due to increased volume of distribution and altered drug pharmacokinetics.

## Ethnicity:
- **Explanation:** Genetic and environmental factors associated with ethnicity can influence drug metabolism, response, and susceptibility to adverse effects.
- **Example:** Certain populations may have higher frequencies of genetic polymorphisms affecting drug metabolism, leading to variability in drug response and dosing requirements.

## Psychological Factors:
- **Explanation:** Psychological factors, such as placebo effects, expectations, and psychological stress, can influence drug efficacy and perceived therapeutic outcomes.
- **Example:** Placebo responses can lead to improvements in symptoms or perceived benefits, even in the absence of active drug treatment.

## Compliance:
- **Explanation:** Patient adherence to prescribed medication regimens can significantly impact drug efficacy and treatment outcomes.
- **Example:** Non-compliance with antihypertensive medications can result in uncontrolled blood pressure and increased risk of cardiovascular events.

## Route of Administration:
- **Explanation:** The route of drug administration can affect drug absorption, distribution, metabolism, and excretion, as well as onset and duration of action.
- **Example:** Intravenous administration provides rapid onset of action for drugs like opioids, while oral administration may result in delayed onset due to absorption from the gastrointestinal tract.

## Environmental Factors:
- **Explanation:** Environmental factors such as temperature, humidity, altitude, and pollution can influence drug stability, absorption, and metabolism.
- **Example:** High-altitude environments can affect drug pharmacokinetics by altering respiratory and cardiovascular function, leading to changes in drug distribution and clearance rates.

## Circadian Rhythms:
- **Explanation:** Biological rhythms, including circadian rhythms, can influence drug metabolism and response, leading to variations in drug efficacy and toxicity over the course of a day.
- **Example:** Corticosteroids may be administered in the morning to coincide with peak endogenous cortisol levels, optimizing anti-inflammatory effects while minimizing adrenal suppression.

## Conclusion:
- These factors highlight the complexity of drug action and underscore the importance of considering individual patient characteristics, environmental factors, and disease states when prescribing and managing medications in clinical practice.

## 109. Explain pharmacogenomics with example? how to apply clinically pharmacogenomics concepts?

- Pharmacogenomics is the study of how genetic variations influence an individual's response to drugs. It combines pharmacology (the study of drugs) with genomics (the study of genes and their functions) to understand how genetic differences affect drug efficacy, safety, and metabolism.
- By identifying genetic variations that influence drug response, pharmacogenomics aims to personalize medicine, optimize drug therapy, and minimize adverse drug reactions.

**Following is an explanation of pharmacogenomics with an example and how it can be applied clinically:**

- **Example:** Consider the drug clopidogrel, commonly prescribed to prevent blood clots in patients with cardiovascular disease.
- Clopidogrel is a prodrug that requires activation by the enzyme CYP2C19 to exert its antiplatelet effects.
- However, individuals with genetic variations that result in reduced CYP2C19 activity may have decreased metabolism of clopidogrel, leading to reduced efficacy and an increased risk of cardiovascular events.

**How to Apply Clinically:**

- **Genetic Testing:** Clinicians can use genetic tests to identify patients with specific genetic variations that may impact drug response. In the case of clopidogrel, testing for CYP2C19 polymorphisms can help identify patients who are poor metabolizers and may require alternative antiplatelet therapy.

- **Personalized Medicine:** Based on the results of genetic testing, clinicians can personalize drug therapy by selecting medications and dosages that are most likely to be effective and safe for individual patients.

- **Example:** Poor metabolizers of clopidogrel may be prescribed alternative antiplatelet agents, such as prasugrel or ticagrelor, which are not dependent on CYP2C19 metabolism for activation.

- **Dose Optimization:** Pharmacogenomic information can guide dose optimization by adjusting drug dosages based on individual genetic profiles. For drugs with narrow therapeutic indices, such as warfarin (an anticoagulant), genetic testing for variants in genes like CYP2C9 and VKORC1 can help determine the optimal dose to achieve therapeutic anticoagulation while minimizing the risk of bleeding or thrombosis.

**Prevention of Adverse Drug Reactions:**

- Pharmacogenomic testing can help identify patients at increased risk of adverse drug reactions due to genetic predispositions.
- **Example:** Testing for HLA-B*5701 can identify individuals at risk of developing severe hypersensitivity reactions to the antiretroviral drug abacavir, allowing clinicians to avoid prescribing it in these patients.

- **Drug Development:** Pharmacogenomics can inform drug development by identifying genetic targets for drug action and predicting individual responses to new medications. By understanding how genetic variations influence drug response, pharmaceutical companies can develop more effective and safer drugs tailored to specific patient populations.

- **Clinical Decision Support:** Integrating pharmacogenomic information into electronic health records and clinical decision support systems can provide real-time guidance to clinicians when prescribing medications. This helps ensure that pharmacogenomic data are effectively utilized in clinical practice to optimize drug therapy and improve patient outcomes.

**Conclusion:**

- Pharmacogenomics plays a crucial role in personalized medicine by identifying genetic variations that influence drug response and guiding clinical decision-making.

- By applying pharmacogenomic concepts clinically, healthcare providers can optimize drug therapy, minimize adverse drug reactions, and improve patient outcomes.

## 110. Explain the effect of pathological status of the patient on drug's action? give suitable examples?

- The pathological status of a patient refers to the presence of underlying diseases or medical conditions that can impact the action of drugs.
- Pathological conditions can affect various aspects of pharmacokinetics and pharmacodynamics, influencing drug absorption, distribution, metabolism, excretion, and response.
- Understanding the pathological status of a patient is essential for healthcare providers to optimize drug therapy and achieve desired treatment outcomes.

Here's how pathological status can affect drug action, along with suitable examples:

- **Altered Absorption:** Pathological conditions affecting the gastrointestinal tract, such as inflammatory bowel disease or gastric ulcers, can impair drug absorption.
- **Example:** Patients with Crohn's disease may have impaired absorption of oral medications due to intestinal inflammation, requiring alternative routes of drug administration or higher doses to achieve therapeutic effects.

- **Altered Distribution:** Pathological conditions affecting blood flow, protein binding, or tissue perfusion can alter drug distribution.
- **Example:** Patients with congestive heart failure may have reduced cardiac output and peripheral perfusion, leading to decreased distribution of drugs to target tissues.

- Adjustments in drug dosing or frequency may be necessary to achieve therapeutic concentrations.

### Altered Metabolism:

- Pathological conditions affecting hepatic function, such as liver cirrhosis or hepatitis, can impair drug metabolism by reducing enzyme activity or altering drug clearance rates.
- **Example:** Patients with liver cirrhosis may have decreased activity of hepatic enzymes involved in drug metabolism, leading to increased systemic exposure to medications like warfarin or benzodiazepines and an increased risk of adverse effects.

### Altered Excretion:

- Pathological conditions affecting renal function, such as chronic kidney disease or acute kidney injury, can impair drug excretion and prolong drug elimination half-life.
- **Example:** Patients with renal impairment may require dosage adjustments for renally eliminated drugs, such as antibiotics or antihypertensive medications, to prevent drug accumulation and toxicity.

### Altered Drug Response:

- Pathological conditions affecting target receptors, signaling pathways, or physiological processes can alter drug response and efficacy.
- **Example:** Patients with diabetes mellitus may have altered insulin sensitivity and glucose metabolism, requiring individualized insulin regimens or antidiabetic medications to achieve glycemic control.

### Disease Progression:

- The progression of a pathological condition over time can alter drug requirements and treatment goals.
- **Example:** Patients with progressive neurodegenerative diseases, such as Alzheimer's disease or Parkinson's disease, may require adjustments in drug therapy as the disease advances and symptoms change.

**Conclusion:**
- The pathological status of a patient can significantly impact the action of drugs by influencing pharmacokinetic and pharmacodynamic processes.
- Healthcare providers should consider the underlying diseases or medical conditions when prescribing medications and adjust drug therapy accordingly to optimize treatment outcomes and minimize the risk of adverse effects.

## 111. What is drug tolerance? Explain different types of drug tolerance with examples?

- Drug tolerance refers to a decrease in the response to a drug following repeated or prolonged exposure, leading to a reduced effectiveness of the drug over time.
- Tolerance can develop to various pharmacological effects of a drug, including therapeutic effects, side effects, and toxic effects.

Following are the different types of drug tolerance, along with examples:

**Pharmacodynamic Tolerance:**
- Pharmacodynamic tolerance occurs when changes in the responsiveness of target receptors or physiological systems result in a decreased response to a drug.
- **Example:** Opioid tolerance develops with chronic use of opioids due to downregulation of opioid receptors and desensitization of opioid signaling pathways. As a result, higher doses of opioids are required to achieve the same analgesic effect over time.

**Metabolic Tolerance:**
- Metabolic tolerance occurs when the body becomes more efficient at metabolizing and eliminating a drug, leading to a decrease in drug concentration at the site of action.
- **Example:** Chronic alcohol consumption induces hepatic enzymes involved in alcohol metabolism, such as alcohol dehydrogenase and cytochrome P450 enzymes.

- As a result, individuals who regularly consume alcohol may develop metabolic tolerance to the sedative effects of alcohol, requiring higher alcohol doses to achieve the same level of intoxication.

**Cellular Tolerance:**
- Cellular tolerance involves adaptations within individual cells or tissues that reduce the cellular response to a drug.
- **Example:** Chronic exposure to beta-adrenergic agonists, such as albuterol, can lead to desensitization of beta-adrenergic receptors on smooth muscle cells in the airways. As a result, individuals with asthma who use beta-agonist inhalers may experience reduced bronchodilation and diminished therapeutic efficacy over time.

**Behavioral Tolerance:**
- Behavioral tolerance occurs when learned behaviors or environmental cues modify the response to a drug, leading to a reduction in drug effects.
- **Example:** Individuals who frequently use stimulant drugs like cocaine may develop behavioral tolerance to the euphoric effects of the drug. They may learn to associate specific environmental cues or rituals with drug use, leading to diminished subjective effects despite consistent drug exposure.

**Cross-Tolerance:**
- Cross-tolerance occurs when tolerance to one drug results in a reduced response to another drug with similar pharmacological properties.
- **Example:** Chronic use of benzodiazepines, such as diazepam, can lead to cross-tolerance to other benzodiazepines due to their shared mechanism of action on gamma-aminobutyric acid (GABA) receptors.
- As a result, individuals who are tolerant to one benzodiazepine may require higher doses of another benzodiazepine to achieve the same sedative effects.

**Conclusion:**

- Drug tolerance refers to a decreased response to a drug following repeated or prolonged exposure.
- Different types of tolerance can occur, including pharmacodynamic, metabolic, cellular, behavioral, and cross-tolerance, each involving specific mechanisms and adaptations that reduce the effectiveness of the drug over time.
- Understanding the mechanisms of tolerance is essential for optimizing drug therapy and managing potential tolerance-related issues in clinical practice.

## 112. Explain tachyphylaxis with example?

- Tachyphylaxis is a rapid and acute decrease in response to a drug following repeated or continuous administration, often occurring within a short period of time.
- Unlike drug tolerance, which develops gradually over time with repeated exposure, tachyphylaxis typically occurs more rapidly, sometimes after just a few doses.
- This phenomenon is thought to involve rapid desensitization or downregulation of receptors or physiological pathways involved in drug response. Here's an explanation of tachyphylaxis with an example:
- **Example of Tachyphylaxis:** Consider the use of topical decongestant nasal sprays, such as oxymetazoline or phenylephrine, for the relief of nasal congestion due to allergies or colds.
- These medications work by constricting blood vessels in the nasal mucosa, reducing swelling and congestion.
- In some cases, individuals who use nasal decongestant sprays for several consecutive days may experience tachyphylaxis, where the effectiveness of the medication rapidly diminishes over time. Initially, the nasal spray provides significant relief from congestion, but with continued use, the duration and magnitude of relief decrease. This occurs because prolonged exposure to the vasoconstrictive effects of the nasal decongestant leads to downregulation of adrenergic receptors in the nasal mucosa, reducing

the responsiveness of blood vessels to the medication. As a result, the nasal spray becomes less effective at relieving congestion, and individuals may experience rebound congestion when the medication wears off, leading to a cycle of increased usage and diminishing efficacy.

- To manage tachyphylaxis with nasal decongestant sprays, healthcare providers may recommend discontinuing use of the medication for a period of time or switching to alternative treatments, such as saline nasal sprays or oral decongestants, to avoid dependence on the vasoconstrictive effects of the medication and prevent rebound congestion.

**Conclusion:**

- Tachyphylaxis refers to a rapid decrease in drug response following repeated administration, often due to desensitization or downregulation of receptors or physiological pathways.
- An example of tachyphylaxis is the diminishing effectiveness of nasal decongestant sprays with prolonged use, leading to rebound congestion and decreased symptom relief.
- Understanding tachyphylaxis is important for healthcare providers to anticipate and manage changes in drug response and optimize treatment outcomes for patients.

## 113. What is drug resistance? Explain drug resistance with examples?

- Drug resistance occurs when microorganisms, such as bacteria, viruses, fungi, or parasites, adapt and develop mechanisms that render them less susceptible or completely resistant to the effects of antimicrobial drugs.
- This phenomenon poses a significant challenge in the treatment of infectious diseases, as it reduces the effectiveness of available medications and complicates patient management. Here's an explanation of drug resistance with examples:

**Antibiotic Resistance:**

- Antibiotic resistance occurs when bacteria develop mechanisms to resist the action of antibiotics, making infections more difficult to treat.

**This can occur through various mechanisms, including:**

**Enzymatic inactivation or modification of antibiotics:**
- Reduced permeability of bacterial cell membranes, preventing antibiotics from entering the cell.
- Efflux pumps that actively pump antibiotics out of bacterial cells.
- Target site modifications that prevent antibiotics from binding to their intended targets.
- **Example:** Methicillin-resistant Staphylococcus aureus (MRSA) is a notorious example of antibiotic resistance.
- MRSA strains have acquired resistance to multiple antibiotics, including methicillin and other beta-lactam antibiotics, making them difficult to treat and leading to severe and sometimes life-threatening infections.

**Antiviral Resistance:**
- Antiviral resistance occurs when viruses develop mutations or acquire genetic changes that reduce their susceptibility to antiviral drugs. This can lead to treatment failure and the persistence or recurrence of viral infections.
- **Example:** Human immunodeficiency virus (HIV) can develop resistance to antiretroviral drugs used to treat HIV/AIDS. Mutations in the viral genome can confer resistance to specific classes of antiretroviral drugs, such as nucleoside reverse transcriptase inhibitors (NRTIs) or protease inhibitors (PIs), limiting treatment options for infected individuals.

**Antifungal Resistance:**
- Antifungal resistance refers to the ability of fungi to resist the effects of antifungal drugs, leading to treatment failure and the progression of fungal infections. Resistance mechanisms may involve alterations in fungal cell wall composition, efflux pumps, or target site mutations.
- Example: Candida auris is an emerging multidrug-resistant fungal pathogen that has caused outbreaks of invasive infections in healthcare settings worldwide. C. auris strains are resistant to multiple antifungal drugs, including fluconazole, amphotericin B, and echinocandins, posing challenges for infection control and patient management.

**Antiparasitic Resistance:**
- Antiparasitic resistance occurs when parasites develop mechanisms to evade the effects of antiparasitic drugs, reducing treatment efficacy and increasing the risk of treatment failure.
- **Example:** Plasmodium falciparum, the parasite that causes malaria, has developed resistance to multiple antimalarial drugs, including chloroquine and sulfadoxine-pyrimethamine, in various regions of the world. This has necessitated the use of alternative antimalarial drugs and combination therapies to combat drug-resistant malaria strains.

**Conclusion:**
- Drug resistance is a complex and evolving phenomenon that poses significant challenges in the treatment of infectious diseases.
- Examples of drug resistance include antibiotic resistance in bacteria, antiviral resistance in viruses, antifungal resistance in fungi, and antiparasitic resistance in parasites.
- Understanding the mechanisms of drug resistance and implementing strategies to prevent its emergence and spread are essential for preserving the effectiveness of antimicrobial drugs and combating infectious diseases.

**114. Explain rational drug use with examples?**
- Rational drug use refers to the appropriate, safe, effective, and cost-effective use of medications based on scientific evidence, clinical guidelines, and patient needs.
- It involves selecting the most suitable drug therapy for a specific medical condition, taking into account factors such as diagnosis, patient characteristics, drug efficacy and safety, dosing regimen, and cost considerations.

- Rational drug use aims to optimize therapeutic outcomes, minimize the risk of adverse effects, and ensure the responsible use of healthcare resources.

**Following is an explanation of rational drug use with examples:**

**Selection of Appropriate Drug Therapy:**
- Rational drug use involves selecting the most appropriate medication for a given medical condition based on factors such as efficacy, safety, and patient preferences.
- **Example:** In the treatment of hypertension, guidelines recommend the use of first-line antihypertensive medications such as thiazide diuretics, angiotensin-converting enzyme (ACE) inhibitors, angiotensin II receptor blockers (ARBs), or calcium channel blockers (CCBs) based on individual patient characteristics and comorbidities.

**Individualized Dosing and Monitoring:**
- Rational drug use includes individualizing drug dosing regimens based on patient characteristics such as age, weight, renal function, and comorbidities, and monitoring treatment response and adverse effects.
- **Example:** Warfarin therapy for anticoagulation requires individualized dosing based on patient factors and regular monitoring of international normalized ratio (INR) to ensure therapeutic anticoagulation and minimize the risk of bleeding or thrombosis.

**Avoidance of Polypharmacy and Drug Interactions:**
- Rational drug use involves minimizing polypharmacy and avoiding drug-drug interactions by carefully assessing the need for each medication and considering potential interactions when prescribing multiple drugs.
- **Example:** Older adults are at increased risk of adverse drug reactions due to polypharmacy and drug interactions. Rational drug use in this population may involve deprescribing unnecessary medications and prioritizing the use of drugs with the lowest potential for interactions.

- Rational drug use relies on evidence-based medicine, incorporating the best available scientific evidence, clinical expertise, and patient values and preferences in clinical decision-making.
- **Example:** In the management of type 2 diabetes mellitus, treatment decisions are guided by evidence-based guidelines that recommend lifestyle modifications, metformin therapy as first-line pharmacotherapy, and individualized treatment strategies based on glycemic control goals and patient preferences.

**Cost-Effective Prescribing:**
- Rational drug use considers the cost-effectiveness of drug therapy, balancing the potential benefits of treatment with the economic impact on patients, healthcare systems, and society.
- **Example:** Prescribing generic medications instead of brand-name drugs when clinically appropriate can help reduce healthcare costs without compromising treatment efficacy or safety, promoting rational drug use and cost-effective prescribing practices.

**Conclusion:**
- Rational drug use involves the judicious selection, individualization, and monitoring of drug therapy based on scientific evidence, clinical guidelines, patient needs, and cost considerations.
- Examples of rational drug use include selecting appropriate drug therapy, individualizing dosing regimens, avoiding polypharmacy and drug interactions, using evidence-based medicine, and prescribing cost-effective medications.
- By promoting rational drug use, healthcare providers can optimize therapeutic outcomes, minimize adverse effects, and ensure the responsible use of healthcare resources.

**115. Explain rational prescribing? what are the factors influencing drug prescribing with examples?**
- Rational prescribing refers to the process of selecting and prescribing medications in a manner that is evidence-based, clinically appropriate,

safe, effective, and cost-effective for individual patients. It involves considering various factors that influence drug therapy decisions, including patient characteristics, medical conditions, drug efficacy and safety profiles, dosing regimens, and cost considerations.

- Rational prescribing aims to optimize therapeutic outcomes, minimize the risk of adverse effects, and ensure the responsible use of medications. Here's an explanation of rational prescribing and the factors influencing drug prescribing with examples:

## Patient Characteristics:

- Patient factors such as age, gender, weight, renal and hepatic function, comorbidities, and medication allergies influence drug prescribing decisions.
- **Example:** Prescribing lower doses of medications for elderly patients or those with renal impairment to minimize the risk of adverse effects or drug accumulation.

## Diagnosis and Medical Condition:

- The underlying medical condition or diagnosis guides drug therapy decisions, including the selection of appropriate medications and treatment goals.
- **Example:** Prescribing proton pump inhibitors (PPIs) for the treatment of gastroesophageal reflux disease (GERD) to reduce gastric acid secretion and alleviate symptoms of heartburn and acid reflux.

## Drug Efficacy and Safety Profiles:

- The efficacy and safety profiles of medications, including their mechanism of action, side effect profiles, and potential drug interactions, influence prescribing decisions.
- **Example:** Selecting statin therapy for lipid-lowering in patients with hyperlipidemia based on their proven efficacy in reducing cardiovascular events and their favorable safety profile when used appropriately.

## Guidelines and Evidence-Based Medicine:

- Clinical practice guidelines and evidence-based medicine provide recommendations for drug therapy based on the best available scientific evidence and expert consensus.
- **Example:** Following guidelines from organizations such as the American Diabetes Association (ADA) or the American Heart Association (AHA) for the management of specific medical conditions, such as diabetes or hypertension, to guide drug prescribing decisions.

## Cost Considerations:

- The cost of medications, including out-of-pocket expenses for patients, insurance coverage, and healthcare system costs, influences prescribing decisions.
- **Example:** Prescribing generic medications instead of brand-name drugs when clinically appropriate to reduce healthcare costs and improve medication adherence.

## Drug Formulary and Availability:

- The availability of medications on formularies, drug formularies, and local drug availability may impact prescribing decisions.
- **Example:** Choosing alternative medications from the hospital formulary when specific drugs are not available or are restricted due to formulary limitations.

## Patient Preferences and Adherence:

- Patient preferences, beliefs, cultural considerations, and treatment adherence influence prescribing decisions and treatment outcomes.
- **Example:** Engaging in shared decision-making with patients to discuss treatment options, address concerns, and collaboratively develop a treatment plan that aligns with their preferences and values.

Conclusion:

- Rational prescribing involves considering multiple factors, including patient characteristics, medical conditions, drug efficacy and safety profiles, guidelines, cost considerations, and patient preferences, to select and prescribe medications that are evidence-based, clinically appropriate, safe, effective, and cost-effective for individual patients.
- By addressing these factors, healthcare providers can optimize therapeutic outcomes, minimize the risk of adverse effects, and improve patient satisfaction and adherence to medication therapy.

## 116. What is irrational prescribing? explain factors influencing irrational prescribing with examples?

- Irrational prescribing refers to the inappropriate, suboptimal, or unjustified use of medications, characterized by prescribing practices that deviate from evidence-based guidelines, clinical standards, or best practices. It encompasses prescribing decisions that may lead to ineffective treatment outcomes, unnecessary healthcare costs, patient harm, or antimicrobial resistance.

**Several factors can contribute to irrational prescribing practices, including:**

### Inadequate Knowledge or Training:

- Healthcare providers may lack sufficient knowledge or training in pharmacotherapy, leading to suboptimal prescribing decisions.
- **Example:** Prescribing antibiotics for viral infections, such as the common cold or influenza, despite evidence that antibiotics are ineffective against viral pathogens.

### Pressure from Patients or Caregivers:

- Healthcare providers may face pressure from patients or caregivers to prescribe medications, even when they are not clinically indicated.
- Example: Prescribing opioids for the management of chronic non-cancer pain due to patient insistence, despite concerns about the risks of addiction and overdose.

### Pharmaceutical Marketing and Promotion:

- Pharmaceutical marketing tactics, such as direct-to-consumer advertising or interactions with pharmaceutical representatives, may influence prescribing behavior.
- **Example:** Prescribing brand-name medications over equally effective generic alternatives due to marketing materials or incentives provided by pharmaceutical companies.

### Financial Incentives:

- Financial incentives, reimbursement structures, or incentives tied to prescribing volume or drug utilization may influence prescribing decisions.
- **Example:** Prescribing expensive brand-name medications or unnecessary diagnostic tests to increase revenue or meet performance targets, rather than considering cost-effective treatment options.

### Polypharmacy and Drug Interactions:

- Prescribing multiple medications concurrently (polypharmacy) without considering potential drug interactions or adverse effects can lead to irrational prescribing.
- Example: Prescribing a combination of medications with known drug-drug interactions, such as combining selective serotonin reuptake inhibitors (SSRIs) with monoamine oxidase inhibitors (MAOIs), without adjusting dosages or monitoring for adverse effects.

### Defensive Medicine:

- Fear of litigation or medical malpractice claims may lead healthcare providers to prescribe unnecessary tests, treatments, or medications.
- **Example:** Ordering unnecessary imaging studies or diagnostic tests to avoid potential legal consequences, despite a lack of clinical indication or benefit.

### Patient Expectations and Satisfaction:

- Healthcare providers may prescribe medications to meet patient expectations or improve patient satisfaction, even when they are not medically necessary or appropriate.

- **Example:** Prescribing antibiotics for self-limiting respiratory tract infections to satisfy patient demands for treatment, despite evidence of viral etiology and the limited benefit of antibiotics.

## Conclusion:

- Irrational prescribing occurs when prescribing decisions deviate from evidence-based guidelines, clinical standards, or best practices, leading to ineffective or inappropriate use of medications.
- Factors influencing irrational prescribing include inadequate knowledge or training, pressure from patients or caregivers, pharmaceutical marketing, financial incentives, polypharmacy, defensive medicine, and patient expectations.
- Addressing these factors through education, guideline adherence, regulatory measures, and patient-centered care can help promote rational prescribing practices and improve patient outcomes.

## 117. Explain the methods to reduce irrational prescribing? explain with examples?

- Reducing irrational prescribing requires a multi-faceted approach that involves healthcare providers, patients, policymakers, and healthcare systems.
- Several methods can be employed to promote rational prescribing practices and improve medication use.

**Following are some examples:**

### Continuing Medical Education (CME) and Training:

- Providing healthcare providers with regular CME activities and training sessions on evidence-based prescribing practices can enhance their knowledge and skills in pharmacotherapy.
- **Example:** Offering workshops or online courses on antibiotic stewardship principles and appropriate prescribing practices for common infectious diseases to improve antibiotic prescribing behavior among healthcare providers.

### Clinical Decision Support Systems (CDSS):

- Implementing CDSS within electronic health record (EHR) systems can provide real-time guidance and alerts to healthcare providers at the point of care, promoting adherence to clinical guidelines and evidence-based prescribing.
- **Example:** Integrating drug-drug interaction alerts or allergy warnings into EHR systems to alert prescribers to potential medication interactions or allergies when selecting medications for patients.

### Formulary Restrictions and Utilization Review:

- Implementing formulary restrictions, prior authorization requirements, and utilization review processes for certain medications can help control inappropriate prescribing and promote the use of cost-effective alternatives.
- **Example:** Requiring prior authorization for high-cost medications or specialty drugs to ensure that they are prescribed only when clinically indicated and cost-effective, based on evidence-based guidelines.

### Antibiotic Stewardship Programs:

- Establishing antibiotic stewardship programs in healthcare settings can promote responsible antibiotic prescribing practices, reduce unnecessary antibiotic use, and mitigate the development of antimicrobial resistance.
- **Example:** Implementing guidelines and protocols for the diagnosis and management of common infectious diseases, such as urinary tract infections or respiratory tract infections, to encourage appropriate antibiotic prescribing and de-escalation of therapy based on culture results.

### Prescriber Feedback and Peer Comparisons:

- Providing prescribers with feedback on their prescribing patterns and performance compared to peers can help identify areas for improvement and encourage adherence to prescribing guidelines.
- **Example:** Sending personalized feedback reports to healthcare providers highlighting their prescribing patterns, including rates of

inappropriate antibiotic prescribing or adherence to formulary guidelines, and benchmarking them against peers to promote self-reflection and quality improvement.

**Patient Education and Shared Decision-Making:**
- Educating patients about the risks and benefits of medications, encouraging medication adherence, and involving patients in shared decision-making can empower them to participate in their treatment decisions and reduce unnecessary prescribing.
- **Example:** Providing educational materials or decision aids to patients with chronic conditions, such as diabetes or hypertension, to help them understand their treatment options, risks, and benefits, and collaborate with healthcare providers in developing personalized treatment plans.

**Conclusion:**
- Reducing irrational prescribing requires a comprehensive approach that involves education, decision support, formulary management, antibiotic stewardship, feedback mechanisms, and patient engagement.
- By implementing these methods, healthcare systems can promote rational prescribing practices, improve medication use, and enhance patient outcomes while minimizing the risks associated with inappropriate prescribing.

## 118. Explain the importance of expiry date of drugs? write the method to dispose the drugs with examples?
- The expiry date of drugs, also known as the expiration date, indicates the date until which the manufacturer guarantees the full potency and safety of the medication when stored under proper conditions.
- Understanding and adhering to expiry dates is essential for ensuring the effectiveness and safety of medications.

**Here's why the expiry date of drugs is important:**

- **Efficacy:** Over time, medications may degrade or lose potency, rendering them less effective or ineffective in treating medical conditions. Adhering to expiry dates helps ensure that patients receive medications that maintain their therapeutic efficacy.
- **Safety:** Expired medications may undergo chemical changes that can alter their composition and lead to the formation of harmful by-products or degradation products. Using expired drugs may pose risks of adverse effects or toxic reactions. Adhering to expiry dates helps prevent potential harm to patients.
- **Regulatory Compliance:** Regulatory agencies, such as the U.S. Food and Drug Administration (FDA), require pharmaceutical manufacturers to establish expiry dates based on stability testing and to ensure product quality and safety. Adhering to expiry dates helps healthcare providers and patients comply with regulatory requirements.
- **Quality Assurance:** Expiry dates serve as a quality assurance measure, indicating the period during which medications are expected to meet established standards of quality, purity, and potency. Adhering to expiry dates helps maintain the integrity and reliability of medications.

**To dispose of expired or unused medications safely, follow these methods:**

**Medication Take-Back Programs:**
- Many communities offer medication take-back programs or events where individuals can safely dispose of expired or unused medications at designated collection sites, such as pharmacies, hospitals, or law enforcement agencies.
- **Example:** The U.S. Drug Enforcement Administration (DEA) hosts National Prescription Drug Take Back Day events twice a year, providing opportunities for individuals to safely dispose of unwanted medications.

**Pharmacy Disposal:**

- Some pharmacies accept expired or unused medications for safe disposal. Check with local pharmacies to inquire about their medication disposal policies and whether they offer medication disposal services.
- **Example:** Some chain pharmacies provide medication disposal kiosks or mail-back envelopes for customers to return unused medications for proper disposal.

**Household Disposal:**

- If medication take-back programs or pharmacy disposal options are not available, follow specific guidelines for household disposal to minimize environmental impact and prevent accidental ingestion by children or pets.
- **Example:** Dispose of medications in the household trash by mixing them with undesirable substances, such as coffee grounds or kitty litter, and placing them in a sealed container or bag before discarding in the trash.

**Do Not Flush:**

- Avoid flushing medications down the toilet or drain unless specific disposal instructions indicate it is safe to do so. Flushing medications can contribute to water pollution and environmental contamination.
- **Example:** Certain medications, such as controlled substances or those with specific disposal instructions, may be eligible for flushing according to FDA recommendations. However, always follow specific disposal instructions provided with the medication.

**Conclusion:**

- By adhering to expiry dates and properly disposing of expired or unused medications, individuals can help ensure medication safety, prevent unintended harm, and promote responsible medication use.

**119. What is evidence based medicine? explain with examples?**

- Evidence-based medicine (EBM) is an approach to clinical decision-making that integrates the best available scientific evidence with clinical expertise and patient values and preferences to inform healthcare decisions.
- The practice of evidence-based medicine involves critically appraising and applying relevant research findings to individual patient care situations, with the goal of improving patient outcomes and optimizing healthcare delivery.

**Following is an explanation of evidence-based medicine with examples:**

**Research Evidence:**

- EBM relies on high-quality research evidence from systematic reviews, meta-analyses, randomized controlled trials (RCTs), and other study designs to inform clinical decision-making.
- **Example:** A meta-analysis of RCTs evaluating the efficacy of statin therapy for the prevention of cardiovascular events provides evidence-based recommendations for the use of statins in patients at risk of coronary artery disease.

**Clinical Expertise:**

- EBM recognizes the importance of clinical expertise and judgment in interpreting research evidence and applying it to individual patient cases. Clinical expertise encompasses healthcare providers' knowledge, skills, and experience in diagnosing and treating patients.
- **Example:** A primary care physician uses clinical expertise to tailor evidence-based treatment guidelines for hypertension to meet the specific needs and preferences of an elderly patient with multiple comorbidities and contraindications to certain antihypertensive medications.

**Patient Values and Preferences:**

- EBM emphasizes the importance of considering patient values, preferences, and individual circumstances in clinical decision-making.

- Patient-centered care involves engaging patients in shared decision-making and incorporating their values and preferences into treatment decisions.
- **Example:** A patient with early-stage breast cancer discusses treatment options, including surgery, chemotherapy, and radiation therapy, with their oncologist. The oncologist considers the patient's preferences, lifestyle, and treatment goals when developing an evidence-based treatment plan tailored to the patient's needs.

## Clinical Practice Guidelines:

- EBM is supported by evidence-based clinical practice guidelines developed by expert panels or professional organizations. Clinical practice guidelines provide recommendations for healthcare providers based on systematic reviews of evidence and expert consensus.
- **Example:** The American Diabetes Association (ADA) publishes evidence-based clinical practice guidelines for the management of diabetes mellitus, offering recommendations for screening, diagnosis, and treatment based on the best available research evidence and expert consensus.

## Continuous Learning and Quality Improvement:

- EBM promotes lifelong learning and continuous quality improvement in healthcare practice. Healthcare providers engage in ongoing education, training, and professional development to stay updated on the latest research evidence and best practices.
- **Example:** A multidisciplinary team at a hospital conducts regular morbidity and mortality conferences to review clinical cases, identify opportunities for improvement, and implement evidence-based interventions to enhance patient care and safety.

Conclusion:
- The evidence-based medicine is an approach to clinical decision-making that integrates research evidence, clinical expertise, and patient values and preferences to inform healthcare decisions and improve patient outcomes.

- By applying the principles of evidence-based medicine, healthcare providers can deliver high-quality, patient-centered care that is based on the best available evidence and tailored to individual patient needs.

## 120. What are clinical trials? explain different types of clinical trials, their objectives, methods to conduct the trials?

- Clinical trials are research studies conducted in human volunteers to evaluate the safety, efficacy, and effectiveness of medical interventions, including medications, treatments, procedures, and medical devices.
- Clinical trials are essential for advancing medical knowledge, developing new therapies, improving patient care, and informing clinical practice guidelines.

Following is an overview of different types of clinical trials, their objectives, and methods to conduct the trials:

## Types of Clinical Trials:

### a. Treatment Trials:
- Objective: Treatment trials evaluate the effectiveness and safety of new medications, treatments, or interventions compared to standard or existing therapies.
- **Example:** A randomized controlled trial (RCT) comparing the efficacy and safety of a novel chemotherapy regimen with standard-of-care chemotherapy in patients with advanced lung cancer.

### b. Prevention Trials:
- Objective: Prevention trials assess the efficacy of interventions or strategies to prevent the occurrence or recurrence of diseases or health conditions.
- **Example:** A randomized trial investigating the effectiveness of a new vaccine in preventing human papillomavirus (HPV) infection and subsequent development of cervical cancer in young women.

## c. Diagnostic Trials:

- Objective: Diagnostic trials evaluate the accuracy and reliability of diagnostic tests, biomarkers, or imaging modalities for detecting diseases, conditions, or risk factors.
- **Example:** A diagnostic accuracy study assessing the sensitivity and specificity of a novel blood test for detecting early-stage prostate cancer compared to standard prostate-specific antigen (PSA) testing.

## d. Screening Trials:

- Objective: Screening trials assess the effectiveness of screening programs or strategies for early detection and diagnosis of diseases or health conditions.
- **Example:** A population-based screening trial evaluating the impact of mammography screening on reducing breast cancer mortality in women aged 50-74 years compared to no screening.

## e. Observational Trials:

- Objective: Observational trials observe and analyze the natural course of diseases, treatment outcomes, risk factors, or associations between variables without intervention.
- **Example:** A cohort study examining the long-term health outcomes and quality of life of patients undergoing different surgical procedures for obesity management.

## Methods to Conduct Clinical Trials:

## Study Design:

- Clinical trials are typically designed as randomized controlled trials (RCTs), where participants are randomly assigned to different treatment groups to minimize bias and confounding factors.
- Other study designs include cohort studies, case-control studies, crossover trials, and factorial trials, depending on the research question and objectives.

## b. Informed Consent:

- Participants in clinical trials must provide informed consent before enrollment, indicating their understanding of the study purpose, procedures, risks, benefits, and voluntary participation.
- Informed consent is obtained through a detailed discussion between the investigator and participant, and written documentation is provided to the participant.

## c. Ethical Review:

- Clinical trials must undergo ethical review and approval by institutional review boards (IRBs) or ethics committees to ensure participant safety, protection of rights, and adherence to ethical principles.
- Ethical review assesses the scientific validity, methodological rigor, potential risks, and benefits of the trial, as well as the adequacy of informed consent procedures.

## d. Recruitment and Enrollment:

- Participants are recruited and enrolled in clinical trials based on specific eligibility criteria, including age, gender, medical history, disease stage, and treatment history.
- Recruitment methods may include physician referrals, community outreach, advertisements, and electronic health record screening.

## e. Data Collection and Monitoring:

- Clinical trial data are collected through standardized procedures, including participant assessments, laboratory tests, imaging studies, and medical record review.
- Data quality and integrity are ensured through monitoring by clinical research coordinators, data managers, and independent monitors or auditors.

## f. Statistical Analysis:

- Statistical analysis of clinical trial data involves comparing outcomes between treatment groups using appropriate statistical tests, such as t-tests, chi-square tests, or regression analysis.

- Sample size calculations are performed to determine the number of participants needed to detect a clinically significant difference between treatment groups with sufficient statistical power.

**Conclusion:**
- Clinical trials are research studies conducted in human volunteers to evaluate medical interventions.
- Different types of clinical trials include treatment, prevention, diagnostic, screening, and observational trials, each with specific objectives and methods.
- Clinical trials adhere to ethical principles, involve informed consent, undergo ethical review, recruit participants based on eligibility criteria, collect data, monitor participant safety, and analyze outcomes to generate evidence for informing clinical practice and improving patient care.

**121. What are preclinical studies? Explain different types of studies done while drug development with examples?**

- Preclinical studies are conducted in laboratory settings or animal models before testing a new drug or medical intervention in humans. These studies provide essential preliminary data on the safety, pharmacokinetics, pharmacodynamics, and potential efficacy of the investigational product.
- Preclinical research plays a crucial role in guiding the development and optimization of candidate drugs and informing decisions regarding their progression to clinical trials.

**Following are different types of preclinical studies conducted during drug development, along with examples:**

**In vitro Studies:**
- In vitro studies involve testing the effects of the investigational compound on isolated cells or tissues in controlled laboratory conditions.
- **Examples:** Cell viability assays to assess the cytotoxicity or cell proliferation effects of a drug candidate on cancer cells.
- Enzyme inhibition assays to evaluate the potential of a compound to inhibit specific enzymatic activity relevant to disease pathology.

**In vivo Pharmacology Studies:**
- In vivo pharmacology studies involve administering the investigational compound to laboratory animals to evaluate its pharmacological effects, toxicity, and mechanism of action.
- **Examples:** Pharmacokinetic studies to assess the absorption, distribution, metabolism, and excretion (ADME) of a drug candidate in animal models, such as rats or mice.
- Pharmacodynamic studies to evaluate the physiological or biochemical effects of a drug candidate on disease-related endpoints, such as blood pressure reduction in hypertensive animal models.

**Safety and Toxicology Studies:**
- Safety and toxicology studies assess the potential adverse effects and safety profile of the investigational compound following repeated dosing in animals.
- Examples: Acute toxicity studies to determine the maximum tolerated dose (MTD) and identify acute adverse effects of the drug candidate in animal models.
- Subchronic and chronic toxicity studies to assess the effects of prolonged exposure to the drug candidate on organ systems, histopathology, and systemic toxicity.

**Pharmacokinetic-Pharmacodynamic (PK-PD) Modeling:**

- PK-PD modeling integrates pharmacokinetic and pharmacodynamic data to characterize the relationship between drug exposure and pharmacological response.
- Examples: Dose-response studies to establish the relationship between drug dose, plasma concentration, and therapeutic effect in animal models.

- Modeling and simulation studies to predict optimal dosing regimens and inform dose selection for clinical trials based on preclinical PK-PD relationships.

**Formulation and Drug Delivery Studies:**
- Formulation and drug delivery studies focus on optimizing the formulation, stability, and delivery of the investigational compound to improve its bioavailability, efficacy, and patient compliance.
- **Examples:** Formulation optimization studies to develop novel drug formulations, such as nanoparticles, liposomes, or sustained-release formulations, to enhance drug solubility, stability, and targeting.
- Pharmacokinetic studies to evaluate the pharmacokinetic profile of different drug formulations and delivery routes in animal models and select the most promising formulation for clinical development.

Conclusion:
- Preclinical studies encompass a range of experimental approaches aimed at evaluating the safety, pharmacology, and efficacy of investigational drugs before human testing.
- These studies provide crucial data to support the rational design and optimization of candidate drugs and inform decisions regarding their advancement to clinical trials.

## 122. What is placebo? Explain its clinical significance?

- A placebo is an inactive substance or treatment that resembles a real medical intervention but has no therapeutic effect on the condition being treated.
- In clinical trials, placebos are often used as controls to assess the true efficacy of investigational drugs or interventions by comparing their effects to those of the placebo.

- Placebos are typically formulated to resemble the active treatment in appearance, taste, or administration method to maintain blinding and minimize bias in the study results.

**The clinical significance of placebos lies in their role in research and clinical practice:**

**Research Tool:**
- Placebos serve as essential controls in clinical trials to distinguish between the specific effects of a treatment and the nonspecific effects, such as the placebo effect or natural disease progression.
- By comparing the outcomes of participants receiving the active treatment to those receiving a placebo, researchers can determine whether the treatment has a genuine therapeutic benefit beyond what would be expected from placebo effects or spontaneous improvement.

**Placebo Effect:**
- The placebo effect refers to the phenomenon whereby patients experience improvements in their symptoms or health outcomes after receiving a placebo, often attributed to psychological or physiological factors, such as patient expectations, conditioning, or the therapeutic encounter.
- Understanding and harnessing the placebo effect is essential for optimizing patient care and maximizing treatment outcomes.
- For example, placebo responses observed in clinical trials can inform the design and interpretation of future studies and guide the development of more effective interventions.

**Clinical Practice:**
- Placebos are occasionally used in clinical practice as part of placebo-controlled trials or as adjunctive treatments in certain conditions where no specific treatment is available or when the benefit of the treatment is uncertain.
- In some cases, placebos may be used ethically in clinical practice to manage symptoms or improve patient well-being, particularly when

patients have unmet needs or experience significant distress, and the risks associated with placebo use are minimal.

- However, the use of placebos in clinical practice must be carefully considered, and ethical guidelines must be followed to ensure patient safety, autonomy, and informed consent.

## Conclusion:

- Overall, placebos play a crucial role in clinical research by providing a standard comparator for evaluating the efficacy and safety of new treatments.
- Additionally, understanding the placebo effect is essential for optimizing patient care and harnessing the therapeutic potential of nonspecific factors in clinical practice.

## 123. What is an adverse drug reaction? explain different types of ADRs with examples?

- An adverse drug reaction (ADR) is an unintended and harmful response to a medication or medical intervention that occurs at doses used for treatment, prevention, or diagnosis.
- ADRs can vary in severity and may range from mild and transient side effects to severe and life-threatening reactions.
- Understanding and monitoring ADRs are essential for ensuring patient safety, optimizing medication use, and minimizing harm associated with pharmacotherapy.

**Following are different types of ADRs with examples:**

### Type A (Augmented) Reactions:
- Type A reactions are the most common type of ADRs and typically result from the known pharmacological effects of a medication. These reactions are dose-dependent and predictable based on the drug's known pharmacology.
- Examples: Gastrointestinal upset (e.g., nausea, vomiting, diarrhea) following the administration of nonsteroidal anti-inflammatory drugs (NSAIDs) due to their irritant effect on the gastric mucosa.

- Anticholinergic effects (e.g., dry mouth, constipation, urinary retention) caused by medications with anticholinergic properties, such as tricyclic antidepressants or antipsychotics.

### Type B (Bizarre) Reactions:
- Type B reactions are less common and often unpredictable, occurring independent of the drug's pharmacological effects. These reactions may result from individual patient factors, immunological mechanisms, or idiosyncratic responses.
- **Examples:** Allergic or hypersensitivity reactions, such as skin rash, urticaria, or anaphylaxis, triggered by exposure to medications, including antibiotics (e.g., penicillin) or non-steroidal anti-inflammatory drugs (NSAIDs).
- Drug-induced hepatotoxicity or liver injury, characterized by elevated liver enzymes, jaundice, or fulminant hepatic failure, associated with certain medications, such as acetaminophen, statins, or antiepileptic drugs.

### Type C (Chronic) Reactions:
- Type C reactions are delayed or long-term adverse effects that develop following prolonged or repeated exposure to a medication. These reactions may manifest gradually over time and may require ongoing monitoring.
- **Examples:** Drug-induced osteoporosis or bone loss associated with chronic use of glucocorticoids, such as prednisone, due to their effects on calcium metabolism and bone remodeling.
- Medication-induced endocrine disturbances, such as hypothalamic-pituitary-adrenal (HPA) axis suppression or adrenal insufficiency, resulting from prolonged corticosteroid therapy.

### Type D (Delayed) Reactions:
- Type D reactions occur after a delay following exposure to a medication and may be related to cumulative dose, drug accumulation, or metabolic factors.

- These reactions may not be apparent until days, weeks, or months after initiation of treatment.
- **Examples:** Drug-induced cardiomyopathy or heart failure associated with certain medications, such as anthracycline chemotherapy agents (e.g., doxorubicin), which may manifest months or years after treatment initiation.
- Delayed hypersensitivity reactions, such as drug-induced lupus erythematosus or serum sickness, occurring weeks to months after exposure to specific medications, including anticonvulsants or antihypertensive drugs.

## Type E (End-of-Treatment) Reactions:

- Type E reactions occur upon discontinuation or withdrawal of a medication and may result from rebound effects, withdrawal symptoms, or discontinuation syndromes.
- **Examples:** Rebound hypertension or tachycardia following abrupt discontinuation of beta-blockers, which may occur due to upregulation of adrenergic receptors and increased sympathetic activity.
- Antidepressant discontinuation syndrome characterized by flu-like symptoms, dizziness, anxiety, or insomnia following the abrupt cessation of selective serotonin reuptake inhibitors (SSRIs) or serotonin-norepinephrine reuptake inhibitors (SNRIs).

## Conclusion:

- Adverse drug reactions encompass a wide range of unintended and harmful responses to medications, including dose-dependent effects, unpredictable reactions, long-term adverse effects, delayed manifestations, and reactions associated with treatment discontinuation.
- Understanding the different types of ADRs and their characteristics is crucial for recognizing, managing, and preventing medication-related harm in clinical practice.

## 124. What is pharmacovigilance? Explain the objectives of pharmacovigilance with examples?

- Pharmacovigilance is the science and activities related to the detection, assessment, understanding, and prevention of adverse effects or any other drug-related problems associated with the use of medications or medical interventions.
- Pharmacovigilance plays a critical role in ensuring the safety and efficacy of medications throughout their lifecycle, from pre-market clinical trials to post-marketing surveillance and monitoring.
- The main objectives of pharmacovigilance are to safeguard public health, promote patient safety, and minimize the risks associated with pharmacotherapy.

## Following are the objectives of pharmacovigilance, along with examples:

## Detection of Adverse Drug Reactions (ADRs):

- Pharmacovigilance aims to identify and collect information on adverse effects, unexpected reactions, and potential safety concerns associated with medications.
- **Example:** Healthcare professionals report cases of suspected adverse reactions to national pharmacovigilance centers or regulatory agencies, such as the Food and Drug Administration (FDA) in the United States or the European Medicines Agency (EMA) in Europe, to contribute to the ongoing monitoring of drug safety.

## Assessment of Drug Safety:

- Pharmacovigilance involves evaluating the severity, frequency, and potential causality of reported adverse events to assess the safety profile of medications.
- **Example:** Pharmacovigilance experts conduct systematic reviews and meta-analyses of spontaneous reports, clinical trials, epidemiological studies, and other sources of safety data to assess the overall risk-benefit profile of medications and inform regulatory decisions.

**Understanding of Risk Factors:**

- Pharmacovigilance aims to identify risk factors, predisposing factors, and patient characteristics associated with an increased risk of adverse drug reactions or medication-related problems.
- **Example:** Pharmacovigilance studies investigate factors such as age, gender, comorbidities, concomitant medications, genetic polymorphisms, and pharmacokinetic variability that may influence individual susceptibility to adverse drug reactions.

**Prevention of Medication Errors:**

- Pharmacovigilance efforts include identifying and mitigating medication errors, prescribing errors, medication mix-ups, and other preventable causes of adverse drug events.
- **Example:** Healthcare organizations implement medication safety initiatives, such as computerized physician order entry (CPOE) systems, barcode medication administration (BCMA), and medication reconciliation processes, to reduce the risk of medication errors and adverse events.

**Communication and Education:**

- Pharmacovigilance involves disseminating information on drug safety, risk factors, and regulatory actions to healthcare professionals, patients, and the public to promote awareness, understanding, and appropriate use of medications.
- **Example:** Regulatory agencies issue safety alerts, drug safety communications, and public advisories to healthcare providers and patients regarding emerging safety concerns, label changes, or recalls associated with specific medications.

**Regulatory Decision-Making:**

- Pharmacovigilance provides regulatory agencies and healthcare authorities with evidence-based data and recommendations to support regulatory decision-making, including drug approvals, labeling updates, risk management plans, and post-marketing surveillance requirements.
- **Example:** Regulatory agencies conduct benefit-risk assessments based on pharmacovigilance data and epidemiological evidence to determine the appropriate regulatory actions for medications, such as label warnings, restrictions, or market withdrawals.

**Conclusion:**

- Pharmacovigilance is a multifaceted discipline aimed at monitoring, evaluating, and ensuring the safety of medications throughout their lifecycle.
- By achieving its objectives, pharmacovigilance contributes to the continuous improvement of medication safety, public health protection, and the rational use of medicines.

## 125. What is drug intolerance? Explain type of drug intolerance with examples?

- Drug intolerance refers to a reduced tolerance or sensitivity to a medication, leading to adverse effects or symptoms that limit the tolerability or use of the drug, despite it being prescribed at therapeutic doses.
- Unlike drug allergies, which involve an immune-mediated response, drug intolerance reactions are typically non-immunological and may result from pharmacological, metabolic, or idiosyncratic factors.
- Drug intolerance can manifest as a wide range of adverse reactions, including gastrointestinal upset, central nervous system effects, cardiovascular symptoms, or dermatological manifestations.

**Following are the types of drug intolerance with examples:**

**Gastrointestinal Intolerance:**

- Gastrointestinal intolerance refers to adverse effects affecting the digestive system, such as nausea, vomiting, diarrhea, abdominal pain, or dyspepsia, following the administration of a medication.

- **Example:** Nonsteroidal anti-inflammatory drugs (NSAIDs), such as ibuprofen or aspirin, may cause gastrointestinal intolerance, including dyspepsia or peptic ulcers, due to their irritant effect on the gastric mucosa.

## Central Nervous System (CNS) Intolerance:

- Central nervous system intolerance involves adverse effects affecting the brain or spinal cord, leading to neurological symptoms, cognitive impairment, or mood changes.
- **Example:** Central nervous system side effects of certain medications, such as opioids (e.g., morphine), benzodiazepines (e.g., diazepam), or antiepileptic drugs (e.g., phenytoin), may include sedation, dizziness, confusion, or impaired motor coordination.

## Cardiovascular Intolerance:

- Cardiovascular intolerance refers to adverse effects affecting the heart or blood vessels, resulting in changes in heart rate, blood pressure, or cardiac function.
- **Example:** Beta-blockers, such as propranolol or metoprolol, used to treat hypertension or cardiac arrhythmias, may cause cardiovascular intolerance, including bradycardia, hypotension, or exacerbation of heart failure symptoms.

## Dermatological Intolerance:

- Dermatological intolerance involves adverse reactions affecting the skin, hair, nails, or mucous membranes, resulting in allergic or non-allergic dermatitis, rash, urticaria, or photosensitivity.
- **Example:** Antibiotics, such as penicillins or sulfonamides, may cause dermatological intolerance reactions, including drug-induced rash or allergic contact dermatitis, characterized by erythematous or pruritic skin eruptions.

## Respiratory Intolerance:

- Respiratory intolerance refers to adverse effects affecting the respiratory system, leading to symptoms such as cough, dyspnea, wheezing, or bronchospasm.
- Example: Nonsteroidal anti-inflammatory drugs (NSAIDs) and angiotensin-converting enzyme (ACE) inhibitors may cause respiratory intolerance reactions, including exacerbation of asthma symptoms or bronchospasm in susceptible individuals.

## Renal Intolerance:

- Renal intolerance involves adverse effects affecting kidney function or renal excretion, leading to changes in renal function tests, electrolyte imbalances, or nephrotoxicity.
- **Example:** Nonsteroidal anti-inflammatory drugs (NSAIDs), aminoglycoside antibiotics (e.g., gentamicin), or certain antihypertensive medications may cause renal intolerance reactions, including acute kidney injury or nephrotic syndrome.

## Conclusion:

- Drug intolerance refers to a reduced tolerance or sensitivity to a medication, resulting in adverse effects or symptoms that limit its tolerability or use.
- Drug intolerance reactions can affect various organ systems and may necessitate discontinuation or adjustment of the offending medication to minimize adverse outcomes and ensure patient safety.

## 126. What is idiosyncrasy? explain with example?

- Idiosyncrasy refers to an unusual or abnormal response to a medication or substance that is peculiar to an individual and cannot be predicted based on known pharmacological principles or mechanisms of action.
- Idiosyncratic reactions are typically unpredictable, rare, and unrelated to the dose or pharmacological effects of the drug.
- These reactions may result from genetic factors, metabolic abnormalities, or individual variations in drug metabolism or immune response.

## Following is an example of idiosyncrasy:

- Example: A patient develops a severe and life-threatening hypersensitivity reaction, such as anaphylaxis, shortly after receiving a single dose of a commonly prescribed antibiotic, such as penicillin.
- Despite having no prior history of allergic reactions to penicillin or related antibiotics, the patient experiences a sudden onset of symptoms, including difficulty breathing, swelling of the face and throat, hypotension, and shock.
- Laboratory tests reveal elevated levels of serum tryptase and immunoglobulin E (IgE), indicating an allergic response.
- Further investigation reveals that the patient has a rare genetic polymorphism associated with an increased risk of penicillin hypersensitivity, leading to an idiosyncratic reaction to the antibiotic.

## 127. What is drug allergy or drug hypersensitivity? Explain different types with examples?

- Drug allergy, also known as drug hypersensitivity, refers to an adverse immune-mediated reaction to a medication or substance that involves the body's immune system recognizing the drug as a foreign invader and mounting an allergic response.
- Drug allergies can vary in severity, ranging from mild skin reactions to severe systemic manifestations, including anaphylaxis.

## Following are the different types of drug allergies with examples:

### Immediate-Type Hypersensitivity Reactions:

- Immediate-type hypersensitivity reactions occur rapidly, typically within minutes to hours after exposure to the allergen, and involve the release of histamine and other inflammatory mediators from mast cells and basophils.
- Examples:Anaphylaxis: A severe and potentially life-threatening allergic reaction characterized by systemic symptoms, including difficulty breathing, swelling of the face and throat, hypotension, and shock, occurring shortly after exposure to the allergen (e.g., penicillin, peanuts, shellfish).

- Urticaria (Hives) and Angioedema: Skin reactions characterized by raised, itchy welts (hives) or localized swelling of the skin, lips, or mucous membranes (angioedema), occurring within minutes to hours after exposure to the allergen (e.g., medications, insect stings, foods).

### Delayed-Type Hypersensitivity Reactions:

- Delayed-type hypersensitivity reactions occur more slowly, typically within hours to days after exposure to the allergen, and involve activation of T cells and recruitment of inflammatory cells to the site of exposure.
- **Examples:** Drug-Induced Delayed Hypersensitivity Dermatitis: A type of allergic contact dermatitis characterized by erythematous, pruritic, and sometimes blistering skin lesions occurring 24-72 hours after exposure to the allergen (e.g., topical medications, cosmetics, metals).

### Drug Reaction with Eosinophilia and Systemic Symptoms (DRESS) Syndrome:

- A severe systemic hypersensitivity reaction characterized by fever, rash, eosinophilia, and multiorgan involvement (e.g., liver, kidney, lungs), occurring weeks to months after exposure to the offending drug (e.g., antiepileptic drugs, allopurinol).

### Cytotoxic Hypersensitivity Reactions:

- Cytotoxic hypersensitivity reactions involve the production of antibodies (IgG or IgM) directed against antigens present on the surface of cells or tissues, leading to cell destruction or tissue damage.
- **Examples:** Drug-Induced Immune Hemolytic Anemia: Destruction of red blood cells (hemolysis) resulting from the formation of antibodies against drug-induced antigens on the surface of red blood cells, leading to anemia and associated symptoms (e.g., fatigue, pallor, jaundice) (e.g., penicillin, sulfonamides).

### Drug-Induced Thrombocytopenia:

- Destruction of platelets (thrombocytopenia) caused by drug-induced antibodies targeting platelet antigens, leading to bleeding disorders and petechiae or purpura (e.g., heparin, quinine).

**Immunological Cross-Reactivity:**
- Immunological cross-reactivity refers to the phenomenon whereby antibodies produced in response to one drug or allergen can recognize and react with structurally similar molecules, leading to allergic reactions to related compounds.

- **Example:** Penicillin Allergy Cross-Reactivity: Patients allergic to penicillin may exhibit cross-reactivity with other beta-lactam antibiotics, such as cephalosporins, due to similarities in their chemical structure, leading to allergic reactions to these related antibiotics.

**Conclusion:**
- Drug allergies or hypersensitivity reactions encompass a spectrum of immune-mediated responses to medications, ranging from immediate-type reactions (e.g., anaphylaxis, urticaria) to delayed-type reactions (e.g., delayed hypersensitivity dermatitis, DRESS syndrome) and cytotoxic reactions (e.g., immune hemolytic anemia, thrombocytopenia).
- Recognizing the different types of drug allergies is essential for accurate diagnosis, management, and prevention of adverse reactions in clinical practice.

**128. What is photosensitivity? explain with examples?**
- Photosensitivity, also known as photodermatitis or sun sensitivity, refers to an abnormal skin reaction triggered by exposure to sunlight or ultraviolet (UV) radiation, resulting in an inflammatory response.
- Photosensitivity reactions can manifest as various skin symptoms, including erythema (redness), edema (swelling), blistering, itching, and pain.
- These reactions may occur in individuals with certain underlying conditions, medications, or substances that make the skin more sensitive to UV radiation.

**Following are the examples of photosensitivity:**

**Drug-Induced Photosensitivity:**
- Certain medications, both topical and systemic, can cause photosensitivity reactions when exposed to sunlight or UV radiation. These drugs may directly absorb UV radiation or induce chemical changes in the skin, making it more susceptible to sun damage.
- Examples:Tetracycline antibiotics (e.g., doxycycline): Some tetracycline antibiotics can cause photosensitivity reactions, resulting in a sunburn-like rash on sun-exposed areas of the skin.
- Nonsteroidal anti-inflammatory drugs (NSAIDs) (e.g., ibuprofen): Some NSAIDs can increase the skin's sensitivity to UV radiation, leading to photosensitivity reactions characterized by erythema and blistering.

**Phototoxic Reaction:**
- Phototoxic reactions occur when a substance, such as a medication or chemical, interacts with UV radiation to produce a toxic reaction in the skin. Unlike photoallergic reactions, phototoxic reactions do not involve an immune response.
- Examples: Psoralens (e.g., methoxsalen): Psoralen compounds are used in phototherapy treatments for psoriasis and vitiligo. When combined with UV radiation, psoralens can cause phototoxic reactions, resulting in erythema, blistering, and hyperpigmentation.
- Certain fragrances (e.g., bergamot oil): Some fragrances, such as those containing bergamot oil, can cause phototoxic reactions when applied to the skin and exposed to sunlight, leading to erythema and dermatitis.

**Photoallergic Reaction:**
- Photoallergic reactions occur when a substance, such as a medication or chemical, interacts with UV radiation to induce an immune-mediated allergic response in the skin. These reactions typically require prior sensitization to the substance.

- Examples: Sunscreen ingredients (e.g., benzo-phenones): Some sunscreen ingredients can cause photoallergic reactions in susceptible individuals, resulting in eczema-like dermatitis or erythema on sun-exposed areas.
- Fragrance ingredients (e.g., musk ambrette): Certain fragrance ingredients can cause photoallergic reactions when applied to the skin and exposed to sunlight, leading to pruritic or vesicular eruptions.

**Idiopathic Photosensitivity:**
- Idiopathic photosensitivity refers to photosensitivity reactions that occur without an identifiable cause or underlying condition. These reactions may be triggered by unknown factors or environmental exposures.
- Examples: Polymorphous light eruption (PMLE): PMLE is a common form of idiopathic photosensitivity characterized by itchy or burning rash on sun-exposed areas, typically occurring in spring or early summer.
- Solar urticaria: Solar urticaria is a rare form of idiopathic photosensitivity characterized by the development of hives (urticaria) within minutes of sun exposure, causing itching, swelling, and discomfort.

**Conclusion:**
- Photosensitivity refers to abnormal skin reactions triggered by exposure to sunlight or UV radiation, resulting in erythema, blistering, or other inflammatory responses.
- These reactions can be caused by certain medications, chemicals, or substances, leading to phototoxic or photoallergic reactions, or may occur idiopathically without an identifiable cause.
- Understanding the underlying mechanisms and potential triggers of photosensitivity is essential for accurate diagnosis and management of affected individuals.

## 129. What is drug dependence? Differentiate drug dependence with drug addiction? give examples?

- Drug dependence and drug addiction are related but distinct concepts that describe different aspects of problematic drug use.

**Drug Dependence:**
- Drug dependence refers to a physical or psychological reliance on a drug to function normally. It involves a state of adaptation in which the body has developed tolerance to the drug's effects and experiences withdrawal symptoms upon discontinuation or reduction of the drug.
- Drug dependence can be classified into two main types:
- **a. Physical dependence:** Physical dependence occurs when the body adapts to the presence of a drug, leading to tolerance and withdrawal symptoms upon cessation of drug use. Withdrawal symptoms may include physical discomfort, cravings, and physiological disturbances.
- **b. Psychological dependence:** Psychological dependence involves a strong emotional or psychological desire to use a drug, driven by cravings, compulsive behaviors, and a perceived need for the drug to cope with stress, manage emotions, or experience pleasure.

**Examples of drug dependence:**
- **Opioid dependence:** Individuals who use opioids regularly may develop physical dependence, experiencing tolerance and withdrawal symptoms such as nausea, vomiting, muscle aches, and cravings when they attempt to reduce or stop opioid use.
- **Benzodiazepine dependence:** Prolonged use of benzodiazepines for anxiety or insomnia can lead to physical dependence, characterized by tolerance to the drug's sedative effects and withdrawal symptoms such as anxiety, insomnia, tremors, and seizures upon discontinuation.

**Drug Addiction:**

- Drug addiction, also known as substance use disorder (SUD), is a chronic, relapsing brain disorder characterized by compulsive drug seeking, craving, and use despite harmful consequences. It involves a loss of control over drug use and persistent drug-seeking behavior, often leading to significant social, occupational, and health problems.
- Addiction is driven by complex neurobiological changes in the brain's reward circuitry, involving dysregulation of neurotransmitters such as dopamine, glutamate, and serotonin, which contribute to compulsive drug-seeking behaviors and the reinforcing effects of drugs.
- Addiction encompasses both physical and psychological components, including tolerance, withdrawal, cravings, and maladaptive patterns of drug use.

**Examples of drug addiction:**

- **Cocaine addiction:** Individuals with cocaine addiction may engage in compulsive drug-seeking behaviors, experience intense cravings, and continue using cocaine despite negative consequences such as financial problems, legal issues, and health complications.
- **Alcohol addiction:** Alcohol addiction involves a pattern of excessive alcohol consumption, loss of control over drinking behavior, and continued alcohol use despite adverse effects on physical health, relationships, and social functioning.

**Conclusion:**

- Drug dependence refers to a state of physical or psychological reliance on a drug, characterized by tolerance and withdrawal symptoms, while drug addiction involves compulsive drug-seeking behavior and loss of control over drug use despite negative consequences.
- Both concepts represent different aspects of problematic drug use, with dependence focusing on physiological adaptation to the drug and addiction emphasizing compulsive and maladaptive behaviors associated with drug use disorder.

## 130. What is drug withdrawal reaction? explain with examples?

- Drug withdrawal reaction refers to a set of symptoms that occur after the discontinuation or reduction of a drug to which an individual has developed physical dependence. These symptoms arise due to the body's adaptation to the presence of the drug and can vary in severity depending on factors such as the type of drug, duration of use, dosage, and individual factors.
- Drug withdrawal reactions can be uncomfortable, distressing, and sometimes life-threatening if not managed appropriately.

**Following are examples of drug withdrawal reactions:**

**Opioid Withdrawal:**

- Symptoms of opioid withdrawal typically emerge within hours to days after discontinuing or reducing the dosage of opioids following prolonged use. Opioid withdrawal symptoms can include:

**Flu-like symptoms:**

- Such as nausea, vomiting, diarrhea, abdominal cramps, and muscle aches.
- Autonomic hyperactivity: Including sweating, yawning, lacrimation (tearing), rhinorrhea (runny nose), and pupillary dilation.
- Psychological symptoms: Such as anxiety, agitation, insomnia, irritability, dysphoria, and drug cravings.
- **Example:** A person who has been using heroin regularly suddenly stops using and begins experiencing symptoms such as severe muscle cramps, diarrhea, sweating, and intense cravings for the drug.

**Benzodiazepine Withdrawal:**

- Benzodiazepine withdrawal can occur in individuals who have been using these medications for an extended period, especially at high doses. Symptoms of benzodiazepine withdrawal may include:

- Anxiety and panic attacks: Including feelings of impending doom, restlessness, and heightened arousal.
- **Insomnia and sleep disturbances:** Such as difficulty falling asleep, frequent awakenings, and nightmares.
- **Gastrointestinal symptoms:** Such as nausea, vomiting, and abdominal discomfort.
- **Sensory disturbances:** Including hypersensitivity to light, sound, and touch.
- **Example:** A person who has been taking alprazolam (Xanax) for anxiety for several months suddenly stops taking the medication and experiences severe anxiety, insomnia, and physical discomfort.

## Alcohol Withdrawal:

- Alcohol withdrawal syndrome can occur in individuals with alcohol dependence who abruptly stop drinking or significantly reduce their alcohol intake.
- Symptoms of alcohol withdrawal can range from mild to severe and may include:
- **Tremors (shakes):** Especially in the hands, which may worsen with movement or stress.
- Sweating, tachycardia (rapid heartbeat), and elevated blood pressure.
- Anxiety, agitation, restlessness, and irritability.
- **Hallucinations:** Such as visual or auditory hallucinations, which may occur within 12 to 24 hours after the last drink.
- **Delirium tremens (DTs):** A severe form of alcohol withdrawal characterized by disorientation, confusion, hallucinations, seizures, and autonomic instability, which can be life-threatening.
- **Example:** A chronic heavy drinker abruptly stops consuming alcohol and develops symptoms such as tremors, sweating, anxiety, and hallucinations.

## Conclusion:

- Drug withdrawal reactions occur when an individual abruptly stops or reduces the dosage of a drug to which they have developed physical dependence.

- Symptoms can vary depending on the type of drug and may include physical discomfort, psychological distress, and autonomic disturbances.
- Proper management of drug withdrawal is essential to ensure the safety and well-being of affected individuals.

## 131. What is teratogenecity? explain with examples?

- Teratogenicity refers to the ability of certain substances, such as medications, chemicals, or environmental factors, to cause structural or functional abnormalities in a developing fetus during pregnancy.
- Teratogens interfere with normal fetal development, particularly during critical periods of embryogenesis, leading to congenital malformations, birth defects, or developmental disorders.
- Teratogenic exposure can occur during the pre-implantation stage (before implantation in the uterine wall), embryonic period (weeks 3-8 of gestation), or fetal period (after the embryonic stage).

**Following are examples of teratogens and their potential effects:**

**Thalidomide:**

- Thalidomide is a medication that was once prescribed as a sedative and antiemetic (anti-nausea) drug during pregnancy in the late 1950s and early 1960s. However, it was later discovered to be highly teratogenic, causing a range of severe birth defects known as thalidomide embryopathy.
- **Examples** of thalidomide-induced birth defects include limb abnormalities (phocomelia), where the arms or legs are either absent or shortened, as well as ear, eye, heart, and gastrointestinal malformations.

**Alcohol (Fetal Alcohol Syndrome):**

- Prenatal exposure to alcohol, particularly during the embryonic and early fetal periods, can result in fetal alcohol syndrome (FAS) and related disorders, collectively known as fetal alcohol spectrum disorders (FASDs).

- FAS is characterized by a constellation of physical, neurological, and behavioral abnormalities, including facial dysmorphology (e.g., smooth philtrum, thin upper lip), growth deficiencies, central nervous system impairments (e.g., intellectual disability, learning difficulties), and behavioral problems (e.g., hyperactivity, impulsivity).

## Retinoids (Isotretinoin, Retinoic Acid):

- Retinoids are a class of medications derived from vitamin A that are used to treat acne, psoriasis, and other dermatological conditions. However, retinoids are potent teratogens and are associated with a high risk of causing severe birth defects when taken during pregnancy.
- **Examples** of retinoid-induced birth defects include craniofacial abnormalities (e.g., cleft palate, micrognathia), cardiovascular defects (e.g., ventricular septal defects), and central nervous system malformations (e.g., hydrocephalus, agenesis of the corpus callosum).

## Antiepileptic Drugs (Valproate, Carbamazepine):

- Some antiepileptic medications, such as valproate (valproic acid) and carbamazepine, have been linked to an increased risk of teratogenic effects when used during pregnancy.
- Valproate exposure in utero has been associated with neural tube defects (e.g., spina bifida), facial dysmorphology (e.g., cleft lip, epicanthal folds), developmental delays, and cognitive impairments in offspring.

## Maternal Infections (Rubella, Zika Virus):

- Certain maternal infections, such as rubella (German measles) and Zika virus, can pose a teratogenic risk to the developing fetus if contracted during pregnancy.
- Rubella infection during the first trimester of pregnancy can lead to congenital rubella syndrome, characterized by eye abnormalities (e.g., cataracts, glaucoma), heart defects, hearing loss, and developmental delays.

- Zika virus infection during pregnancy has been associated with microcephaly (small head size), brain abnormalities, and other neurodevelopmental complications in newborns.

Conclusion:
- Teratogenicity refers to the potential of certain substances or factors to cause birth defects or developmental abnormalities in the fetus during pregnancy.
- Examples of teratogens include medications (e.g., thalidomide, retinoids), chemicals (e.g., alcohol), maternal infections (e.g., rubella, Zika virus), and environmental factors that can disrupt normal fetal development.
- It's essential for pregnant individuals to avoid exposure to known teratogens and to consult with healthcare providers regarding the safety of medications and other substances during pregnancy.

## 132. What is carcinogenicity and mutagenecity? explain with examples?

- Carcinogenicity and mutagenicity are both terms used to describe the ability of substances to cause cancer or genetic mutations, respectively. While closely related, they refer to slightly different aspects of the potential harm caused by certain agents.

## Carcinogenicity:

- Carcinogenicity refers to the ability of substances to cause cancer or promote the development of tumors in living organisms, including humans.
- Carcinogens can act through various mechanisms, including damaging DNA, altering gene expression, or disrupting cellular processes involved in cell growth and proliferation.
- **Examples of carcinogens:** Tobacco smoke: Cigarette smoke contains numerous carcinogenic compounds, including polycyclic aromatic hydrocarbons (PAHs), nitrosamines, and benzene, which can lead to various cancers, such as lung, bladder, and pancreatic cancer.

- Asbestos: Asbestos fibers, commonly found in construction materials, can cause mesothelioma (a cancer of the lining of the lungs or abdomen), lung cancer, and other respiratory cancers when inhaled.
- Benzene: Benzene, a solvent and industrial chemical, is known to cause leukemia and other hematopoietic cancers.

## Mutagenicity:

- Mutagenicity refers to the ability of substances to induce genetic mutations in cells, leading to changes in DNA sequence or structure. Mutagens can disrupt the normal genetic code and may increase the risk of cancer or other genetic disorders by altering the functioning of genes involved in cell growth, repair, or regulation.
- **Examples of mutagens:** Ultraviolet (UV) radiation: Exposure to UV radiation from sunlight or tanning beds can cause mutations in skin cells, leading to skin cancer, including melanoma, squamous cell carcinoma, and basal cell carcinoma.
- **Certain chemicals:** Various chemicals, such as certain pesticides, industrial solvents, and aromatic amines, have mutagenic properties and can increase the risk of cancer or genetic abnormalities.
- **Ionizing radiation:** Ionizing radiation from sources such as X-rays, gamma rays, and radioactive materials can induce mutations in DNA and increase the risk of cancer, particularly in tissues that are sensitive to radiation exposure.
- It's important to note that some substances may exhibit both carcinogenic and mutagenic properties, as genetic mutations can contribute to the development of cancer.
- Additionally, not all mutagens are carcinogens, and not all carcinogens are mutagens.

## Conclusion:

- Both carcinogenicity and mutagenicity are significant concerns for public health and regulatory agencies, which assess the potential risks associated with exposure to these substances and implement measures to mitigate harm.

- **133. What is iatrogenic disease or drug induced disease? give examples?**

- Iatrogenic disease, also known as drug-induced disease or iatrogenesis, refers to any illness or adverse condition that arises as a result of medical treatment or intervention, including the use of medications.
- These conditions may occur due to the intended effects of treatment, unintended side effects, or errors in medical practice. Iatrogenic diseases can range from mild and reversible to severe and life-threatening.

**Following are the examples of iatrogenic diseases or drug-induced conditions:**

**Drug-induced liver injury (DILI):**
- Many medications, including prescription drugs, over-the-counter medications, and herbal supplements, can cause liver damage or liver dysfunction as an adverse drug reaction. This can manifest as hepatotoxicity, hepatitis, or liver failure.
- 
- **Examples** of drugs associated with DILI include acetaminophen (in cases of overdose), certain antibiotics (e.g., isoniazid, amoxicillin-clavulanate), statins (e.g., atorvastatin), and certain herbal supplements (e.g., kava).

**Drug-induced nephrotoxicity:**
- Some medications can cause kidney damage or impairment of kidney function, leading to acute kidney injury or chronic kidney disease. Nephrotoxic drugs can affect various parts of the kidneys, including the tubules, glomeruli, or renal vasculature.
- 
- **Examples** of drugs known to cause nephrotoxicity include nonsteroidal anti-inflammatory drugs (NSAIDs), such as ibuprofen and naproxen, certain antibiotics (e.g., vancomycin, aminoglycosides), contrast agents used in imaging procedures, and certain chemotherapeutic agents.

**Drug-induced cardiotoxicity:**
- Certain medications can have adverse effects on the heart, leading to cardiotoxicity, arrhythmias, heart failure, or myocardial damage. Cardiotoxic drugs can disrupt the normal electrical conduction of the heart or impair cardiac function.

- **Examples** of drugs associated with cardiotoxicity include certain chemotherapeutic agents (e.g., anthracyclines such as doxorubicin), antipsychotic medications (e.g., haloperidol), certain antibiotics (e.g., macrolides), and some herbal supplements (e.g., ephedra).

**Drug-induced hematologic disorders:**
- Some medications can cause abnormalities in blood cells or disrupt the normal functioning of the hematologic system, leading to anemia, thrombocytopenia, leukopenia, or other hematologic disorders.

- **Examples** of drugs associated with hematologic toxicity include certain chemotherapeutic agents (e.g., methotrexate, cisplatin), anticoagulants (e.g., heparin), antiplatelet agents (e.g., clopidogrel), and certain antibiotics (e.g., sulfonamides).

**Drug-induced metabolic disorders:**
- Certain medications can disrupt normal metabolic processes in the body, leading to alterations in glucose metabolism, lipid metabolism, electrolyte balance, or hormonal regulation.

- **Examples** of drugs associated with metabolic disorders include corticosteroids (which can cause hyperglycemia, fluid retention, and electrolyte imbalances), antipsychotic medications (which can cause weight gain and dyslipidemia), and some antiretroviral drugs used in HIV treatment (which can cause dyslipidemia and insulin resistance).

- These examples highlight the diverse range of iatrogenic diseases or drug-induced conditions that can occur as a result of medical treatment.

- It's essential for healthcare providers to be aware of the potential risks associated with medications and to monitor patients closely for signs of adverse drug reactions or iatrogenic effects.

- Additionally, patients should communicate any concerns or symptoms they experience while taking medications to their healthcare providers for appropriate evaluation and management.

## 134. What are the phases of clinical trials? explain the importance of each phase of clinical trial with examples?

- Clinical trials typically progress through several phases, each with its own objectives and importance in evaluating the safety and efficacy of a new medical intervention. Here are the typical phases:

**Phase 0:**
- This phase is not always included in every clinical trial, but when it is, it involves a very small number of participants and aims to gather preliminary data on how the drug or treatment behaves in the body.
- It's often exploratory and helps researchers decide whether to move forward with larger trials.
- Phase 0 trials may involve microdosing, where subtherapeutic doses of the drug are administered to observe its pharmacokinetics.

**Phase I:**
- Phase I trials involve a small group of healthy volunteers (sometimes patients with the condition of interest) to evaluate the safety, dosage range, and potential side effects of the drug or treatment.
- The main goal is to determine the maximum tolerated dose (MTD) and identify any adverse effects. These trials are usually not designed to evaluate effectiveness but rather safety.
- **Example**: A pharmaceutical company develops a new cancer drug and conducts a Phase I trial to determine the highest dose that can be given safely without severe side effects.

**Phase II**:

- In Phase II trials, the drug or treatment is administered to a larger group of patients with the condition being studied to further evaluate its safety and efficacy.
- These trials aim to determine the optimal dose and to gather preliminary data on effectiveness. Phase II trials provide more information about potential benefits and risks.
- **Example**: Continuing with the cancer drug example, Phase II trials may involve administering the drug to a larger group of cancer patients to assess its effectiveness in shrinking tumors or improving survival rates.

**Phase III**:

- Phase III trials are large-scale studies involving hundreds to thousands of patients.
- They aim to confirm the effectiveness of the drug or treatment, monitor side effects, compare it to commonly used treatments or a placebo, and collect information that will allow the drug or treatment to be used safely.
- Phase III trials provide the most robust evidence of efficacy and safety.
- **Example**: If the cancer drug has shown promise in Phase II, Phase III trials may compare it to standard treatments or placebos in a larger population to confirm its efficacy in improving survival rates and quality of life.

**Phase IV**:

- Also known as post-marketing surveillance trials, Phase IV trials occur after the drug or treatment has been approved and is on the market.
- These trials monitor the long-term safety and effectiveness of the treatment in larger, more diverse patient populations over an extended period.
- Phase IV trials may also identify rare side effects that were not apparent in earlier phases due to the smaller sample sizes.

- **Example**: After the cancer drug is approved and in use, Phase IV trials may continue to monitor patients over several years to detect any unexpected long-term side effects or to assess its effectiveness in real-world settings.

**Conclusion:**

- Each phase of clinical trials plays a crucial role in the drug development process, from initial safety evaluations to establishing effectiveness and long-term safety profiles.
- Without these phases, it would be challenging to ensure that new treatments are safe and effective for widespread use in patient populations.

## 135. What are the different types of transmembrane drug transport systems available? explain with examples?

- Transmembrane drug transport systems are mechanisms that facilitate the movement of drugs across cell membranes.
- These systems are essential for drug absorption, distribution, and elimination within the body.
- Several types of transmembrane drug transport systems exist, each with unique characteristics and functions. Here are some of the main types:

- **Passive Diffusion**: Passive diffusion is the simplest form of transmembrane drug transport, where drugs move across cell membranes along a concentration gradient, from an area of high concentration to an area of low concentration.
- Example: Lipophilic drugs, such as benzodiazepines, can easily diffuse through cell membranes and reach their target sites.

- **Facilitated Diffusion**: Facilitated diffusion involves the movement of drugs across cell membranes with the help of carrier proteins, but unlike active transport, it does not require energy expenditure.

- **Example:** Glucose transporter proteins facilitate the movement of glucose across cell membranes down its concentration gradient.

- **Active Transport**: Active transport is a process that moves drugs against their concentration gradient, requiring energy in the form of ATP (adenosine triphosphate).
- **Example:** P-glycoprotein (P-gp) is a well-known drug efflux transporter that actively pumps drugs out of cells, contributing to multidrug resistance in cancer cells.

- **Ion Channels**: Ion channels are membrane-spanning proteins that allow specific ions to pass through, influencing cellular functions and drug transport.
- **Example:** Voltage-gated calcium channels play a crucial role in neuronal signaling and can be targeted by drugs such as calcium channel blockers for hypertension and cardiac arrhythmias.

- **Endocytosis and Exocytosis**: Endocytosis involves the uptake of substances into cells by engulfing them in vesicles formed from the cell membrane, while exocytosis is the process of releasing substances from cells by fusing vesicles with the cell membrane.
- **Example:** Macrophages utilize endocytosis to engulf pathogens or foreign particles, and certain drugs can exploit this mechanism for targeted delivery.

- **Transporter Proteins**: Transporter proteins facilitate the movement of specific molecules across cell membranes by binding to them and undergoing conformational changes.
- **Example:** Organic anion transporters (OATs) are responsible for the uptake of various organic anions, including some drugs like penicillin, from the bloodstream into renal tubular cells for excretion in urine.

**Conclusion:**

- Understanding the various transmembrane drug transport systems is crucial for pharmacokinetic studies, drug development, and optimizing drug delivery strategies to enhance therapeutic efficacy while minimizing adverse effects.

## 135. Explain targeted drug delivery with examples?

- Targeted drug delivery refers to the delivery of drugs specifically to their intended target sites within the body, such as diseased tissues or cells, while minimizing exposure to healthy tissues.
- This approach enhances the therapeutic efficacy of drugs while reducing systemic side effects.
- Several strategies are employed for targeted drug delivery, some of which are outlined below with examples:

- **Passive Targeting**: Passive targeting takes advantage of physiological differences between diseased and healthy tissues, such as differences in vascular permeability or the presence of specific receptors.

- **Example:** The enhanced permeability and retention (EPR) effect is commonly exploited in cancer therapy.
- Tumors often have leaky blood vessels and impaired lymphatic drainage, leading to the accumulation of macromolecules and nanoparticles within the tumor tissue.
- Chemotherapeutic agents encapsulated within liposomes or nanoparticles can passively accumulate in tumors, leading to higher drug concentrations at the site of action.

- **Active Targeting**: Active targeting involves the use of ligands, such as antibodies, peptides, or small molecules, that specifically bind to receptors or antigens overexpressed on diseased cells or tissues.

- **Example:** Monoclonal antibodies conjugated to cytotoxic agents can selectively target cancer cells that express specific surface antigens.
- For instance, trastuzumab (Herceptin) targets HER2-positive breast cancer cells, leading to the delivery of cytotoxic drugs specifically to cancer cells while sparing healthy tissues.

- **Prodrug Strategy**: Prodrugs are inactive forms of drugs that undergo chemical modification or enzymatic activation to release the active drug at the target site.

- **Example:** Enzyme-targeted prodrug therapy involves conjugating a drug to a substrate that is selectively cleaved by an enzyme overexpressed in diseased tissues.
- For instance, Cytosine deaminase (CD) enzyme converts the prodrug 5-fluorocytosine (5-FC) into the active chemotherapeutic agent 5-fluorouracil (5-FU) specifically within tumor cells, leading to localized cytotoxicity.

- **Nanotechnology-Based Delivery Systems**: Nanoparticles can be engineered to encapsulate drugs, protect them from degradation, and facilitate targeted delivery to specific tissues or cells.

- **Example:** Polymeric nanoparticles or liposomes loaded with anti-inflammatory drugs can be designed to target inflamed tissues in diseases like rheumatoid arthritis.
- These nanoparticles can exploit the increased vascular permeability and expression of inflammatory markers to accumulate at sites of inflammation and release the drug locally.

- **Gene Therapy**: Gene delivery vectors can be engineered to specifically target diseased cells or tissues for the delivery of therapeutic genes or RNA molecules.

- **Example:** Adenoviral vectors modified to express therapeutic genes can be targeted to cancer cells by incorporating tumor-specific promoters.

- Upon infection of cancer cells, the viral vectors deliver therapeutic genes, such as tumor suppressors or suicide genes, leading to selective tumor cell death.

- These examples illustrate how targeted drug delivery strategies can improve the therapeutic index of drugs by enhancing their specificity and efficacy while minimizing off-target effects, ultimately improving patient outcomes.

**137. What is mechanism of drug action? what are the different methods through which drug can act? explain ten methods with example?**

- The mechanism of drug action refers to the specific biochemical or physiological processes through which a drug produces its effects in the body.
- Drugs can act through various mechanisms, targeting specific molecular targets, biochemical pathways, or physiological processes.

**Following are ten common methods through which drugs can act, along with examples:**

- **Receptor Agonism:** Drugs can bind to specific receptors on cell membranes and mimic the action of endogenous ligands, thereby activating the receptor and eliciting a biological response.

- **Example:** Beta-adrenergic agonists like albuterol bind to beta-adrenergic receptors in the airway smooth muscle, leading to bronchodilation and relief of asthma symptoms.

- **Receptor Antagonism**: Drugs can bind to receptors without activating them, thereby blocking the action of endogenous ligands or other agonist drugs.

- **Example:** Beta-blockers such as propranolol bind to beta-adrenergic receptors in the heart, blocking the effects of adrenaline and reducing heart rate and blood pressure.

- **Enzyme Inhibition**: Drugs can inhibit the activity of enzymes, disrupting biochemical pathways or metabolic processes in the body.

- **Example:** Acetylcholinesterase inhibitors like donepezil inhibit the breakdown of acetylcholine, thereby increasing the levels of this neurotransmitter in the brain and improving cognitive function in Alzheimer's disease.

- **Ion Channel Modulation**: Drugs can modulate the activity of ion channels, affecting the flow of ions across cell membranes and altering cellular excitability.

- **Example:** Calcium channel blockers such as diltiazem block calcium channels in cardiac muscle cells, leading to vasodilation and decreased heart rate, which is beneficial in treating hypertension and angina.

- **Altering Neurotransmitter Levels**: Drugs can affect neurotransmitter levels in the nervous system by modulating synthesis, release, reuptake, or degradation of neurotransmitters.

- **Example:** Selective serotonin reuptake inhibitors (SSRIs) like sertraline inhibit the reuptake of serotonin in the brain, increasing serotonin levels and improving mood in depression and anxiety disorders.

- **DNA Binding**: Certain drugs can bind to DNA, interfering with DNA replication, transcription, or repair processes.

- **Example:** Anthracycline antibiotics such as doxorubicin intercalate into DNA strands, inhibiting DNA replication and leading to cell death in rapidly dividing cancer cells.

- **Modulation of Signal Transduction Pathways**: Drugs can modulate intracellular signaling pathways, influencing gene expression, cell proliferation, differentiation, or survival.

- Example: Tyrosine kinase inhibitors like imatinib inhibit the activity of specific tyrosine kinases involved in aberrant signaling pathways in cancer cells, leading to inhibition of cell proliferation and tumor growth.

- **Inhibition of Protein Synthesis**: Drugs can inhibit the synthesis of proteins by targeting ribosomes or other components of the protein synthesis machinery.

- **Example:** Aminoglycoside antibiotics such as gentamicin bind to bacterial ribosomes, disrupting protein synthesis and leading to bacterial cell death.

- **Allosteric Modulation**: Drugs can bind to allosteric sites on receptors or enzymes, modulating their activity without directly competing with endogenous ligands or substrates.

- **Example:** Benzodiazepines like diazepam bind to allosteric sites on GABA receptors, potentiating the effects of the neurotransmitter GABA and producing sedative and anxiolytic effects.

- **Induction of Cellular Responses**: Drugs can induce specific cellular responses or gene expression changes through activation of intracellular signaling pathways or transcription factors.

- **Example:** Glucocorticoids such as prednisone bind to cytoplasmic receptors, leading to translocation to the nucleus and regulation of gene expression, which is beneficial in suppressing inflammation and immune responses.

**Conclusion:**
- These examples illustrate the diverse ways in which drugs can act in the body, highlighting the importance of understanding their mechanisms of action for effective therapeutic intervention.

## 138. Explain agonist, partial agonist, inverse agonist, antagonist of drugs with examples?

- Understanding the concepts of agonists, partial agonists, inverse agonists, and antagonists is crucial in pharmacology as they describe different interactions between drugs and their target receptors.

**Following is an explanation of each term with examples:**

- **Agonist**: An agonist is a drug that binds to a receptor and activates it, eliciting a biological response similar to that of the endogenous ligand for that receptor.

- **Example:** Morphine is an agonist of opioid receptors in the central nervous system. By binding to these receptors, morphine produces analgesia (pain relief) and other effects characteristic of opioids.

- **Partial Agonist**: A partial agonist is a drug that binds to a receptor and activates it, but produces a submaximal response compared to a full agonist, even when all receptor sites are occupied.

- **Example:** Buprenorphine is a partial agonist of opioid receptors. It produces less analgesia and respiratory depression compared to full opioid agonists like morphine, making it useful in opioid addiction treatment due to its lower abuse potential and milder withdrawal symptoms.

- **Inverse Agonist**: An inverse agonist is a drug that binds to a receptor and induces an effect opposite to that of an agonist, by stabilizing the inactive conformation of the receptor.

- **Example:** Beta-blockers like propranolol are inverse agonists at beta-adrenergic receptors. Instead of stimulating the receptor like agonists do, they reduce heart rate and blood pressure by inhibiting the basal activity of beta receptors.

- **Antagonist**: An antagonist is a drug that binds to a receptor but does not activate it, thereby blocking the action of agonists or other substances that normally activate the receptor.

- **Example:** Naloxone is an antagonist of opioid receptors. It competes with opioids like morphine for binding to opioid receptors but does not activate them. Naloxone is used to reverse opioid overdose by displacing opioids from their receptors and restoring normal respiration.

**Conclusion:**

- Agonists activate receptors and produce a response.
- Partial agonists activate receptors but produce a weaker response than full agonists.
- Inverse agonists bind to receptors and produce an effect opposite to that of agonists.
- Antagonists bind to receptors but do not activate them, blocking the actions of agonists.
- These concepts are fundamental in understanding the effects of drugs on biological systems and are essential in drug development and therapeutic interventions.

## 139. Explain the regulation of receptors and functions of receptors with examples?

- Receptors are proteins or protein complexes located on the surface of cells or within cells that bind to specific molecules, such as neurotransmitters, hormones, or drugs, and initiate cellular responses.
- The regulation of receptors involves mechanisms that control their expression, activity, and localization in response to various internal and external signals.

**Following is an explanation of the regulation of receptors and their functions, along with examples:**

- **Regulation of Receptor Expression**: Cells can regulate the expression of receptors by adjusting the rate of receptor synthesis and degradation in response to various stimuli.

- **Example:** Upregulation of beta-adrenergic receptors in response to chronic sympathetic stimulation. This adaptation occurs in conditions like heart failure, where increased sympathetic activity leads to increased expression of beta-adrenergic receptors in cardiac myocytes, enhancing the heart's responsiveness to catecholamines.

- **Desensitization and Downregulation**: Prolonged or repeated exposure to agonists can lead to desensitization or downregulation of receptors, reducing the cell's responsiveness to the agonist.

- **Example:** Tolerance to opioids develops with chronic opioid use due to desensitization and downregulation of opioid receptors. This leads to decreased analgesic effects and may require higher doses to achieve the same therapeutic effect.

- **Internalization and Recycling**: Receptors can undergo internalization, where they are endocytosed into the cell following activation by agonists. Internalized receptors can be either recycled back to the cell surface or targeted for degradation.

- **Example:** Endocytosis of insulin receptors following insulin binding. Internalization of insulin receptors allows for the downregulation of receptor signaling after insulin stimulation, contributing to the regulation of glucose homeostasis.

- **Receptor Phosphorylation**: Receptor phosphorylation is a post-translational modification that can regulate receptor activity, localization, and downstream signaling pathways.

- **Example:** Phosphorylation of receptor tyrosine kinases (RTKs) upon ligand binding. Phosphorylation of RTKs leads to activation of intracellular signaling pathways involved in cell growth, proliferation, and differentiation.

**Heterologous Desensitization**:
- Activation of one type of receptor can lead to desensitization of another type of receptor through cross-talk between signaling pathways.

- **Example:** Activation of beta-adrenergic receptors leading to desensitization of adenosine receptors. Beta-adrenergic receptor activation can stimulate adenylyl cyclase activity, leading to increased levels of cyclic AMP (cAMP) and subsequent activation of protein kinase A (PKA), which phosphorylates and desensitizes adenosine receptors.

Functions of receptors include:
- Sensing and responding to extracellular signals.
- Initiating intracellular signaling cascades.
- Regulating gene expression and cellular processes.
- Mediating the effects of neurotransmitters, hormones, and drugs on cells and tissues.

**Conclusions:**
- Understanding the regulation and functions of receptors is essential for elucidating cellular signaling pathways, developing pharmacological interventions, and treating various diseases.

### 140. Explain drug selectivity with examples?

- Drug selectivity refers to the degree to which a drug interacts selectively with its intended target or targets in the body, while minimizing interactions with other molecules or receptors.
- Selective drugs are designed to exert their therapeutic effects by binding specifically to their target molecules, which are typically proteins involved in disease pathways or physiological processes.

**Following is an explanation of drug selectivity with examples:**

- **Specificity for Target Receptors**: Selective drugs bind with high affinity and specificity to their target receptors, minimizing off-target effects.

- **Example:** Selective serotonin reuptake inhibitors (SSRIs) such as fluoxetine are antidepressants that specifically inhibit the reuptake of serotonin by binding to serotonin transporters in the brain. By selectively targeting serotonin transporters, SSRIs increase serotonin levels in synaptic clefts, alleviating symptoms of depression without significant interactions with other neurotransmitter systems.

- **Tissue Selectivity**: Some drugs exhibit selectivity for specific tissues or organs within the body, targeting receptors or molecules predominantly expressed in those tissues.

- **Example:** Beta-2 adrenergic agonists like salbutamol are bronchodilators used to relieve bronchoconstriction in asthma. These drugs selectively activate beta-2 adrenergic receptors predominantly expressed in bronchial smooth muscle cells, leading to relaxation of airway smooth muscle and bronchodilation without significant effects on beta-1 adrenergic receptors in the heart.

- **Isoform Selectivity**: Isoform-selective drugs target specific isoforms or subtypes of receptors or enzymes, allowing for more precise modulation of cellular functions.

- **Example:** COX-2 selective nonsteroidal anti-inflammatory drugs (NSAIDs) such as celecoxib selectively inhibit the cyclooxygenase-2 (COX-2) enzyme, which is upregulated at sites of inflammation. By sparing COX-1, which plays a protective role in the gastrointestinal tract, COX-2 selective NSAIDs reduce the risk of gastrointestinal side effects compared to non-selective NSAIDs.

- Drugs may selectively target specific signaling pathways or molecular cascades involved in disease processes while sparing unrelated pathways.

- **Example:** Tyrosine kinase inhibitors (TKIs) like imatinib selectively inhibit the activity of BCR-ABL tyrosine kinase, which drives the proliferation of leukemia cells in chronic myeloid leukemia (CML). By specifically targeting the BCR-ABL pathway, imatinib suppresses leukemia cell growth with minimal effects on normal cells.

- **Subtype Selectivity**: Some drugs exhibit selectivity for specific subtypes of receptors within a receptor family, allowing for modulation of distinct physiological functions.

- **Example:** Beta-blockers like atenolol selectively block beta-1 adrenergic receptors, which are primarily located in cardiac tissue. By selectively antagonizing beta-1 receptors, atenolol reduces heart rate and blood pressure without affecting beta-2 receptors in bronchial smooth muscle.

- **Genetic Selectivity**: Advances in pharmacogenomics enable the development of drugs tailored to individuals based on their genetic makeup, enhancing selectivity and efficacy while minimizing adverse effects.

- **Example:** Targeted therapies like trastuzumab (Herceptin) are used to treat HER2-positive breast cancer, which overexpresses the HER2 receptor. Trastuzumab selectively targets HER2-positive cancer cells while sparing normal cells, leading to improved outcomes in patients with this genetic subtype of breast cancer.

- Overall, drug selectivity is a crucial consideration in drug development and therapy, as selective drugs can provide effective treatment with fewer side effects and improved patient outcomes.

**141. Explain drug antagonism with ten different types with examples?**

- Drug antagonism refers to the phenomenon where one drug interferes with the activity of another drug or endogenous substance, resulting in a reduction or blockade of its effects. There are various types of drug antagonism, each involving different mechanisms.

**Following are ten different types of drug antagonism with examples:**

- **Competitive Antagonism**: Competitive antagonists compete with agonists for binding to the same receptor site. They do not activate the receptor but prevent agonists from binding, reducing the response.

- **Example:** Naloxone competes with opioids like morphine for binding to opioid receptors. By blocking opioid binding, naloxone reverses the effects of opioids, such as respiratory depression and analgesia.

- **Non-competitive Antagonism**: Non-competitive antagonists bind to a different site on the receptor than the agonist, leading to a conformational change in the receptor that reduces its responsiveness to agonists.

- **Example:** Phenoxybenzamine irreversibly binds to alpha-adrenergic receptors, leading to inhibition of sympathetic responses. It is used to block the effects of catecholamines in conditions like pheochromocytoma.

- **Physiological Antagonism**: Physiological antagonists produce opposing effects through different mechanisms without directly interacting with each other.

- **Example:** Histamine and adrenaline have opposing effects on smooth muscle contraction. Histamine causes bronchoconstriction, while adrenaline causes bronchodilation.

- These two substances exert physiological antagonism on airway smooth muscle.

- **Chemical Antagonism**: Chemical antagonists neutralize the effects of agonists by forming chemical complexes with them, rendering them inactive.

- **Example:** Chelating agents like EDTA bind to metal ions such as calcium, magnesium, or zinc, forming stable complexes. In cases of heavy metal poisoning, EDTA chelation therapy removes toxic metals from the body by forming inert complexes with them.

- **Functional Antagonism**: Functional antagonists produce effects opposite to those of agonists by activating different receptors or pathways that counteract the effects of the agonist.

- **Example:** Beta-adrenergic agonists like isoproterenol cause bronchodilation by activating beta-2 adrenergic receptors. Conversely, muscarinic agonists like acetylcholine cause bronchoconstriction by activating muscarinic receptors. Isoproterenol and acetylcholine exert functional antagonism on airway smooth muscle tone.

- **Allosteric Antagonism**: Allosteric antagonists bind to allosteric sites on receptors, modulating receptor activity and reducing the responsiveness to agonists.

- **Example:** Benzodiazepines like diazepam enhance the inhibitory effects of gamma-aminobutyric acid (GABA) by binding to allosteric sites on GABA-A receptors. Flumazenil is an allosteric antagonist that reverses the effects of benzodiazepines by competitively displacing them from GABA-A receptors.

- **Physicochemical Antagonism**: Physicochemical antagonists interact with agonists through physical or chemical mechanisms that neutralize their effects without binding to receptors.

- Example: Magnesium sulfate can precipitate calcium salts in the gastrointestinal tract, reducing the absorption of calcium-based antacids. This physicochemical interaction results in antagonism of antacid effects.

- **Inverse Agonism**: Inverse agonists bind to receptors and induce effects opposite to those of agonists, reducing the constitutive activity of receptors.

- **Example:** Propranolol is a beta-adrenergic inverse agonist that reduces basal activity of beta-adrenergic receptors. By blocking the constitutive activity of beta receptors, propranolol lowers heart rate and blood pressure.

- **Tachyphylaxis**: Tachyphylaxis refers to a rapid decrease in response to a drug upon repeated administration, which may occur due to receptor desensitization or downregulation.

- **Example:** Continuous administration of nitroglycerin leads to rapid tolerance or tachyphylaxis due to desensitization of vascular smooth muscle to its vasodilatory effects, requiring dose escalation to maintain therapeutic efficacy.

- **Metabolic Antagonism**: Metabolic antagonists inhibit or accelerate the metabolism of agonists, altering their concentration or duration of action in the body.

- **Example:** Ethanol competes with methanol for alcohol dehydrogenase enzymes in the liver. Ethanol metabolism generates non-toxic metabolites, while methanol metabolism produces toxic metabolites. Ethanol serves as a metabolic antagonist by competitively inhibiting methanol metabolism and reducing its toxicity.

- These examples illustrate various types of drug antagonism and their mechanisms, highlighting the complex interactions between drugs and their targets in the body.

## 142. Explain 20 different factors that influence the method of action of the drug with examples?

- The method of action of a drug can be influenced by a wide range of factors, including pharmacokinetic properties, pharmacodynamic interactions, patient characteristics, and environmental factors.

**Following are 20 different factors that can influence the method of action of a drug, along with examples:**

- **Chemical Structure**: The chemical structure of a drug determines its interactions with target receptors or enzymes.

- **Example:** The beta-lactam ring structure of penicillin antibiotics allows them to bind to and inhibit bacterial cell wall synthesis.

- **Route of Administration**:The route of administration affects the rate and extent of drug absorption, distribution, and metabolism.

- **Example:** Intravenous administration of a drug bypasses first-pass metabolism, resulting in rapid onset of action compared to oral administration.

- **Bioavailability**: Bioavailability refers to the fraction of an administered drug that reaches systemic circulation unchanged.

- **Example:** Food intake can affect the bioavailability of certain drugs. For instance, the absorption of some antibiotics may be reduced when taken with food due to interactions with dietary components.

- **Drug Formulation**: The formulation of a drug can influence its release profile, stability, and absorption characteristics.

- **Example:** Extended-release formulations of medications like metformin provide prolonged drug action, allowing for once-daily dosing and improved patient adherence.

- **Drug Interactions**: Interactions between drugs can alter their pharmacokinetics or pharmacodynamics, affecting their method of action.

- **Example:** Concurrent administration of warfarin and nonsteroidal anti-inflammatory drugs (NSAIDs) can increase the risk of bleeding due to potentiation of anticoagulant effects.

- **Dose and Dosage Regimen**: The dose and dosing schedule of a drug influence its concentration-time profile and therapeutic effects.

- **Example:** High doses of opioids can lead to respiratory depression, while lower doses may provide effective pain relief with fewer side effects.

- **Patient Factors**: Individual patient characteristics, such as age, weight, genetics, and comorbidities, can affect drug response.

- **Example:** Genetic polymorphisms in drug-metabolizing enzymes can influence the metabolism and efficacy of drugs like clopidogrel, an antiplatelet agent used in cardiovascular disease.

- **Disease State:** Disease states can alter drug metabolism, distribution, and target receptor expression, affecting drug efficacy and safety.

- **Example:** Liver cirrhosis can impair drug metabolism and clearance, leading to increased risk of adverse effects with certain medications like benzodiazepines.

- **Drug Tolerance**: Prolonged exposure to certain drugs can lead to tolerance, requiring higher doses to achieve the same therapeutic effects.

- **Example:** Chronic opioid use can result in tolerance to analgesic effects, necessitating dose escalation for pain management.

- **Drug Resistance**: Development of resistance mechanisms in pathogens or cancer cells can render drugs ineffective.

- **Example:** Antibiotic resistance in bacteria, such as methicillin-resistant Staphylococcus aureus (MRSA), limits the efficacy of certain antibiotics and requires alternative treatment strategies.

- **pH and Ionization**: pH conditions in the body can affect the ionization state of drugs, influencing their solubility, absorption, and distribution.

- **Example:** Acidic drugs like aspirin are more ionized in alkaline environments, reducing their absorption in the acidic stomach but increasing absorption in the alkaline small intestine.

- **Drug Formulation Excipients**: Excipients in drug formulations can affect drug solubility, stability, and absorption.

- **Example:** Some patients may experience allergic reactions to excipients like lactose or gluten in drug formulations, necessitating alternative formulations.

- **Drug Metabolism**: Metabolism of drugs by enzymes, primarily in the liver, can affect their bioavailability and duration of action.

- **Example:** Cytochrome P450 enzymes metabolize many drugs, and genetic variations in these enzymes can lead to interindividual differences in drug metabolism and response.

- **Drug Transporters**: Membrane transporters play a role in the absorption, distribution, and excretion of drugs, influencing their pharmacokinetics.

- **Example:** P-glycoprotein (P-gp) transports drugs across cell membranes and can affect drug absorption and distribution. Inhibition of P-gp can increase drug bioavailability.

- **Age and Developmental Stage**: Age-related changes in physiology, organ function, and drug metabolism can impact drug response.

- **Example:** Neonates and infants have immature renal function, leading to reduced drug clearance and increased risk of toxicity with certain medications like aminoglycoside antibiotics.

- **Sex Differences**: Biological differences between sexes can affect drug pharmacokinetics and pharmacodynamics.

- **Example:** Women may require lower doses of certain drugs like zolpidem due to differences in drug metabolism and sensitivity to central nervous system depressant effects.

- **Drug Allergies and Hypersensitivity**: Allergic reactions to drugs can lead to immune-mediated responses, affecting drug efficacy and safety.

- Example: Anaphylaxis is a severe allergic reaction that can occur in response to drugs like penicillin, leading to life-threatening symptoms such as difficulty breathing and low blood pressure.

- **Patient Compliance and Adherence**: Patient adherence to prescribed medication regimens can influence drug effectiveness and treatment outcomes.

- **Example:** Poor adherence to antihypertensive medications can result in inadequate blood pressure control and increased risk of cardiovascular events.

- **Environmental Factors**: Environmental factors such as temperature, humidity, and altitude can affect drug stability and absorption.

- **Example:** High-altitude environments can alter drug absorption and metabolism due to changes in gastrointestinal motility and blood flow, affecting drug efficacy.

- **Psychological and Behavioral Factors**: Psychological and behavioral factors, such as placebo effects and patient expectations, can influence drug response.

- **Example:** The placebo effect can lead to improvements in symptoms or outcomes in patients receiving inactive treatments due to psychological factors like expectancy and conditioning.

- These factors highlight the complexity of drug action and the importance of considering multiple variables in optimizing drug therapy for individual patients.

## 143. Explain twenty different types of adverse drug reactions with examples?

- Adverse drug reactions (ADRs) are unintended and harmful effects resulting from the use of medications, which can occur at therapeutic doses.

- ADRs can manifest in various ways and are classified into different types based on their clinical manifestations and underlying mechanisms. Here are twenty different types of adverse drug reactions, along with examples:

- **Allergic Reactions**: Allergic reactions involve an immune-mediated response to a drug, resulting in symptoms such as rash, itching, hives, or anaphylaxis.

- **Example:** Anaphylaxis due to penicillin allergy, characterized by severe respiratory distress, hypotension, and urticaria shortly after drug administration.

- **Idiosyncratic Reactions**: Idiosyncratic reactions are unpredictable and uncommon adverse effects that occur in susceptible individuals and are not related to the pharmacological action of the drug.

- **Example:** Hemolytic anemia in individuals with glucose-6-phosphate dehydrogenase (G6PD) deficiency after exposure to certain drugs like primaquine or sulfonamides.

- **Drug Hypersensitivity Syndrome (DRESS)**: Drug reaction with eosinophilia and systemic symptoms (DRESS) is a severe and potentially life-threatening hypersensitivity reaction characterized by fever, rash, eosinophilia, and multi-organ involvement.

- **Example:** DRESS syndrome associated with antiepileptic drugs like phenytoin, carbamazepine, or lamotrigine, presenting with rash, fever, and organ dysfunction.

- **Stevens-Johnson Syndrome (SJS) and Toxic Epidermal Necrolysis (TEN)**: SJS and TEN are severe mucocutaneous reactions characterized by blistering and detachment of the skin and mucous membranes, often with systemic symptoms.

- **Example:** SJS/TEN associated with medications like sulfonamides, allopurinol, or antiepileptic drugs, leading to widespread skin detachment and potential mortality.

- **Photosensitivity Reactions**: Photosensitivity reactions occur when a drug sensitizes the skin to sunlight or ultraviolet (UV) radiation, leading to skin reactions upon sun exposure.

- **Example:** Phototoxic reactions with tetracycline antibiotics, resulting in exaggerated sunburn-like reactions upon exposure to sunlight.

- **Drug-induced Liver Injury (DILI)**: DILI encompasses a spectrum of liver disorders ranging from asymptomatic transaminase elevations to acute liver failure, which can result from drug toxicity or idiosyncratic reactions.

- **Example:** Acute hepatitis due to overdose of acetaminophen, leading to hepatocellular necrosis and liver failure.

- **Nephrotoxicity**: Nephrotoxicity refers to kidney damage caused by medications, resulting in impaired renal function and potential kidney failure.

- **Example:** Acute kidney injury (AKI) associated with nonsteroidal anti-inflammatory drugs (NSAIDs) due to renal vasoconstriction and decreased renal blood flow.

- **Cardiotoxicity**: Cardiotoxicity involves adverse effects on the cardiovascular system, such as arrhythmias, myocardial damage, or heart failure, caused by medications.

- Example: QT prolongation and torsades de pointes with certain medications like antiarrhythmics (e.g., quinidine, amiodarone) or antibiotics (e.g., macrolides, fluoroquinolones).

- **Neurotoxicity**: Neurotoxicity refers to adverse effects on the nervous system, including symptoms such as cognitive impairment, peripheral neuropathy, seizures, or psychiatric disturbances.

- **Example:** Peripheral neuropathy associated with certain chemotherapy drugs like vincristine or cisplatin, resulting in numbness, tingling, and weakness in the extremities.

- **Endocrine Dysfunction**: Endocrine dysfunction involves hormonal imbalances or disturbances caused by medications, leading to conditions such as hypothyroidism, hyperglycemia, or adrenal insufficiency.

- **Example:** Glucocorticoid-induced hyperglycemia in patients receiving long-term corticosteroid therapy, resulting in insulin resistance and hyperglycemia.

- **Gastrointestinal Reactions**: Gastrointestinal reactions encompass adverse effects on the digestive system, including symptoms such as nausea, vomiting, diarrhea, or gastrointestinal bleeding.

- **Example:** Gastric ulcers and gastrointestinal bleeding associated with NSAIDs due to inhibition of prostaglandin synthesis and disruption of gastric mucosal integrity.

- **Respiratory Reactions**: Respiratory reactions involve adverse effects on the respiratory system, such as bronchospasm, pulmonary fibrosis, or respiratory depression.

- Example: Bronchospasm and wheezing in patients with asthma or chronic obstructive pulmonary disease (COPD) triggered by beta-blockers like propranolol or nonselective NSAIDs.

- **Hematological Reactions**: Hematological reactions involve adverse effects on the blood or blood-forming organs, leading to abnormalities such as anemia, thrombocytopenia, or leukopenia.

- **Example:** Agranulocytosis associated with antithyroid drugs like propylthiouracil or methimazole, resulting in severe neutropenia and increased risk of infections.

- **Musculoskeletal Reactions**: Musculoskeletal reactions encompass adverse effects on the musculoskeletal system, including symptoms such as myalgia, arthralgia, or musculoskeletal pain.

- **Example:** Statin-induced myopathy characterized by muscle pain, weakness, and elevated creatine kinase levels in patients receiving statin therapy for dyslipidemia.

- **Ocular Toxicity**: Ocular toxicity involves adverse effects on the eyes or visual system, resulting in symptoms such as blurred vision, visual disturbances, or retinal damage.

- **Example:** Chloroquine or hydroxychloroquine-induced retinopathy, leading to irreversible retinal damage and vision loss in patients receiving long-term treatment for malaria or autoimmune diseases.

- **Immunosuppression**: Immunosuppression refers to suppression of the immune system by medications, increasing susceptibility to infections or malignancies.

- **Example:** Opportunistic infections such as Pneumocystis jirovecii pneumonia (PCP) in patients receiving immunosuppressive therapy with corticosteroids or immunosuppressants following organ transplantation.

- **Reproductive Toxicity**: Reproductive toxicity involves adverse effects on reproductive organs or fertility, including effects on gonads, sexual function, or pregnancy outcomes.

- **Example:** Teratogenic effects of isotretinoin (Accutane) in pregnant women, leading to congenital malformations and fetal abnormalities when used during pregnancy.

- **Psychiatric Reactions**: Psychiatric reactions encompass adverse effects on mental health or behavior, including symptoms such as depression, anxiety, or psychosis.

- **Example:** Antidepressant-induced sexual dysfunction, including decreased libido, anorgasmia, or erectile dysfunction, associated with selective serotonin reuptake inhibitors (SSRIs) or serotonin-norepinephrine reuptake inhibitors (SNRIs).

- **Metabolic Disturbances**: Metabolic disturbances involve alterations in metabolic processes or disturbances in electrolyte balance caused by medications.

- **Example:** Hyperkalemia associated with potassium-sparing diuretics like spironolactone or angiotensin-converting enzyme (ACE) inhibitors, leading to increased serum potassium levels and potential cardiac arrhythmias.

- **Secondary Neoplasms**: Some medications may increase the risk of secondary malignancies or carcinogenesis through various mechanisms.

- Example: Long-term use of alkylating agents like cyclophosphamide or radiation therapy can increase the risk of secondary malignancies, such as leukemia or solid tumors, due to DNA damage and mutagenic effects.

- These examples illustrate the diverse spectrum of adverse drug reactions, highlighting the importance of monitoring for and managing ADRs to optimize patient safety and therapeutic outcomes.

- **144. Explain 10 methods through which drug toxicities can be treated with examples?**

- Treating drug toxicities involves managing the adverse effects caused by medications to minimize harm and restore physiological function. There are various methods for treating drug toxicities, depending on the specific toxic effects and underlying mechanisms.

**Following are ten methods through which drug toxicities can be treated, along with examples:**

- **Discontinuation of the Offending Drug**: Discontinuing the administration of the causative drug is often the first step in managing drug toxicities, allowing the body to metabolize and eliminate the drug.

- **Example:** Discontinuation of acetaminophen in cases of acetaminophen overdose to prevent further hepatotoxicity and liver damage.

- **Supportive Care**: Supportive care aims to maintain vital functions and provide symptomatic relief while the body metabolizes and eliminates the toxic drug.

- **Example:** Intravenous fluids and electrolyte replacement to manage dehydration and electrolyte imbalances in patients with diuretic-induced dehydration.

- **Gastric Decontamination**: Gastric decontamination techniques aim to reduce the absorption of the toxic drug from the gastrointestinal tract, typically through methods such as gastric lavage or administration of activated charcoal.

- Example: Activated charcoal administration following ingestion of a toxic substance to adsorb the drug in the gastrointestinal tract and prevent systemic absorption.

- **Enhanced Elimination**: Enhanced elimination techniques aim to increase the removal of the toxic drug from the body, often through mechanisms such as hemodialysis, hemoperfusion, or urinary alkalinization.

- **Example:** Hemodialysis for the removal of water-soluble toxins like methanol or ethylene glycol in cases of severe poisoning.

- **Antidotes**: Antidotes are specific agents that counteract the toxic effects of a drug by either antagonizing its action, enhancing its metabolism, or neutralizing its effects.

- **Example:** Naloxone as an antidote for opioid overdose, reversing respiratory depression and central nervous system depression by competitively antagonizing opioid receptors.

- **Symptomatic Treatment**: Symptomatic treatment involves addressing specific symptoms or complications associated with drug toxicities to alleviate discomfort and prevent further harm.

- **Example:** Administration of antiemetics like ondansetron to manage nausea and vomiting in patients experiencing chemotherapy-induced nausea and vomiting (CINV).

- **Chelation Therapy**: Chelation therapy involves the administration of chelating agents that bind to toxic metals or minerals, facilitating their elimination from the body.

- **Example:** Dimercaprol (BAL) or succimer (DMSA) for the treatment of heavy metal poisoning, such as lead or arsenic toxicity.

- **Hormonal Support**: Hormonal support may be necessary in cases where drug toxicities affect endocrine function, requiring supplementation or replacement of deficient hormones.

- **Example:** Glucocorticoid replacement therapy in patients with adrenal insufficiency due to long-term corticosteroid use or adrenal suppression.

- **Fluid and Electrolyte Management**: Fluid and electrolyte management is crucial in treating drug toxicities that disrupt fluid balance or electrolyte levels, helping to restore homeostasis.

- **Example:** Calcium gluconate administration to counteract the cardiotoxic effects of hyperkalemia or calcium channel blocker toxicity by stabilizing cardiac cell membranes.

- **Mechanical Ventilation**: Mechanical ventilation may be necessary in cases of severe respiratory depression or failure caused by drug toxicities, providing respiratory support until the effects of the toxic drug wear off.

- **Example:** Intubation and mechanical ventilation in patients with opioid overdose or sedative overdose causing respiratory depression and hypoxemia.

- These methods represent various strategies for managing drug toxicities, with treatment approaches tailored to the specific toxic effects, severity of toxicity, and individual patient characteristics.

- Prompt recognition and appropriate intervention are essential for optimizing outcomes and minimizing morbidity and mortality associated with drug toxicities.

## 145. Explain side effect, secondary effect, toxic effect with examples?

- Understanding the distinctions between side effects, secondary effects, and toxic effects is important in pharmacology and medicine, as they describe different types of adverse outcomes associated with drug use.

**Following is an explanation of each term with examples:**

- **Side Effect**: A side effect is an unintended and usually mild or tolerable effect of a drug that occurs at therapeutic doses. Side effects are often predictable based on the pharmacological actions of the drug and may or may not be related to the drug's primary therapeutic effect.

- **Example:** Drowsiness caused by first-generation antihistamines like diphenhydramine used to treat allergy symptoms. While the primary therapeutic effect is antihistaminic, drowsiness is a common side effect due to the drugs' sedative properties.

- **Secondary Effect**: A secondary effect refers to an unintended consequence of a drug's primary action or mechanism of action, which may or may not be adverse. Unlike side effects, secondary effects can encompass both beneficial and harmful outcomes.

- **Example:** The antihypertensive drug minoxidil was initially developed as a vasodilator but was found to have a secondary effect of promoting hair growth. While hair growth is not the intended therapeutic effect, it is considered a beneficial secondary effect in the treatment of alopecia.

- **Toxic Effect**: A toxic effect occurs when a drug produces harmful or adverse effects on the body, typically at doses higher than those used for therapeutic purposes. Toxic effects can range from mild to severe and may result from overdosage, impaired drug metabolism, or individual susceptibility.

- **Example:** Acetaminophen overdose can lead to hepatotoxicity and acute liver failure due to the toxic metabolite N-acetyl-p-benzoquinone imine (NAPQI) produced during metabolism. While acetaminophen is safe at therapeutic doses, excessive ingestion can result in severe hepatotoxicity and potentially fatal outcomes.

**Conclusion:**

- Side effects are unintended and usually mild adverse effects that occur at therapeutic doses, secondary effects encompass both beneficial and harmful outcomes related to a drug's primary action, and toxic effects are harmful or adverse effects that occur at doses higher than therapeutic levels.

- Understanding these terms helps healthcare professionals assess and manage the risks associated with drug therapy, ensuring the safe and effective use of medications.

## 146. Explain the general management of poisoning with examples?

- Managing poisoning involves assessing and treating individuals who have been exposed to toxic substances, whether accidentally, intentionally, or occupationally. The general management of poisoning typically follows a systematic approach that includes assessment, stabilization, decontamination, supportive care, specific antidote administration, and monitoring.

**Following is an overview of the general management of poisoning, along with examples:**

- **Assessment**: Obtain a thorough history, including the substance involved, route of exposure, quantity ingested, and timing of exposure. Perform a physical examination to assess the patient's vital signs, level of consciousness, and any signs or symptoms of toxicity.

- Example: A patient presents to the emergency department with symptoms of opioid overdose. History reveals recent ingestion of an unknown quantity of prescription opioids obtained from a friend.

- **Stabilization**: Address immediate life-threatening conditions and  stabilize the patient's vital signs. Provide supportive measures such as airway management, oxygen supplementation, and intravenous fluids as needed.

- **Example:** Administer naloxone to reverse respiratory depression and improve airway patency in a patient with opioid overdose.

- **Decontamination**: Initiate decontamination measures to prevent further absorption of the toxic substance. This may involve gastric lavage, administration of activated charcoal, or removal of contaminated clothing.

- **Example:** Administer activated charcoal to a patient who ingested a large quantity of acetaminophen to reduce absorption and enhance elimination of the toxic drug.

- **Supportive Care**: Provide supportive care to manage symptoms and complications associated with poisoning. This may include monitoring vital signs, administering oxygen therapy, correcting electrolyte imbalances, and maintaining hemodynamic stability.

- **Example:** Monitor and manage electrolyte abnormalities, such as hyperkalemia, in a patient with digoxin toxicity, as hyperkalemia can exacerbate cardiac toxicity.

- **Specific Antidote Administration**: Administer specific antidotes when available and indicated to counteract the effects of certain toxic substances. Antidotes work by either neutralizing the toxic agent, enhancing its elimination, or reversing its effects on target organs.

- **Example:** Administer intravenous naloxone to reverse respiratory depression and central nervous system depression in a patient with opioid overdose.

- **Enhanced Elimination**: Consider enhanced elimination techniques, such as hemodialysis or urinary alkalinization, to accelerate the removal of certain toxic substances from the body.

- **Example:** Initiate hemodialysis in a patient with severe lithium toxicity to enhance elimination and reduce serum lithium levels.

- **Monitoring**: Monitor the patient closely for changes in clinical status, vital signs, laboratory parameters, and toxicological effects. Adjust treatment interventions as necessary based on ongoing assessment.

- **Example:** Monitor liver function tests and coagulation studies in a patient with acetaminophen overdose to assess for hepatotoxicity and coagulopathy.

- **Disposition**: Determine the appropriate disposition of the patient based on their clinical status, response to treatment, and risk of complications. This may involve admission to the hospital for further observation and management or discharge with appropriate follow-up care.

- **Example:** Admit a patient with severe organophosphate poisoning to the intensive care unit for close monitoring and supportive care due to the risk of respiratory failure and cardiovascular collapse.

**Conclusion:**

- The general management of poisoning involves a systematic approach that includes assessment, stabilization, decontamination, supportive care, specific antidote administration, enhanced elimination, monitoring, and disposition.
- Prompt recognition and appropriate intervention are essential for optimizing outcomes and minimizing morbidity and mortality associated with poisoning.

**147. Discuss the differences between prescription and non-prescription drugs? add a note on OTC drugs?**

- Prescription and non-prescription drugs, also known as over-the-counter (OTC) drugs, differ primarily in terms of accessibility, regulation, and the conditions for which they are used. Here are the key differences:

- **Regulation and Accessibility**:

- **Prescription Drugs**: These are medications that can only be obtained with a prescription from a licensed healthcare professional, such as a doctor or nurse practitioner.
- Prescription drugs are typically more potent, have a higher potential for side effects, and may require monitoring by a healthcare provider.

- **Non-Prescription Drugs (OTC)**: These are medications that are available for purchase without a prescription.
- They are generally considered safe for use without medical supervision and are intended for self-diagnosed conditions or minor ailments.
- OTC drugs are regulated by government agencies to ensure their safety and efficacy, but they are usually less potent than prescription drugs.

- **Use and Indications**:

- **Prescription Drugs**: These are often used to treat more serious or complex medical conditions that require professional diagnosis, monitoring, and management. They may include antibiotics, antidepressants, opioids, chemotherapy drugs, and other medications that require careful oversight.

- **Non-Prescription Drugs (OTC)**: These are typically used to relieve symptoms of common, self-limiting conditions such as headaches, allergies, colds, coughs, indigestion, and minor aches and pains.

- They are designed for short-term use and are not intended to treat chronic or severe health issues.

- **Safety and Potential Risks**:

- **Prescription Drugs**: Because they are often more potent and targeted to specific conditions, prescription drugs carry a higher risk of adverse effects and interactions.
- They require careful consideration of dosage, administration, and potential side effects under the supervision of a healthcare professional.

- **Non-Prescription Drugs (OTC)**: These medications are generally considered safe when used as directed, but they still carry risks of side effects, interactions, and misuse.
- Consumers should carefully read and follow the instructions on OTC drug labels and consult a pharmacist or healthcare provider if they have any questions or concerns.

- **Cost and Insurance Coverage**:

- **Prescription Drugs**: These medications tend to be more expensive than OTC drugs due to their higher potency, specialized formulations, and the need for professional oversight.
- Depending on the healthcare system and insurance coverage, patients may bear a significant portion of the cost.

- **Non-Prescription Drugs (OTC)**: These medications are typically more affordable and widely available since they do not require a prescription.
- Many OTC drugs are available in generic forms, further reducing costs for consumers.

Conclusion:
- Prescription drugs are more tightly regulated and require a prescription from a healthcare provider for purchase, while non-prescription drugs (OTC) are available without a prescription for self-diagnosed conditions or minor ailments.

- Both types of drugs have their own set of benefits, risks, and appropriate uses, and consumers should use them responsibly and as directed.

## 148. Discuss the method through which receptors are regulated with examples?

- Receptors, which are proteins located on the surface or within cells, play a crucial role in transmitting signals within the body.
- The regulation of receptors is essential for maintaining normal physiological function and responding appropriately to various stimuli.
- Receptor regulation can occur through several mechanisms, including desensitization, internalization, downregulation, upregulation, and allosteric modulation.

**Following is the discussion of these mechanisms with examples:**

- **Desensitization**: Desensitization refers to a decrease in the responsiveness of receptors to continuous or prolonged exposure to an agonist (a molecule that activates the receptor).

- **Example:** Beta-adrenergic receptors in response to continuous exposure to adrenaline during stress. Over time, these receptors become less responsive to adrenaline to prevent excessive stimulation.

- **Internalization**: Internalization involves the removal of receptors from the cell surface by endocytosis, leading to a decrease in the number of receptors available for signaling.

- **Example:** Endocytosis of receptors involved in neurotransmission, such as the dopamine receptors, after prolonged exposure to dopamine. This process helps regulate neurotransmitter signaling and prevent overstimulation.

- **Downregulation**: Downregulation refers to a decrease in the total number of receptors expressed by a cell in response to prolonged exposure to high concentrations of agonists.

- **Example:** Chronic exposure to opioids can lead to downregulation of opioid receptors in the brain. This downregulation may contribute to the development of tolerance, requiring higher doses of opioids to achieve the same effect.

- **Upregulation**: Upregulation involves an increase in the total number of receptors expressed by a cell in response to low concentrations of agonists or prolonged exposure to antagonists (molecules that block the receptor).

- **Example:** Upregulation of insulin receptors on target cells in response to chronic hyperglycemia (high blood sugar levels). This helps enhance the cellular response to insulin and maintain glucose homeostasis.

- **Allosteric Modulation**: Allosteric modulation refers to the binding of a molecule to a site on the receptor distinct from the agonist-binding site, leading to changes in receptor activity.

- **Example:** Benzodiazepines act as positive allosteric modulators of GABA-A receptors. They bind to a site on the receptor complex and enhance the inhibitory effects of the neurotransmitter gamma-aminobutyric acid (GABA), resulting in sedative and anxiolytic effects.

**Conclusion**
- The regulation of receptors is a dynamic process that helps maintain cellular responsiveness to stimuli and ensures proper physiological function.
- Dysregulation of receptor signaling can contribute to various diseases and conditions, highlighting the importance of understanding these regulatory mechanisms for developing effective therapeutics.

**149. What are the functions of receptors? explain with examples?**

- Receptors are specialized proteins located on the surface or within cells that recognize and bind to specific molecules, known as ligands, initiating a cellular response.
- These responses can range from changes in membrane potential to alterations in gene expression, ultimately leading to various physiological effects.
- The functions of receptors are diverse and crucial for proper cellular communication and organismal homeostasis.

**Following are some key functions of receptors explained with examples:**

- **Signal Transduction**: Receptors transmit signals from the extracellular environment to the intracellular space, initiating a cascade of cellular events.

- **Example:** G protein-coupled receptors (GPCRs) respond to ligands such as neurotransmitters, hormones, and photons.
- Upon ligand binding, GPCRs activate intracellular signaling pathways, leading to diverse physiological responses.
- For instance, beta-adrenergic receptors respond to adrenaline, leading to increased heart rate and contractility.

- **Sensory Perception**: Receptors in sensory organs detect various stimuli from the environment, allowing organisms to perceive and respond to changes in their surroundings.

- **Example:** Photoreceptors in the retina, such as rhodopsin, detect light stimuli.
- When light activates rhodopsin, it triggers a signaling cascade that ultimately leads to changes in membrane potential, initiating visual perception.

- **Regulation of Neurotransmission**: Receptors mediate the effects of neurotransmitters, regulating neuronal communication and synaptic transmission.

- **Example:** Acetylcholine receptors at neuromuscular junctions respond to acetylcholine released by motor neurons, leading to muscle contraction. Dysfunction of these receptors can result in neuromuscular disorders such as myasthenia gravis.

- **Hormonal Regulation**: Receptors for hormones mediate the effects of endocrine signals, regulating various physiological processes throughout the body.

- **Example:** Insulin receptors on target cells respond to insulin released by the pancreas in response to elevated blood glucose levels. Insulin binding to its receptors promotes glucose uptake by cells, regulating blood sugar levels.

- **Immune Response Modulation**: Receptors on immune cells recognize foreign antigens and modulate immune responses, including inflammation and immune cell activation.

- **Example:** Toll-like receptors (TLRs) recognize pathogen-associated molecular patterns (PAMPs) present on microbes. Activation of TLRs initiates innate immune responses, such as the production of inflammatory cytokines, helping to combat infections.

- **Cellular Growth and Differentiation**:

- Receptors regulate processes such as cell proliferation, differentiation, and apoptosis, influencing tissue development and homeostasis.

- Example: Growth factor receptors, such as the epidermal growth factor receptor (EGFR), respond to growth factors by activating signaling pathways that promote cell growth and division.

- Dysregulation of EGFR signaling is implicated in cancer development and progression.

**Conclusion:**
- Receptors play diverse and essential roles in cellular communication, sensory perception, physiological regulation, and immune responses.
- Their functions are tightly regulated and finely tuned to maintain organismal homeostasis and respond appropriately to environmental stimuli.
- Dysfunctional receptors can contribute to various diseases and disorders, highlighting their importance as therapeutic targets in medicine.

**150. Explain non receptor mediated drug's action with examples?**

- Non-receptor mediated drug actions refer to mechanisms through which drugs exert their effects without directly binding to specific receptors.
- Instead, these drugs typically act through physical or chemical interactions with cellular components, leading to physiological changes.

**Following are some common examples of non-receptor mediated drug actions:**

- **Antacids**: Antacids such as aluminum hydroxide and magnesium hydroxide neutralize gastric acid in the stomach by chemically reacting with it, rather than interacting with specific receptors.
- This action helps alleviate symptoms of heartburn and indigestion.

- **Antacids as Laxatives**: Magnesium hydroxide, when used in higher doses, acts as an osmotic laxative.
- It draws water into the intestine through osmosis, leading to increased intestinal motility and softer stools, thus relieving constipation.

- **Antibiotics**: Some antibiotics, such as polymyxins, disrupt bacterial cell membranes by interacting with phospholipids, causing leakage of cellular contents and ultimately bacterial cell death.

- This action is not receptor-mediated but rather based on physical disruption of bacterial cell structures.

- **Chelating Agents**: Chelating agents like ethylenediaminetetraacetic acid (EDTA) bind to metal ions, forming stable complexes.
- EDTA is used in medicine to treat heavy metal poisoning by binding to toxic metals such as lead or mercury and facilitating their excretion from the body.

- **Antiseptics and Disinfectants**: Antiseptics and disinfectants such as alcohol (ethanol) and hydrogen peroxide exert their antimicrobial effects by denaturing proteins and disrupting cell membranes of microorganisms.
- This action is not receptor-mediated but rather based on chemical interactions with microbial components.

- **Osmotic Diuretics**: Osmotic diuretics like mannitol increase urine volume and decrease fluid accumulation in tissues by exerting osmotic pressure in the renal tubules.
- This osmotic effect prevents water reabsorption and promotes water excretion, leading to increased urine output.

- **Local Anesthetics**: Local anesthetics such as lidocaine block voltage-gated sodium channels in nerve membranes, preventing the generation and propagation of action potentials.
- While this action does involve binding to a specific target (sodium channels), it is considered non-receptor mediated because it does not involve interaction with a traditional receptor site.

**Conclusion:**
- In summary, non-receptor mediated drug actions involve mechanisms where drugs exert their effects through physical or chemical interactions with cellular components or physiological processes, rather than through specific receptor binding.

- These actions play important roles in pharmaco-therapy and can be exploited for therapeutic purposes in various medical conditions.

## 151. Explain dose response curve with examples?

- A dose-response curve is a graphical representation of the relationship between the dose or concentration of a drug or stimulus and the magnitude of the response it produces in a biological system.
- These curves provide valuable information about the potency, efficacy, and potential side effects of drugs, as well as the dose range required to achieve therapeutic effects.

**Following is an explanation of dose-response curves with examples:**

- **Increasing Dose and Response**: In a typical dose-response curve, as the dose of a drug increases, the magnitude of the response also increases.
- This relationship is often characterized by a sigmoidal (S-shaped) curve, indicating that there is a threshold dose below which no response occurs, followed by a range where the response increases steeply with increasing dose, and finally reaching a plateau where further increases in dose produce little to no additional response.

- **Potency**: Potency refers to the amount of drug required to produce a given effect. Drugs with higher potency require lower doses to produce a certain level of response compared to less potent drugs. This is reflected in dose-response curves by shifts along the dose axis.

- **Example:** Consider two pain relievers, aspirin and ibuprofen. If aspirin is more potent than ibuprofen, the dose-response curve for aspirin will be shifted to the left along the dose axis, indicating that lower doses of aspirin are needed to achieve the same level of pain relief as higher doses of ibuprofen.

- **Efficacy**: Efficacy refers to the maximum effect that a drug can produce, regardless of dose. Drugs with higher efficacy produce a greater maximal response compared to drugs with lower efficacy. This is reflected in dose-response curves by differences in the height of the plateau phase.

- **Example:** Consider two antihypertensive drugs, Drug A and Drug B. If Drug A has higher efficacy than Drug B, the plateau phase of the dose-response curve for Drug A will be higher, indicating that Drug A can lower blood pressure to a greater extent compared to Drug B, even at maximal doses.

- **Therapeutic Index**: The therapeutic index is the ratio of the dose of a drug that produces a therapeutic effect to the dose that produces toxic effects. Drugs with a higher therapeutic index have a wider margin of safety.

- **Example:** A dose-response curve for a pain reliever may show that a certain dose provides effective pain relief without causing significant side effects, indicating a wide therapeutic index. In contrast, if higher doses produce severe side effects without significantly increasing the therapeutic effect, the therapeutic index would be narrow.

- **Side Effects**: Dose-response curves can also reveal the occurrence of side effects at higher doses of a drug. Side effects may manifest as additional responses beyond the desired therapeutic effect or as toxic effects.

- **Example:** A dose-response curve for an antihistamine may show that at low doses, the drug effectively reduces allergy symptoms without causing significant drowsiness (a common side effect). However, at higher doses, drowsiness becomes more pronounced, indicating the occurrence of a side effect.

- Overall, dose-response curves provide valuable information about the relationship between drug dose and response, helping clinicians determine appropriate dosing regimens, assess drug potency and efficacy, and evaluate the risk-benefit profile of medications.

## 152. Differentiate efficacy and potency with examples?

- Efficacy and potency are both important concepts in pharmacology that describe different aspects of a drug's effectiveness, but they refer to distinct properties:

- **Efficacy**: Efficacy refers to the maximum effect that a drug can produce, regardless of the dose. It represents the intrinsic ability of a drug to elicit a response from its target.
- In other words, efficacy describes how well a drug can activate its target receptors or produce the desired therapeutic effect.
- Efficacy is often measured by the height of the plateau phase of a dose-response curve, where further increases in dose do not result in additional response.
- A drug with high efficacy will produce a greater maximal response, while a drug with low efficacy will produce a smaller maximal response.

- **Example:** Morphine is a highly efficacious opioid analgesic, meaning it can produce strong pain relief even at moderate doses. Its maximal analgesic effect is high, making it a potent pain reliever.

- **Potency**: Potency refers to the amount or concentration of a drug required to produce a specific effect of a given magnitude. It represents the dose-response relationship of a drug.
- Potency is a measure of the drug's strength or activity relative to its concentration or dose.
- Potency is often determined by comparing the doses of different drugs required to produce the same level of effect.

- Potency is typically measured by the position of a drug's dose-response curve along the dose axis. A drug with higher potency requires a lower dose to produce the same effect compared to a drug with lower potency.

- **Example:** Fentanyl is a synthetic opioid analgesic that is more potent than morphine. This means that fentanyl produces the same level of pain relief at lower doses compared to morphine. In other words, fentanyl has a higher potency but may not necessarily have higher efficacy than morphine.

**Conclusion:**

- Efficacy refers to the maximal effect a drug can produce, while potency refers to the dose or concentration of a drug required to produce a specific effect.
- A drug with high efficacy will produce a greater maximal response, while a drug with high potency will produce the same response at lower doses.
- Understanding both efficacy and potency is crucial for selecting appropriate drugs and dosing regimens in clinical practice.

## 153. Explain drug selectivity and specificity with examples?

- Drug selectivity and specificity are both important concepts in pharmacology that describe the ability of a drug to target specific receptors or biological pathways while minimizing effects on other receptors or pathways.
- Although these terms are often used interchangeably, they have slightly different meanings:

- **Drug Selectivity**: Drug selectivity refers to the ability of a drug to interact predominantly with a specific target or receptor subtype, while having minimal effects on other targets or receptors.
- Selective drugs are designed to exert their effects primarily at the desired site of action, reducing the risk of unwanted side effects.

- Selectivity can be achieved through structural modifications of the drug molecule to enhance affinity for the target receptor or to reduce affinity for off-target receptors.

- **Example:** Beta-blockers used in the treatment of hypertension and cardiac conditions are designed to selectively block beta-adrenergic receptors in the heart, thereby reducing heart rate and blood pressure. Selective beta-blockers such as metoprolol primarily target beta-1 adrenergic receptors in the heart, leading to cardiac effects, while minimizing effects on beta-2 adrenergic receptors in the lungs to avoid bronchoconstriction.

- **Drug Specificity**: Drug specificity refers to the degree to which a drug interacts exclusively with a single target or receptor subtype, with minimal interactions with other receptors or targets.
- Highly specific drugs exhibit binding and activity only at their intended target, without significant interactions with unrelated receptors or biological systems.
- Specificity can be assessed through pharmacological studies evaluating the binding affinity and functional activity of a drug at different receptors or targets.

- **Example:** Enzyme inhibitors used in cancer therapy often aim for high specificity to target key enzymes involved in tumor growth and proliferation, such as tyrosine kinases. Drugs like imatinib specifically inhibit the activity of the BCR-ABL tyrosine kinase, which is characteristic of chronic myeloid leukemia (CML), leading to selective inhibition of leukemia cell growth while sparing normal cells.

## Conclusion:
- Drug selectivity and specificity both describe the ability of a drug to interact with specific targets or receptors.
- Drug selectivity emphasizes the preferential interaction with a particular target over others, while drug specificity focuses on the exclusivity of the drug's interaction with its intended target.

- Both concepts are important considerations in drug design and development to optimize therapeutic efficacy and minimize side effects.

## 154. Explain the effect of kidney disease and liver disease on drug's action with examples?

- Kidney disease and liver disease can both have significant effects on the pharmacokinetics (absorption, distribution, metabolism, and excretion) and pharmacodynamics (the drug's effects on the body) of medications, potentially altering their action, efficacy, and safety profiles.

**Following is an explanation of the effects of kidney and liver disease on drug action, along with examples:**

**Kidney Disease**:
- **Pharmacokinetic Effects**: Decreased renal function in kidney disease can impair the elimination of drugs primarily excreted by the kidneys, leading to drug accumulation and potential toxicity.
- Drugs that are renally cleared may require dose adjustments or extended dosing intervals in patients with kidney disease to prevent excessive accumulation.

- **Example:** Digoxin, a medication used to treat heart failure, is primarily eliminated by the kidneys. In patients with kidney disease, impaired renal function can lead to digoxin accumulation, increasing the risk of toxicity such as arrhythmias.

- **Pharmacodynamic Effects**: Changes in kidney function can alter the sensitivity of the body to certain drugs, affecting their efficacy or side effect profile.

- **Example:** Aminoglycoside antibiotics, such as gentamicin, exhibit nephrotoxicity and ototoxicity.

- In patients with impaired kidney function, the risk of nephrotoxicity increases, necessitating careful monitoring of drug levels and renal function.

**Liver Disease**:

- **Pharmacokinetic Effects**: Liver disease can impair drug metabolism and clearance, leading to decreased drug metabolism and potentially increased systemic drug concentrations.
- Drugs that undergo hepatic metabolism may require dose adjustments in patients with liver disease to avoid drug accumulation and toxicity.
- **Example:** Warfarin, an oral anticoagulant, undergoes extensive hepatic metabolism. In patients with liver disease, impaired metabolism can lead to increased warfarin levels and an elevated risk of bleeding complications.

- **Pharmacodynamic Effects**: Liver disease can alter the expression or function of drug targets, affecting the drug's efficacy or safety profile.
- **Example:** Benzodiazepines, such as diazepam, are metabolized in the liver and exert their effects through modulation of gamma-aminobutyric acid (GABA) receptors in the brain. In patients with liver disease, impaired drug metabolism may lead to prolonged sedation and increased risk of respiratory depression due to enhanced drug effects.

**Conclusion**:

- Kidney disease and liver disease can both impact the pharmacokinetics and pharmacodynamics of medications, influencing their action, efficacy, and safety profiles.
- Healthcare providers need to consider these factors when prescribing medications to patients with impaired kidney or liver function and may need to adjust drug doses or choose alternative medications to optimize therapeutic outcomes and minimize the risk of adverse effects.
- Regular monitoring of renal and hepatic function, as well as drug levels when appropriate, is essential in managing patients with kidney or liver disease.

## 155. What are the uses of drugs? explain with examples?

- Drugs are substances that have medicinal properties and are used for various purposes in healthcare to prevent, diagnose, treat, or manage diseases, symptoms, and conditions.
- They can exert their effects on specific targets within the body to produce therapeutic outcomes.

**Following are some common uses of drugs explained with examples:**

- **Treatment of Acute and Chronic Diseases**: Drugs are frequently used to treat both acute and chronic diseases, including infections, cardiovascular disorders, respiratory conditions, autoimmune diseases, and cancer.

- **Example:** Antibiotics such as amoxicillin are used to treat bacterial infections like pneumonia, while antihypertensive medications such as lisinopril are prescribed to manage chronic conditions like hypertension.

- **Symptom Relief**: Drugs are used to alleviate symptoms associated with various medical conditions, such as pain, fever, inflammation, cough, congestion, nausea, and insomnia.

- **Example:** Nonsteroidal anti-inflammatory drugs (NSAIDs) like ibuprofen are used to reduce pain and inflammation associated with conditions such as arthritis, while antihistamines such as diphenhydramine can relieve symptoms of allergies, including sneezing and itching.

- **Prevention of Diseases and Conditions**: Drugs are used for preventive purposes to reduce the risk of developing certain diseases or conditions, including vaccines to prevent infectious diseases and medications to lower the risk of cardiovascular events or osteoporotic fractures.

- **Example:** The influenza vaccine is administered annually to prevent seasonal flu infections, while statin medications like atorvastatin are prescribed to lower cholesterol levels and reduce the risk of heart attacks and strokes.

- **Management of Chronic Conditions**: Drugs play a critical role in managing chronic conditions that require ongoing treatment and monitoring, such as diabetes, asthma, epilepsy, and mental health disorders.

- **Example:** Insulin and oral hypoglycemic agents such as metformin are used to manage blood sugar levels in patients with diabetes, while inhaled corticosteroids and bronchodilators are prescribed to control symptoms and prevent exacerbations in patients with asthma.

- **Supportive Care**: Drugs are used to provide supportive care to patients undergoing medical treatments, such as chemotherapy, radiation therapy, or surgery, to manage side effects, relieve symptoms, and improve quality of life.

- **Example:** Antiemetic medications like ondansetron are administered to prevent nausea and vomiting associated with chemotherapy, while opioids such as morphine are used to relieve pain following surgery.

- **Diagnostic Purposes**: Drugs are sometimes used diagnostically to help identify or evaluate certain medical conditions, such as contrast agents used in imaging studies or medications used in provocative testing.

- **Example:** Contrast agents like iodine-based dyes are injected intravenously during computed tomography (CT) scans to enhance visualization of blood vessels, organs, and tissues, aiding in the diagnosis of various conditions such as tumors or vascular abnormalities.

**Conclusion:**
- Drugs have diverse uses in healthcare, including the treatment of diseases, symptom relief, prevention of illnesses, management of chronic conditions, supportive care, and diagnostic purposes.
- Healthcare providers carefully select and prescribe medications based on the patient's medical history, diagnosis, and individual needs, aiming to achieve optimal therapeutic outcomes while minimizing risks and adverse effects.

## 156. While studying drugs, what factors should be kept in mind as a student of pharmacology?

- As a student of pharmacology, there are several important factors to consider while studying drugs.
- Understanding these factors will help you develop a comprehensive understanding of pharmacology and its applications in healthcare.

**Following are some key considerations:**

- **Mechanism of Action**: Learn how drugs interact with biological targets (receptors, enzymes, ion channels, etc.) to produce their effects. Understanding the mechanism of action provides insights into drug efficacy, selectivity, and potential side effects.

- **Pharmacokinetics**: Study the absorption, distribution, metabolism, and excretion (ADME) of drugs in the body. Factors such as bioavailability, half-life, and drug clearance influence dosing regimens, drug interactions, and therapeutic monitoring.

- **Pharmacodynamics**: Understand how drugs produce physiological effects and how these effects are quantified and measured. Consider concepts such as dose-response relationships, drug-receptor interactions, and therapeutic indices.

- **Drug Classes and Categories**: Familiarize yourself with different classes of drugs, their primary indications, mechanisms of action, and common side effects.

- Classify drugs based on their pharmacological properties (e.g., antibiotics, analgesics, anti-hypertensives).

- **Therapeutic Uses**: Learn about the therapeutic uses of drugs for various medical conditions, including both acute and chronic diseases. Understand the rationale behind drug selection, dosing, and treatment algorithms.

- **Adverse Effects**: Be aware of potential adverse effects associated with drug therapy, including side effects, drug interactions, allergic reactions, and toxicity. Recognize the importance of monitoring and managing adverse drug reactions.

- **Patient Factors**: Consider patient-specific factors that influence drug therapy, such as age, gender, genetics, comorbidities, organ function, and concomitant medications. Individualize treatment plans based on patient characteristics and clinical status.

- **Drug Development and Regulation**: Understand the drug development process, including preclinical studies, clinical trials, and regulatory approval. Learn about drug regulation agencies, drug scheduling, and post-marketing surveillance.

- **Evidence-Based Medicine**: Evaluate the strength of evidence supporting drug efficacy and safety. Critically appraise scientific literature, clinical trials, meta-analyses, and practice guidelines to make informed decisions about drug therapy.

- **Ethical and Legal Considerations**: Recognize ethical principles and legal regulations governing drug research, prescribing practices, and patient care. Understand the importance of patient autonomy, informed consent, and adherence to professional standards.

- **Emerging Trends and Innovations**: Stay informed about emerging trends, advances, and innovations in pharmacology, including new drug developments, pharmacogenomics, personalized medicine, and drug repurposing.

## Conclusion:

- By keeping these factors in mind and integrating them into your study of pharmacology, you can develop a comprehensive understanding of drugs and their applications in healthcare, preparing you for a career in pharmacy, medicine, research, or other related fields.

## 157. What are the factors that influence the selection of route of drug administration?

- The selection of the route of drug administration is influenced by several factors, including the characteristics of the drug, the patient's condition, the desired onset and duration of action, and practical considerations.

**Following are the key factors that influence the selection of the route of drug administration:**

**Drug Properties**:
- **Chemical Properties**: The solubility, stability, and formulation of the drug influence its suitability for different routes of administration. For example, lipid-soluble drugs are well-suited for transdermal or oral administration, while hydrophilic drugs may require parenteral routes.

- **Half-Life**: The drug's pharmacokinetic properties, including its half-life, determine the frequency and timing of dosing. Drugs with short half-lives may require frequent administration or continuous infusion.

**Patient Factors**:

- **Age**: The age of the patient can affect the route of administration. For example, oral routes may be preferred in adults, while pediatric or geriatric patients may require alternative routes due to swallowing difficulties or reduced gastric motility.

- **Condition**: The patient's medical condition, co-morbidities, and physiological status influence the route of administration. Patients with gastro-intestinal disorders may have impaired absorption, necessitating parenteral routes.

**Onset and Duration of Action**:

- **Onset of Action**: The desired onset of action influences the choice of route. Some routes, such as intravenous or inhalation, provide rapid onset of action, while others, such as oral or transdermal, may have slower onset.

- **Duration of Action**: The desired duration of action affects the selection of sustained-release formulations or continuous infusion methods to maintain therapeutic drug levels over an extended period.

**Therapeutic Goal**:

- **Local vs. Systemic Effects**: The intended site of action—local or systemic—guides the selection of the route. For localized effects, topical or regional routes may be preferred, while systemic effects may require oral, parenteral, or inhalation routes.

- **Target Tissue or Organ**: The specific target tissue or organ influences the route of administration.
- For example, drugs targeting the central nervous system may require routes that bypass the blood-brain barrier, such as intrathecal or intranasal administration.

**Patient Preference and Compliance**:

- **Patient Preference**: Patient preferences, comfort level, and ability to adhere to the prescribed regimen may influence the choice of route. Some patients may prefer oral routes for convenience, while others may prefer injections or topical formulations.

- **Compliance**: The ease of administration and frequency of dosing impact patient compliance. Complex dosing regimens or invasive routes may affect patient adherence to therapy.

**Safety and Risk of Complications**:

- **Risk of Adverse Effects**: The route's safety profile and risk of adverse effects, including local irritation, tissue damage, or systemic toxicity, are considerations in route selection. Intravenous routes carry a higher risk of infection or thrombosis compared to oral or transdermal routes.

- **Skill and Training**: The availability of trained healthcare professionals to administer certain routes, such as intravenous or intramuscular injections, influences route selection in clinical settings.

**Cost and Accessibility**:

- **Cost of Administration**: The cost of drug administration, including equipment, supplies, and personnel, affects route selection. Some routes may be more cost-effective or accessible than others.

- **Availability of Formulations**: The availability of appropriate drug formulations, such as oral tablets, injectable solutions, or transdermal patches, influences route selection based on practical considerations.

- **Conclusion:**
- By considering these factors, healthcare providers can make informed decisions regarding the most appropriate route of drug administration for each patient and therapeutic scenario, optimizing drug efficacy, safety, and patient adherence to treatment.

## 158. How to assess the safety of the drugs? explain with examples?

- Assessing the safety of drugs involves evaluating their potential risks, adverse effects, and toxicity profiles to ensure that their benefits outweigh their potential harms.
- Several methods and tools are used to assess drug safety throughout the drug development process and during clinical use.

**Following is how drug safety is assessed, along with examples:**

- **Preclinical Studies**: Before drugs are tested in humans, preclinical studies are conducted to assess their safety in laboratory and animal models.

- **Examples:** Toxicity studies assess the effects of drugs on various organ systems, including the cardiovascular, respiratory, hepatic, renal, and nervous systems.
- Genotoxicity studies evaluate the potential for drugs to cause DNA damage or mutations. These studies help identify potential safety concerns early in the drug development process.

- **Clinical Trials**: Clinical trials are conducted in human subjects to evaluate the safety, efficacy, and pharmacokinetics of drugs.

- **Examples:** Phase I trials assess the safety and pharmacokinetics of drugs in healthy volunteers, determining the maximum tolerated dose and identifying potential adverse effects.

- Phase II and III trials evaluate the safety and efficacy of drugs in larger patient populations with the target disease, monitoring adverse events and comparing outcomes with placebo or standard treatments.

- **Post-Marketing Surveillance**: Once drugs are approved for marketing, post-marketing surveillance (also known as pharmacovigilance) monitors their safety in real-world clinical practice.

- **Examples:** Adverse event reporting systems collect and analyze reports of suspected adverse drug reactions (ADRs) from healthcare professionals, patients, and regulatory agencies.
- Signal detection methods identify potential safety signals or trends in adverse event data that may indicate previously unrecognized risks associated with drugs.

- **Risk Management Plans**: Regulatory agencies may require risk management plans (RMPs) for certain drugs with known or potential safety concerns to minimize risks and ensure safe use.

- **Examples:** Risk minimization measures may include restricted distribution programs, medication guides, patient education materials, and additional monitoring requirements.
- For example, isotretinoin, a drug used to treat severe acne, is subject to a risk management program called iPLEDGE, which includes mandatory patient education, pregnancy testing, and contraception counseling to prevent fetal exposure and birth defects.

- **Meta-Analysis and Systematic Reviews**: Meta-analysis and systematic reviews of clinical trial data can provide comprehensive assessments of drug safety across multiple studies.

- **Examples:** Meta-analyses may synthesize data from randomized controlled trials to evaluate the overall risk of specific adverse events associated with a drug compared to placebo or other treatments.

- Systematic reviews may also assess the quality and reliability of evidence supporting drug safety claims.

- **Pharmacogenomics**: Pharmacogenomic testing evaluates genetic factors that influence individual variability in drug response and susceptibility to adverse effects.

- **Examples:** Genetic testing for drug-metabolizing enzymes (e.g., CYP2D6, CYP2C19) or drug transporters (e.g., ABCB1) can help identify patients at increased risk of adverse reactions or therapeutic failure due to genetic polymorphisms.

- For example, patients with certain genetic variants in the CYP2D6 gene may be at increased risk of QT prolongation and torsades de pointes when treated with QT-prolonging drugs such as certain antidepressants and antipsychotics.

**Conclusion:**
- By employing these methods and tools, healthcare professionals and regulatory agencies can comprehensively assess the safety of drugs, identify potential risks, and take appropriate measures to minimize harm to patients.

### 159. What is signal detection in pharmacovigilance? How to identify signal? explain with example?

- Signal detection in pharmacovigilance refers to the process of identifying potential safety signals or trends in adverse event data that may indicate previously unrecognized risks associated with drugs. It involves analyzing large volumes of spontaneous reports, clinical trial data, electronic health records, and other sources of pharmacovigilance data to identify patterns of adverse events that warrant further investigation.

- The goal of signal detection is to proactively identify and assess potential safety concerns associated with drugs, allowing for timely risk evaluation and risk management interventions.

**Following is how signal detection is typically conducted and how signals are identified:**

- **Data Collection**: Pharmacovigilance databases collect spontaneous reports of adverse drug reactions (ADRs) submitted by healthcare professionals, patients, and pharmaceutical companies.

- These reports include information such as the suspected drug, the adverse event(s), patient demographics, concomitant medications, and clinical outcomes.

- Other sources of pharmacovigilance data may include clinical trial databases, electronic health records, prescription databases, medical literature, social media, and regulatory databases.

- **Data Mining and Analysis**: Pharmacovigilance data are analyzed using statistical and data mining techniques to detect potential safety signals.

- Various quantitative methods, such as disproportionality analysis, Bayesian data mining, and time-to-onset analysis, are used to identify statistically significant associations between drugs and adverse events that may represent potential safety signals.

- Data are stratified by factors such as drug, adverse event, patient demographics, and time period to identify patterns or clusters of events that may be indicative of drug-related risks.

- **Signal Evaluation**: Identified signals undergo further evaluation to assess their clinical significance, causality, and potential implications for patient safety.

- Signal evaluation may involve reviewing additional data sources, conducting literature reviews, consulting subject matter experts, and considering biological plausibility.

- Signals are assessed in the context of known drug safety profiles, regulatory requirements, and public health priorities to prioritize signals for further investigation.

- **Risk Assessment and Management**: Once signals are confirmed and validated, they undergo risk assessment to determine the magnitude and nature of the associated risk.

- Risk management measures, such as changes to product labeling, communication to healthcare professionals and patients, post-marketing studies, or regulatory actions, may be implemented to mitigate identified risks and optimize the safe use of drugs.

- **Example:** Suppose a pharmacovigilance database receives an increased number of spontaneous reports of a rare adverse event, such as liver injury, associated with a specific medication (e.g., Drug X).
- Signal detection methods are applied to analyze the data and identify whether there is a disproportionate reporting of liver injury with Drug X compared to other drugs.
- Statistical analysis reveals a statistically significant association between Drug X and liver injury, suggesting a potential safety signal.
- Signal evaluation is then conducted to assess the clinical significance, causality, and potential risks associated with this signal.
- If the signal is confirmed and validated, regulatory agencies may take appropriate risk management actions, such as updating the drug's labeling to include warnings about liver injury or requiring additional post-marketing surveillance.

## 160. What is pharmacovigilance? explain the components/objectives of pharmacovigilance program of India?

- Pharmacovigilance is the science and activities related to the detection, assessment, understanding, and prevention of adverse effects or any other drug-related problems associated with the use of medications.
- It plays a crucial role in ensuring the safety of pharmaceutical products throughout their lifecycle, from preclinical development through post-marketing surveillance.
- The components and objectives of the pharmacovigilance program in India are outlined by the Central Drugs Standard Control Organization (CDSCO), which is the national regulatory authority for pharmaceuticals and medical devices.

**The main objectives and components of the pharmacovigilance program in India include:**

**Adverse Drug Reaction (ADR) Reporting:**
- **Objective:** To facilitate the reporting and monitoring of adverse drug reactions (ADRs) by healthcare professionals, patients, and pharmaceutical companies.

- **Components:** Establishment of the Pharmacovigilance Program of India (PvPI) to oversee ADR reporting and monitoring activities.

- Development and maintenance of a national ADR database to collect, collate, and analyze ADR reports from various sources.

- Promotion of ADR reporting through educational initiatives, training programs, and awareness campaigns targeting healthcare professionals, patients, and the public.

**Signal Detection and Evaluation:**
- **Objective:** To identify potential safety signals or trends in ADR data that may indicate previously unrecognized risks associated with medications.

- **Components:** Data analysis and signal detection methods to identify statistically significant associations between drugs and adverse events.

- Signal evaluation and assessment of the clinical significance, causality, and potential implications of identified signals for patient safety.

- Prioritization of signals for further investigation, risk assessment, and risk management actions.

**Risk Assessment and Risk Management:**
- **Objective:** To assess the magnitude and nature of identified risks associated with medications and implement risk management measures to mitigate these risks.

- **Components:** Risk assessment of identified safety signals to determine the severity, frequency, and preventability of adverse events.

- **Implementation** of risk management strategies, such as changes to product labeling, communication to healthcare professionals and patients, post-marketing studies, and regulatory actions, to minimize identified risks and optimize the safe use of medications.

**Quality Assurance and Compliance:**

- **Objective:** To ensure the quality, integrity, and compliance of pharmacovigilance activities with regulatory requirements and international standards.

- **Components:** Establishment of pharmacovigilance quality systems and standard operating procedures (SOPs) to govern pharmacovigilance processes and activities.

- Conduct of audits, inspections, and assessments to monitor compliance with pharmacovigilance regulations and guidelines.

- Continuous improvement initiatives to enhance the effectiveness and efficiency of pharmacovigilance systems and practices.

**Communication and Information Exchange:**

- **Objective:** To facilitate communication and information exchange regarding drug safety issues among stakeholders, including healthcare professionals, patients, regulatory authorities, and pharmaceutical companies.

- **Components:** Dissemination of drug safety information, alerts, and updates through newsletters, bulletins, websites, and other communication channels.

- Collaboration with international pharmacovigilance networks and regulatory agencies to share information, best practices, and experiences in drug safety monitoring and risk management.

- Provision of training and educational resources to enhance pharmacovigilance knowledge and skills among healthcare professionals and stakeholders.

**Conclusion:**

- Overall, the pharmacovigilance program in India aims to promote the safe and effective use of medications by systematically monitoring and evaluating drug safety issues, identifying and mitigating potential risks, and ensuring timely communication of relevant information to healthcare professionals, patients, and regulatory authorities.

**161. How to identify and prevent the risks of drugs? explain with examples?**

- Identifying and preventing the risks of drugs is a critical aspect of pharmacovigilance, ensuring the safe and effective use of medications. Several strategies and measures can be employed to identify and mitigate drug-related risks.

**Here's how risks of drugs can be identified and prevented, along with examples:**

- **Preclinical Studies and Risk Assessment:** Before drugs are tested in humans, preclinical studies assess their safety profile in laboratory and animal models. These studies help identify potential toxicities, adverse effects, and other safety concerns.

- **Example:** Preclinical toxicology studies may identify hepatotoxicity (liver toxicity) associated with a new drug candidate, prompting further investigation and potential modification of the drug's chemical structure or dosing regimen to mitigate the risk of liver injury.

- **Clinical Trials and Risk Evaluation**: Clinical trials evaluate the safety and efficacy of drugs in human subjects, providing valuable data on adverse reactions and safety profiles.
- Rigorous monitoring and assessment of adverse events are conducted throughout clinical development.

- **Example:** During Phase III clinical trials of a new antidepressant medication, increased suicidality (suicidal thoughts or behavior) is observed in a subset of patients.
- This safety signal prompts further evaluation and labeling changes to include warnings about the risk of suicidality in the drug's prescribing information.

- **Post-Marketing Surveillance and Signal Detection**: Post-marketing surveillance (pharmacovigilance) monitors the safety of drugs in real-world clinical practice, detecting and assessing adverse drug reactions (ADRs) and safety signals that may not have been identified during preclinical or clinical testing.

- **Example:** Post-marketing surveillance data reveal an increased risk of cardiovascular events (e.g., heart attacks, strokes) associated with a widely used nonsteroidal anti-inflammatory drug (NSAID).
- This safety signal prompts regulatory action, such as label warnings or contraindications in certain patient populations, to minimize the risk of cardiovascular complications.

- **Risk Minimization Strategies**: Risk minimization strategies aim to reduce or mitigate identified risks associated with drug therapy through targeted interventions, educational initiatives, and regulatory measures.

- **Example:** A risk minimization program is implemented for a teratogenic (pregnancy) drug, involving educational materials, counseling, and pregnancy testing requirements to prevent fetal exposure and birth defects in women of childbearing age.

- **Labeling and Packaging Changes**: Product labeling and packaging are important tools for communicating drug risks and safety information to healthcare professionals and patients. Labeling updates, warnings, contraindications, and precautions help ensure informed decision-making and safe use of medications.

- **Example:** Following the identification of a serious adverse reaction associated with a medication, the drug's label is revised to include a black box warning—a prominent warning highlighting the drug's significant risks—to alert prescribers and patients about the potential dangers.

- **Educational Initiatives and Healthcare Provider Training**: Educational programs and training initiatives aim to enhance healthcare professionals' awareness, knowledge, and understanding of drug risks, adverse effects, and safety monitoring practices.

- **Example:** Continuing medical education (CME) programs provide healthcare professionals with updates on drug safety issues, evidence-based guidelines, and best practices for identifying, managing, and reporting adverse drug reactions.

**Conclusion:**
- By employing these strategies and measures, stakeholders in healthcare, including regulatory agencies, pharmaceutical companies, healthcare professionals, and patients, can work together to identify, evaluate, and mitigate the risks associated with drug therapy, ensuring the safe and effective use of medications.

## 162. Explain drug drug interaction with example?

- Drug-drug interactions occur when the effects of one drug are altered by the presence of another drug, leading to potentially harmful or beneficial effects.

- These interactions can occur through various mechanisms, including pharmacokinetic interactions (affecting drug absorption, distribution, metabolism, or excretion) or pharmacodynamic interactions (altering drug effects at the site of action).

**Following is an explanation of drug-drug interactions with an example:**

**Example of a Pharmacokinetic Drug-Drug Interaction:**

- **Drug Combination**: Warfarin (an anticoagulant) + Amiodarone (an antiarrhythmic)

- **Mechanism**: Amiodarone inhibits the metabolism of warfarin by interfering with the activity of cytochrome P450 enzymes (specifically CYP2C9 and CYP3A4) in the liver, which are responsible for metabolizing warfarin.

- **Effect**: As a result of the inhibition of warfarin metabolism, the plasma concentration of warfarin increases, leading to enhanced anticoagulant effects and an increased risk of bleeding.

- **Clinical Implications**: Patients taking warfarin and amiodarone concurrently require careful monitoring of their international normalized ratio (INR) and may need a reduction in warfarin dosage to avoid excessive anticoagulation and bleeding complications.

**Example of a Pharmacodynamic Drug-Drug Interaction:**

- 
- **Drug Combination**: Benzodiazepines (e.g., diazepam) + Opioids (e.g., morphine)

- **Mechanism**: Both benzodiazepines and opioids exert sedative effects on the central nervous system (CNS). When taken together, their CNS depressant effects are additive, leading to increased sedation, respiratory depression, and the risk of overdose.

- **Effect**: Concurrent use of benzodiazepines and opioids can potentiate respiratory depression and increase the risk of respiratory arrest, particularly in vulnerable populations such as elderly patients or those with respiratory conditions.

- **Clinical Implications**: Healthcare providers should exercise caution when prescribing benzodiazepines and opioids together, considering the potential for additive CNS depression and respiratory depression. Patients should be monitored closely for signs of sedation, respiratory depression, and overdose.

**Conclusion:**

- These examples illustrate how drug-drug interactions can result in altered pharmacokinetics or pharmacodynamics, leading to significant clinical consequences.
- Healthcare providers need to be aware of potential drug interactions when prescribing medications and consider factors such as patient-specific characteristics, dosing regimens, and monitoring requirements to minimize the risk of adverse effects and optimize therapeutic outcomes.
- Additionally, patients should inform their healthcare providers about all medications they are taking, including prescription drugs, over-the-counter medications, supplements, and herbal products, to help identify and prevent potential drug interactions.

**163. Explain various types of drug drug interactions with examples?**

- Drug interactions occur when two or more drugs interact with each other, altering their effectiveness or causing unexpected side effects.
- These interactions can occur due to various mechanisms, including pharmacokinetic interactions (changes in drug absorption, distribution, metabolism, and excretion) and pharmacodynamic interactions (alterations in drug effects at the site of action).

**Here are some common types of drug interactions along with examples:**

**Pharmacokinetic Interactions**:

- **Absorption Interactions**: One drug may affect the absorption of another drug from the gastrointestinal tract.

- For example, calcium supplements can interfere with the absorption of antibiotics like tetracycline.

- **Distribution Interactions**: Drugs may compete for binding sites on plasma proteins, altering the distribution of one or both drugs.

- For instance, nonsteroidal anti-inflammatory drugs (NSAIDs) may displace warfarin from plasma proteins, increasing its anticoagulant effect.

- **Metabolic Interactions**: Some drugs can induce or inhibit drug-metabolizing enzymes, affecting the metabolism of other drugs.

- For example, grapefruit juice inhibits the CYP3A4 enzyme, leading to increased blood levels of certain drugs like statins and calcium channel blockers.

- **Excretion Interactions**: Drugs can interfere with each other's elimination through renal or hepatic excretion pathways.

- For instance, probenecid inhibits the renal excretion of penicillin, leading to increased penicillin levels in the blood.

**Pharmacodynamic Interactions**:

- **Additive Effects**: Two drugs with similar pharmacological effects may produce an enhanced effect when taken together.

- For example, combining alcohol with sedatives like benzodiazepines can lead to increased CNS depression.

- **Synergistic Effects**: Some drug combinations may result in a greater-than-expected effect.

- For instance, combining opioids with benzodiazepines can lead to respiratory depression, which is more pronounced than when either drug is used alone.

- **Antagonistic Effects**: Drugs may counteract each other's effects, reducing overall efficacy.

- For example, taking a stimulant like caffeine with sedatives may reduce the sedative effect of the latter.

- **Idiosyncratic Interactions**: These are unpredictable interactions resulting from unique individual responses to drug combinations.

- For example, combining certain antidepressants with sympathomimetic agents can lead to serotonin syndrome in susceptible individuals.

**Pharmaceutical Interactions**:

- **Chemical Incompatibility**: Some drugs may interact at a chemical level when mixed together, leading to the formation of precipitates or degradation products.

- For example, mixing amphotericin B with saline can lead to precipitation.

- **Physical Incompatibility**: Drugs may interact physically, causing changes in solubility, pH, or stability.

- For instance, mixing insulin with certain other drugs in the same syringe can lead to denaturation or aggregation of insulin molecules.

**Conclusion:**

- Understanding these various types of drug interactions is crucial for healthcare professionals to prevent adverse effects and ensure optimal therapeutic outcomes when managing patients on multiple medications.
- It's essential for patients to inform their healthcare providers about all the medications they are taking, including prescription drugs, over-the-counter medications, and dietary supplements, to minimize the risk of harmful interactions.

## 164. What is drug disease interaction? explain various types of drug disease interactions with examples?

- Drug-disease interactions occur when a medication prescribed to treat one condition exacerbates or interferes with the management of another existing medical condition.
- These interactions can complicate treatment regimens and may lead to worsened symptoms or adverse effects.
- Understanding drug-disease interactions is crucial for healthcare professionals to make informed decisions about medication therapy.

**Following are various types of drug-disease interactions with examples:**

**Exacerbation of Existing Disease:**

- **Asthma Exacerbation**: Non-selective beta-blockers, such as propranolol, can worsen asthma symptoms by causing bronchoconstriction. Prescribing propranolol to a patient with asthma can lead to increased respiratory distress.

- **Heart Failure Exacerbation**: NSAIDs can cause sodium and water retention and exacerbate heart failure symptoms by increasing blood pressure and reducing renal blood flow. Prescribing NSAIDs to a patient with heart failure can lead to fluid retention and worsening heart failure.

**Interference with Disease Management:**

- **Diabetes Management**: Certain medications, like corticosteroids and diuretics, can raise blood glucose levels and interfere with diabetes management.
- Prescribing corticosteroids to a patient with diabetes can lead to hyperglycemia and difficulty controlling blood sugar levels.

- **Hypertension Management**: NSAIDs can reduce the effectiveness of antihypertensive medications by causing sodium and water retention and antagonizing the effects of diuretics. Prescribing NSAIDs to a patient with hypertension can lead to elevated blood pressure and inadequate control of hypertension.

**Compromised Immune Response:**

- **Infection Risk**: Immunosuppressive medications, such as corticosteroids and certain biologic agents, can increase the risk of infections by suppressing the immune response. Prescribing corticosteroids to a patient with an active infection can delay healing and increase the risk of complications.

- **Vaccine Efficacy**: Immunosuppressive medications can reduce the efficacy of vaccines by impairing the immune response. Administering live vaccines to patients on immunosuppressive therapy may result in inadequate protection. For example, administering the varicella vaccine to a patient receiving high-dose corticosteroids may not confer sufficient immunity against chickenpox.

**Organ Dysfunction or Failure:**

- **Renal Impairment**: NSAIDs can worsen renal function by reducing renal blood flow and causing sodium and water retention. Prescribing NSAIDs to a patient with renal impairment can lead to acute kidney injury or exacerbation of chronic kidney disease.

- **Hepatic Impairment**: Certain medications, such as acetaminophen and statins, can cause hepatotoxicity and worsen liver function in patients with liver disease. Prescribing these medications to patients with hepatic impairment can lead to liver damage and hepatic decompensation.

**Electrolyte Imbalance**:

- **Potassium Imbalance**: Potassium-sparing diuretics, such as spironolactone, can increase serum potassium levels and cause hyperkalemia, which can be dangerous, especially in patients with renal impairment or heart disease. Prescribing spironolactone to patients with these conditions can lead to life-threatening cardiac arrhythmias.

Conclusion:
- Understanding these drug-disease interactions is essential for healthcare professionals to optimize medication therapy and minimize the risk of adverse outcomes in patients with multiple medical conditions.
- It underscores the importance of a comprehensive medication review and individualized treatment plans tailored to each patient's specific needs and medical history.

**165. What are the factors that influence the drug drug interaction and drug disease interaction? explain with examples?**

- Several factors can influence the occurrence and severity of drug-drug interactions (DDIs) and drug-disease interactions (DDIs). These factors can vary widely and may include pharmacokinetic and pharmacodynamic properties of drugs, patient characteristics, and underlying medical conditions.

**Following are some key factors that influence these interactions, along with examples:**

- **Pharmacokinetic Factors**:

- **Absorption**: Drugs that alter gastrointestinal pH or motility can affect the absorption of other medications. For example, antacids can reduce the absorption of certain antibiotics like tetracycline.

- **Distribution**: Drugs that bind extensively to plasma proteins may compete for binding sites, leading to altered distribution. For instance, NSAIDs can displace warfarin from plasma proteins, increasing its free fraction and risk of bleeding.

- **Metabolism**: Drugs that induce or inhibit cytochrome P450 enzymes can affect the metabolism of other drugs.
- For example, rifampin induces CYP3A4 and can reduce the effectiveness of oral contraceptives metabolized by this enzyme.

- **Excretion**: Drugs that affect renal or hepatic clearance can alter the elimination of other medications.
- For instance, probenecid inhibits the renal excretion of penicillin, leading to increased penicillin levels in the blood.

**Pharmacodynamic Factors**:

- **Receptor Interactions**: Drugs that act on the same or related receptors can have additive or synergistic effects.
- For example, combining opioids with benzodiazepines can lead to increased respiratory depression due to synergistic effects on the central nervous system.

- **Enzyme Inhibition/Induction**: Drugs that inhibit or induce specific enzymes can alter the pharmacodynamic effects of other medications.
- For instance, combining selective serotonin reuptake inhibitors (SSRIs) with monoamine oxidase inhibitors (MAOIs) can lead to serotonin syndrome due to excessive serotonin accumulation.

- **Electrolyte Imbalance**: Some medications can affect electrolyte levels, leading to pharmacodynamic interactions.
- For example, loop diuretics can cause hypokalemia, which can potentiate the risk of cardiac arrhythmias when combined with drugs that also affect cardiac conduction.

**Patient-related Factors**:

- **Genetic Variability**: Genetic polymorphisms in drug-metabolizing enzymes or drug transporters can influence individual responses to medications.
- For example, individuals with reduced CYP2C19 activity may have increased exposure to clopidogrel, affecting its antiplatelet efficacy.

- **Age**: Pharmacokinetic and pharmacodynamic parameters can change with age, affecting drug interactions.
- Elderly patients may be more susceptible to drug interactions due to changes in organ function and polypharmacy.

- **Renal or Hepatic Impairment**: Impaired renal or hepatic function can alter drug metabolism and excretion, increasing the risk of drug interactions.
- For example, patients with renal impairment may be at higher risk of toxicity when taking medications eliminated primarily by the kidneys.

**Disease-related Factors**:

- **Organ Dysfunction**: Underlying medical conditions affecting organ function can alter drug metabolism and clearance, increasing the risk of interactions.
- For example, liver disease can impair the metabolism of certain medications, leading to increased drug levels and toxicity.

- **Electrolyte Imbalance**: Some diseases, such as heart failure or renal disease, can lead to electrolyte imbalances that can potentiate drug interactions.

- For example, patients with heart failure are at increased risk of hyperkalemia when taking potassium-sparing diuretics.

**Conclusion:**

- Understanding these factors is crucial for healthcare professionals to identify and manage potential drug interactions effectively, optimize therapy, and minimize the risk of adverse outcomes in patients receiving multiple medications or with complex medical conditions.
- It emphasizes the importance of comprehensive medication reviews and individualized treatment plans tailored to each patient's specific needs and risk factors.

## 166. Explain drug food interaction with examples?

- Drug-food interactions occur when certain foods or beverages interfere with the absorption, metabolism, or effectiveness of medications.
- These interactions can lead to altered drug levels in the body, potentially affecting therapeutic outcomes or increasing the risk of adverse effects.

**Following are some common types of drug-food interactions with examples:**

**Altered Absorption**:

- **Calcium and Dairy Products**: Calcium-containing foods and dairy products can reduce the absorption of certain antibiotics, such as tetracyclines and fluoroquinolones.
- These drugs form insoluble complexes with calcium ions, reducing their bioavailability. Therefore, it's recommended to take these antibiotics at least 2 hours before or after consuming calcium-rich foods.

- **High-Fiber Foods**: High-fiber foods can delay the absorption of certain medications, such as digoxin and some antidepressants. Fiber can bind to drugs in the gastrointestinal tract, reducing their absorption and effectiveness.

- Patients may be advised to take these medications away from high-fiber meals to ensure adequate absorption.

**Effects on Metabolism**:

- **Grapefruit Juice**: Grapefruit juice contains compounds that inhibit the activity of cytochrome P450 enzymes in the intestine, particularly CYP3A4.
- This can lead to increased blood levels of certain medications, such as statins (e.g., simvastatin) and calcium channel blockers (e.g., felodipine), increasing the risk of toxicity. Patients taking medications affected by grapefruit juice should avoid consuming it or consult their healthcare provider for guidance.

- **Tyramine-containing Foods**: Tyramine-rich foods, such as aged cheeses, cured meats, and fermented foods, can interact with monoamine oxidase inhibitors (MAOIs), leading to hypertensive crisis.
- MAOIs inhibit the breakdown of tyramine, causing an excessive release of norepinephrine, which can elevate blood pressure dangerously. Patients prescribed MAOIs are typically advised to avoid tyramine-rich foods.

**Alteration of Drug Effects**:

- **Vitamin K-rich Foods**: Vitamin K-rich foods, such as leafy green vegetables, can antagonize the effects of oral anticoagulants like warfarin. Vitamin K is essential for the synthesis of clotting factors, and consuming large amounts can counteract the anticoagulant effects of warfarin.
- Patients on warfarin therapy are often advised to maintain consistent intake of vitamin K-containing foods to avoid fluctuations in anticoagulant efficacy.

- **Alcohol**: Alcohol can potentiate the sedative effects of central nervous system depressants, such as benzodiazepines and opioids, leading to increased drowsiness, impaired coordination, and respiratory depression.
- Patients should avoid alcohol while taking these medications to prevent adverse effects and minimize the risk of accidents or overdose.

**Delayed Gastric Emptying**:

- **High-fat Meals**:  High-fat meals can delay gastric emptying and affect the absorption of certain medications, such as delayed-release formulations or drugs with narrow therapeutic windows.
- For example, taking enteric-coated aspirin with a high-fat meal can delay its onset of action, potentially reducing its effectiveness in preventing cardiovascular events.
- Patients may be advised to take these medications on an empty stomach or with a light meal to optimize absorption.

- Patients should be educated about potential drug-food interactions associated with their medications and advised on appropriate dietary modifications to minimize risks and optimize therapeutic outcomes.
- Healthcare providers should review patients' dietary habits and medication regimens regularly to identify and manage potential interactions effectively.

## 167. Explain drug herbal drug interaction with examples?

- Drug-herbal interactions occur when herbal supplements or natural products interact with prescription or over-the-counter medications, leading to altered therapeutic effects, increased side effects, or decreased drug efficacy.
- These interactions can be unpredictable and may pose risks to patient safety. Here are some common examples of drug-herbal interactions:

**St. John's Wort (Hypericum perforatum)**:
- **Interaction with Antidepressants**: St. John's Wort is known to induce the activity of cytochrome P450 enzymes, particularly CYP3A4 and CYP2C9.

- This can lead to accelerated metabolism and decreased blood levels of various medications, including selective serotonin reuptake inhibitors (SSRIs) and serotonin-norepinephrine reuptake inhibitors (SNRIs), reducing their efficacy in treating depression.

- **Interaction with Oral Contraceptives**: St. John's Wort can also reduce the effectiveness of hormonal contraceptives by increasing their metabolism, potentially leading to contraceptive failure and unintended pregnancies. Women using oral contraceptives should be cautioned against concurrent use of St. John's Wort.

**Ginkgo Biloba**:
- **Interaction with Anticoagulants**: Ginkgo biloba has antiplatelet and anticoagulant properties, which can increase the risk of bleeding when taken concurrently with anticoagulant medications like warfarin or antiplatelet drugs like aspirin.
- Combining these agents can lead to excessive bleeding and should be avoided or closely monitored.

- **Interaction with Antidepressants**: Ginkgo biloba may interact with certain antidepressants, such as selective serotonin reuptake inhibitors (SSRIs), leading to an increased risk of serotonin syndrome—a potentially life-threatening condition characterized by agitation, confusion, rapid heart rate, and high blood pressure.

**Garlic (Allium sativum)**:
- **Interaction with Anticoagulants**: Garlic supplements can inhibit platelet aggregation and enhance the anticoagulant effects of medications like warfarin, leading to an increased risk of bleeding.
- Patients taking anticoagulants should use garlic supplements cautiously and inform their healthcare provider.

- **Interaction with Antihypertensive Medications**: Garlic may have hypotensive effects and can potentiate the effects of antihypertensive medications, leading to excessively low blood pressure.
- Patients on antihypertensive therapy should be cautious when using garlic supplements, especially in high doses.

**Ginseng (Panax ginseng)**:
- **Interaction with Warfarin**: Ginseng may interact with warfarin and other anticoagulants, potentially increasing the risk of bleeding. Ginseng contains compounds that inhibit platelet aggregation and can interfere with coagulation pathways.
- Patients taking warfarin should use ginseng cautiously and be monitored for signs of bleeding.

- **Interaction with Diabetes Medications**: Ginseng may lower blood glucose levels and can potentiate the effects of diabetes medications, leading to hypoglycemia.
- Patients with diabetes should monitor their blood sugar closely when using ginseng supplements.

**Echinacea**:
- **Interaction with Immunosuppressants**: Echinacea may stimulate the immune system and interfere with the efficacy of immunosuppressive medications used to prevent organ rejection in transplant recipients.
- Concurrent use of echinacea and immunosuppressants can lead to transplant rejection and should be avoided.

- **Interaction with Antiviral Medications**: Echinacea may interact with antiviral medications, potentially reducing their effectiveness in treating viral infections such as HIV or herpes.
- Patients on antiviral therapy should consult their healthcare provider before using echinacea supplements.

**Conclusion:**

- These examples highlight the importance of considering potential interactions between herbal supplements and medications when managing patients' health.
- Patients should be advised to inform their healthcare providers about all herbal products they are taking to prevent adverse effects and ensure safe and effective treatment.
- Healthcare professionals should also stay informed about emerging evidence regarding drug-herbal interactions to provide evidence-based recommendations to patients.

## 168. Explain external drug drug interaction with examples?

- External drug-drug interactions refer to interactions that occur when two or more drugs are applied externally to the body, such as topically or locally, and interact with each other.
- While most drug interactions are commonly associated with oral or systemic administration, external drug interactions can also occur and may result in altered therapeutic effects or increased risk of adverse reactions.

**Following are some examples of external drug-drug interactions:**

**Topical Corticosteroids and Topical Calcineurin Inhibitors:**

- **Interaction**: When topical corticosteroids (e.g., hydrocortisone) are used concomitantly with topical calcineurin inhibitors (e.g., tacrolimus or pimecrolimus), there may be an increased risk of skin atrophy, striae, and other local adverse effects.

- **Explanation**: Both corticosteroids and calcineurin inhibitors have immunosuppressive and anti-inflammatory effects, and their combined use may potentiate these effects, leading to more pronounced adverse reactions on the skin.

**Topical Antifungal Agents and Topical Steroids:**

- **Interaction**: Topical antifungal agents (e.g., clotrimazole or miconazole) used concurrently with topical corticosteroids may reduce the efficacy of the corticosteroids.

- **Explanation**: Antifungal agents can alter the permeability of the skin barrier, potentially reducing the absorption and effectiveness of corticosteroids.
- This interaction may result in inadequate control of inflammation and symptoms associated with dermatitis or eczema.

**Topical Antibiotics and Topical Steroids:**

- **Interaction**: Concurrent use of topical antibiotics (e.g., neomycin or bacitracin) with topical corticosteroids may increase the risk of skin sensitization or contact dermatitis.

- **Explanation**: Topical antibiotics can disrupt the integrity of the skin barrier and may enhance the penetration of corticosteroids into the skin, increasing the likelihood of adverse reactions such as irritation or allergic contact dermatitis.

**Topical Anesthetics and Vasoconstrictors:**

- **Interaction**: When topical anesthetics (e.g., lidocaine) are combined with vasoconstrictors (e.g., epinephrine), there may be an increased risk of systemic absorption and cardiovascular effects.

- **Explanation**: Vasoconstrictors like epinephrine can reduce local blood flow and delay the systemic absorption of topical anesthetics.
- However, if the vasoconstrictor effect is overwhelmed or if there are breaks in the skin barrier, systemic absorption of the anesthetic may increase, potentially leading to systemic toxicity or adverse cardiovascular effects.

**Topical Salicylic Acid and Topical Resorcinol**:

- **Interaction**: Concurrent use of topical salicylic acid and topical resorcinol may increase the risk of skin irritation and chemical burns.

- **Explanation**: Salicylic acid and resorcinol are both keratolytic agents commonly used in acne and wart treatments.
- Using them together may lead to excessive exfoliation and irritation of the skin, particularly in sensitive areas.

**Conclusion:**
- These examples illustrate that external drug-drug interactions can occur when medications are applied topically or locally.
- Healthcare professionals should be aware of potential interactions between externally applied drugs and consider factors such as skin integrity, absorption rates, and the likelihood of systemic effects when prescribing or recommending combination therapies for dermatological conditions.
- Patients should also be educated about the importance of following treatment guidelines and reporting any adverse reactions or unexpected symptoms to their healthcare provider.

### 169. Explain internal drug drug interactions with examples?

- Internal drug-drug interactions occur when two or more drugs interact within the body, leading to alterations in their pharmacokinetics or pharmacodynamics.
- These interactions can result in changes in drug efficacy, increased risk of adverse effects, or altered therapeutic outcomes.

**Following are some examples of internal drug-drug interactions:**

**Additive Effects**:
**Combining Sedatives**: When two sedative drugs, such as benzodiazepines (e.g., diazepam) and opioids (e.g., oxycodone), are taken together, they can have additive central nervous system depressant effects.
- This can lead to increased sedation, respiratory depression, and the risk of overdose.

- **Combining Antihypertensives**: Concurrent use of different classes of antihypertensive medications, such as beta-blockers (e.g., metoprolol) and diuretics (e.g., hydrochlorothiazide), can lead to additive blood pressure-lowering effects.
- While this can be beneficial in some cases, it may also increase the risk of hypotension and orthostatic hypotension.

**Synergistic Effects**:

- **Combining Anticoagulants**: Combining oral anticoagulants, such as warfarin, with antiplatelet agents, such as aspirin or clopidogrel, can result in synergistic effects leading to an increased risk of bleeding.
- These drugs affect different components of the coagulation cascade, and their combined use can potentiate the anticoagulant effect.

- **Combining SSRIs and MAOIs**: Selective serotonin reuptake inhibitors (SSRIs) and monoamine oxidase inhibitors (MAOIs) are antidepressants that affect serotonin levels in the brain.
- Concurrent use of these medications can lead to serotonin syndrome, a potentially life-threatening condition characterized by agitation, confusion, rapid heart rate, and high blood pressure.

**Antagonistic Effects**:

- **Combining Levothyroxine and Calcium Supplements**: Calcium supplements can interfere with the absorption of levothyroxine, a thyroid hormone replacement medication.

- Taking calcium supplements with levothyroxine can reduce its absorption and efficacy, leading to inadequate thyroid hormone levels.

- **Combining Levodopa and Antipsychotics**: Antipsychotic medications, particularly dopamine antagonists, can antagonize the effects of levodopa, a medication used to treat Parkinson's disease.
- This can lead to reduced effectiveness of levodopa in controlling motor symptoms associated with Parkinson's disease.

**Pharmacokinetic Interactions**:

- **CYP450 Enzyme Interactions**: Many drugs are metabolized by cytochrome P450 (CYP450) enzymes in the liver.
- Concurrent use of drugs that inhibit or induce these enzymes can affect the metabolism and blood levels of other medications.
- For example, fluoxetine (a CYP2D6 inhibitor) can increase the blood levels of certain tricyclic antidepressants metabolized by the same enzyme, leading to enhanced therapeutic effects or increased risk of toxicity.

- **Renal Clearance Interactions**: Drugs that affect renal function or compete for renal excretion pathways can alter the elimination of other medications.
- For example, NSAIDs can reduce renal blood flow and impair renal function, leading to decreased clearance of lithium, potentially increasing the risk of lithium toxicity.

**Conclusion**:
- Understanding internal drug-drug interactions is essential for healthcare professionals to optimize medication therapy, minimize the risk of adverse effects, and ensure safe and effective treatment for patients receiving multiple medications.
- It emphasizes the importance of comprehensive medication reviews, patient education, and close monitoring for signs of interactions or adverse reactions.

## 170. Explain in-vitro drug drug interaction with examples?

- In vitro drug-drug interactions (DDIs) refer to interactions between drugs that occur in laboratory settings outside the body, typically using isolated biological components or cell-based assays.
- These experiments aim to understand how drugs interact with each other at a molecular level, influencing factors such as drug metabolism, transport, and receptor binding.

**Following are some examples of in vitro drug-drug interactions:**

**Enzyme Inhibition Studies**:
- **Example**: Researchers conduct in vitro experiments to assess the potential of one drug to inhibit the activity of drug-metabolizing enzymes, such as cytochrome P450 (CYP) enzymes.
- This is often done using liver microsomes or recombinant enzyme systems.
- The test drug is incubated with a substrate of the target enzyme, and the extent of inhibition is measured.

- **Outcome**: For instance, in vitro studies have shown that fluoxetine, an antidepressant, inhibits CYP2D6 enzyme activity.
- This inhibition can lead to decreased metabolism of other drugs that are substrates for CYP2D6, potentially resulting in increased plasma concentrations and adverse effects when these drugs are co-administered with fluoxetine.

**Enzyme Induction Studies**:

- **Example**: In vitro experiments can also investigate the ability of a drug to induce the expression of drug-metabolizing enzymes.
- This is often evaluated using cell-based assays or liver microsomes, where the test drug is incubated with the cells or microsomes, and changes in enzyme expression or activity are measured.

- **Outcome**: Rifampin, an antibiotic, is known to induce the expression of CYP3A4 enzyme. In vitro studies have demonstrated that rifampin treatment increases the activity of CYP3A4, leading to enhanced metabolism of drugs metabolized by this enzyme, such as oral contraceptives and certain antiviral medications.

**Drug Transporter Interactions**:

- **Example**: In vitro assays can assess the impact of one drug on drug transporters, such as P-glycoprotein (P-gp) or organic anion transporting polypeptides (OATPs).
- This is often performed using cell-based systems or membrane vesicles containing the transporter proteins, where the test drug is added, and changes in transporter activity or substrate uptake are measured.

- **Outcome**: Verapamil, a calcium channel blocker, is a known inhibitor of P-gp. In vitro studies have shown that verapamil inhibits the efflux function of P-gp, leading to increased intracellular concentrations of P-gp substrates like digoxin and certain anticancer drugs.

**Receptor Binding Studies**:

- **Example**: In vitro experiments can investigate the binding affinity and activity of a drug at specific receptors using radioligand binding assays or functional assays with recombinant cell lines expressing the target receptor. These studies help elucidate the interactions between drugs and their target receptors.

- **Outcome**: For example, in vitro receptor binding studies have been used to assess the interactions between benzodiazepines and gamma-aminobutyric acid (GABA) receptors. These studies provide insights into the pharmacological effects of benzodiazepines and their potential for interactions with other GABAergic drugs.

**Conclusion:**

- In vitro drug-drug interaction studies provide valuable insights into the mechanisms underlying drug interactions and help predict potential interactions that may occur in vivo.
- However, it's essential to interpret these findings in the context of clinical data and consider factors such as drug concentrations, tissue distribution, and patient variability when assessing the relevance of in vitro results to clinical practice.

## 171. Explain in-vivo drug drug interaction with examples?

- In vivo drug-drug interactions (DDIs) refer to interactions that occur within the body when two or more drugs are administered simultaneously or sequentially to an individual.
- These interactions can lead to changes in drug pharmacokinetics (absorption, distribution, metabolism, excretion) or pharmacodynamics (effects at the site of action), affecting the therapeutic efficacy or safety of the drugs involved.

**Following are some examples of in vivo drug-drug interactions:**

- **Pharmacokinetic Interactions**:

- **Example**: Co-administration of grapefruit juice with certain medications can inhibit the activity of intestinal cytochrome P450 3A4 (CYP3A4) enzymes, leading to decreased metabolism and increased systemic exposure of the drugs.
- This interaction has been observed with statins like simvastatin and calcium channel blockers like felodipine, resulting in elevated plasma concentrations and an increased risk of adverse effects, such as myopathy or hypotension.

- **Outcome**: In vivo studies have demonstrated that consuming grapefruit juice with these medications can significantly increase their bioavailability and systemic exposure, potentially leading to dose-dependent toxicities or adverse reactions.

- **Pharmacodynamic Interactions**:

- **Example**: Concurrent administration of nonsteroidal anti-inflammatory drugs (NSAIDs) and oral anticoagulants like warfarin can increase the risk of bleeding due to additive effects on platelet function and coagulation.
- NSAIDs inhibit platelet aggregation and may also interfere with the metabolism of warfarin, leading to enhanced anticoagulant effects and an increased risk of bleeding events.

- **Outcome**: In vivo studies and clinical observations have confirmed that co-administration of NSAIDs with warfarin can potentiate the anticoagulant effect of warfarin, resulting in prolonged prothrombin time (PT) and increased bleeding risk, particularly in elderly patients or those with pre-existing bleeding disorders.

## Metabolic Interactions:

- **Example**: Concurrent use of selective serotonin reuptake inhibitors (SSRIs) and monoamine oxidase inhibitors (MAOIs) can lead to serotonin syndrome—a potentially life-threatening condition characterized by altered mental status, autonomic instability, and neuromuscular hyperactivity.
- SSRIs increase serotonin levels by inhibiting its reuptake, while MAOIs block its breakdown, leading to excessive serotonin accumulation in the brain.

- **Outcome**: In vivo studies and clinical reports have documented cases of serotonin syndrome in patients co-administered SSRIs and MAOIs, highlighting the importance of avoiding this combination due to the increased risk of severe adverse effects.

## Renal Interactions:

- **Example**: Co-administration of nephrotoxic drugs, such as aminoglycoside antibiotics and loop diuretics, can potentiate renal toxicity and increase the risk of acute kidney injury (AKI).

- Aminoglycosides impair renal function by inducing nephrotoxicity, while loop diuretics further exacerbate renal injury by causing electrolyte imbalances and intrarenal vasoconstriction.

- **Outcome**: In vivo studies and clinical observations have shown that combining nephrotoxic drugs can lead to additive renal toxicity, resulting in decreased glomerular filtration rate (GFR), electrolyte abnormalities, and AKI, particularly in susceptible populations such as the elderly or patients with pre-existing renal impairment.

## Conclusion:

- These examples demonstrate the diverse mechanisms through which in vivo drug-drug interactions can occur and highlight the importance of considering potential interactions when prescribing multiple medications to patients.
- Healthcare professionals should be vigilant in assessing patients' medication regimens, identifying potential interactions, and implementing appropriate management strategies to optimize therapeutic outcomes and minimize the risk of adverse effects.

## 172. Why drugs should not be mixed before administration in infusion bottles? explain with examples?

- Mixing drugs before administration in infusion bottles can lead to chemical or physical incompatibilities between the drugs, potentially resulting in reduced drug efficacy, precipitation of drug particles, or formation of toxic by-products.

**Following are some reasons why drugs should not be mixed before administration in infusion bottles, along with examples:**

**Chemical Incompatibilities**:

- **Example**: Mixing calcium-containing solutions with phosphate-containing solutions can lead to the formation of insoluble calcium phosphate precipitates.
- This can occur when calcium chloride and potassium phosphate are mixed to prepare intravenous (IV) solutions.
- The formation of precipitates can occlude IV lines or catheters, leading to infusion-related complications such as blockages or embolisms.

**Physical Incompatibilities**:

- **Example**: Mixing drugs with different pH levels or solubilities can result in physical incompatibilities, leading to changes in drug stability or precipitation.
- For instance, mixing ceftriaxone (a cephalosporin antibiotic) with calcium-containing solutions can lead to the formation of ceftriaxone-calcium precipitates, potentially reducing the effectiveness of the antibiotic and causing infusion-related reactions such as phlebitis or thrombophlebitis.

**Therapeutic Incompatibilities**:

- **Example**: Combining drugs with antagonistic pharmacological effects in the same infusion bottle can lead to therapeutic incompatibilities.
- For instance, mixing benzodiazepines (sedatives) with beta-blockers (antihypertensives) in the same IV solution can result in decreased sedative effects due to the antagonistic actions of beta-blockers on benzodiazepine receptors. This can compromise the desired therapeutic outcomes of both drugs.

**Microbial Contamination**:

- **Example**: Preparing multi-drug infusion solutions in advance increases the risk of microbial contamination, as it provides an optimal environment for microbial growth.
- Bacterial or fungal contamination of the infusion solution can lead to serious infections in patients receiving IV therapy.
- For instance, mixing antibiotics with lipid emulsions in advance can provide nutrients for microbial growth and increase the risk of contamination.

**Drug Stability**:

- **Example**: Some drugs are chemically unstable when mixed with other drugs or diluents, leading to degradation or loss of potency over time.
- For example, mixing insulin with certain IV fluids or medications can alter its stability and bioavailability, resulting in decreased efficacy in controlling blood glucose levels.

**Conclusion**:
- To mitigate the risks associated with mixing drugs in infusion bottles, healthcare providers should adhere to established guidelines and recommendations for drug compatibility and stability.
- This may involve preparing drugs separately and administering them sequentially through the same IV line or using dedicated infusion lines for incompatible drugs.
- Additionally, regular monitoring for signs of infusion-related complications and microbial contamination is essential to ensure patient safety during IV therapy.

### 173. Why expired drugs should not be used? explain with examples?

- Expired drugs should not be used because their safety, efficacy, and potency may be compromised over time, posing potential risks to patients. Here are several reasons why expired drugs should be avoided, along with examples:

**Decreased Efficacy**:
- **Example**: Antibiotics, such as amoxicillin, lose potency over time due to degradation of the active ingredients.

- Using expired antibiotics can result in inadequate treatment of bacterial infections, leading to treatment failure and the development of antibiotic-resistant bacteria.
- For instance, if expired amoxicillin is used to treat a bacterial infection, the reduced potency may not effectively eradicate the bacteria, allowing them to persist and potentially lead to worsening of the infection.

### Loss of Stability:
- **Example**: Insulin formulations can lose stability over time, resulting in changes in potency and effectiveness.
- Expired insulin may have decreased activity, leading to inadequate control of blood glucose levels in diabetic patients.
- If expired insulin is used, patients may experience hyperglycemia or hypoglycemia due to the unpredictable effects of the degraded insulin.

### Potential Toxicity:
- **Example**: Expired tetracycline antibiotics can degrade into toxic compounds, such as epimerized degradation products or degradation products with nephrotoxic properties.
- Using expired tetracyclines can increase the risk of adverse effects, such as kidney damage or gastrointestinal disturbances.
- Ingestion of degraded tetracycline products can result in severe toxicity and exacerbation of pre-existing health conditions.

### Microbial Contamination:
- **Example**: Expired sterile injectable medications, such as intravenous (IV) fluids or medications, may be more susceptible to microbial contamination over time.
- Using expired IV fluids or medications can increase the risk of bloodstream infections or sepsis in patients receiving intravenous therapy.
- Microbial contamination of expired IV fluids can introduce pathogens into the bloodstream, leading to serious systemic infections and septic complications.

### Lack of Quality Assurance:

- **Example**: Expired drugs may not meet the standards of quality, purity, and potency required for safe and effective use.
- Over time, exposure to environmental factors such as heat, humidity, and light can degrade the chemical stability of drugs, rendering them less effective or potentially harmful.
- Without assurance of quality, expired drugs cannot reliably provide the intended therapeutic benefits to patients.

### Conclusion:
- In summary, using expired drugs can pose significant risks to patient safety and may result in treatment failure, adverse effects, or serious complications.
- Healthcare providers should adhere to expiration dates and guidelines for drug storage and disposal to ensure the safe and effective use of medications.
- Proper disposal of expired drugs helps prevent their inadvertent use and reduces the risk of harm to patients.

### 174. What are the adverse effects caused by expired drugs? explain with examples?

- Expired drugs can potentially cause various adverse effects due to changes in their chemical composition, potency, and stability over time.

**Following are some adverse effects that can be caused by expired drugs, along with examples:**

### Decreased Efficacy:
- **Example**: Expired antibiotics, such as amoxicillin or ciprofloxacin, may lose potency and become less effective in treating bacterial infections.
- Inadequate treatment with expired antibiotics can lead to incomplete eradication of bacteria, allowing them to proliferate and potentially cause persistent or recurrent infections.

- This can result in prolonged illness, complications, or the development of antibiotic-resistant strains of bacteria.

**Toxicity**:
- **Example**: Expired tetracycline antibiotics, such as doxycycline or minocycline, can degrade into toxic compounds, including epimerized degradation products or degradation products with nephrotoxic properties.
- Using expired tetracyclines can increase the risk of adverse effects such as kidney damage, liver toxicity, or gastrointestinal disturbances.
- Ingestion of degraded tetracycline products can result in severe toxicity and exacerbation of pre-existing health conditions.

**Allergic Reactions**:
- **Example**: Expired medications containing preservatives or other inactive ingredients may undergo chemical changes that can trigger allergic reactions in susceptible individuals.
- For instance, expired eye drops containing preservatives like benzalkonium chloride may degrade into compounds that cause ocular irritation, redness, or allergic conjunctivitis when applied to the eyes.
- Allergic reactions to expired medications can manifest as skin rashes, itching, swelling, or respiratory symptoms such as wheezing or difficulty breathing.

**Microbial Contamination**:
- **Example**: Expired sterile injectable medications, such as intravenous (IV) fluids or medications, may be more susceptible to microbial contamination over time.
- Using expired IV fluids or medications can increase the risk of bloodstream infections or sepsis in patients receiving intravenous therapy.
- Microbial contamination of expired IV fluids can introduce pathogens into the bloodstream, leading to serious systemic infections and septic complications.

**Treatment Failure**:
**Example**: Expired insulin formulations may

have decreased stability and potency, resulting in inadequate control of blood glucose levels in diabetic patients.
- Using expired insulin can lead to treatment failure, hyperglycemia, or hypoglycemia due to the unpredictable effects of the degraded insulin.
- Inadequate glycemic control can increase the risk of long-term complications of diabetes, such as cardiovascular disease, neuropathy, or retinopathy.

**Conclusion:**
- These examples illustrate the potential adverse effects that can result from the use of expired drugs.
- Healthcare providers should educate patients about the importance of adhering to expiration dates and guidelines for drug storage and disposal to prevent the inadvertent use of expired medications and minimize the risk of harm.
- Proper disposal of expired drugs helps ensure patient safety and prevent adverse outcomes associated with expired medications.

## 175. What are the advantages and disadvantages of fixed dose combinations? explain with examples?
- Fixed dose combinations (FDCs) involve combining two or more active pharmaceutical ingredients (APIs) in a single dosage form at fixed doses. There are advantages and disadvantages associated with FDCs:

**Advantages of Fixed Dose Combinations (FDCs):**

- **Simplified Dosage Regimen**: FDCs can simplify treatment regimens by combining multiple medications into a single dosage form.
- This can improve medication adherence, particularly in patients who require multiple drugs to manage chronic conditions.
- For example, combining antihypertensive agents like amlodipine and lisinopril into a single tablet simplifies dosing for patients with hypertension.

- **Synergistic Effects**: FDCs can harness the synergistic effects of multiple drugs to enhance therapeutic efficacy. By combining drugs with complementary mechanisms of action, FDCs can achieve better treatment outcomes compared to monotherapy. For instance, combining two antiretroviral drugs with different targets in HIV treatment can enhance viral suppression and reduce the risk of drug resistance.

- **Reduced Risk of Medication Errors**: FDCs reduce the likelihood of medication errors associated with prescribing, dispensing, and administering multiple drugs separately. By providing a single dosage form containing all necessary medications, FDCs minimize the risk of dosing errors and improve patient safety.

- **Convenience**: FDCs offer convenience to patients by reducing the number of pills they need to take each day. This can improve treatment adherence and patient satisfaction, particularly in individuals who have difficulty managing complex medication regimens. For example, FDCs containing a combination of antidiabetic agents simplify treatment for patients with type 2 diabetes.

## Disadvantages of Fixed Dose Combinations (FDCs):

- **Limited Dosing Flexibility**: FDCs have fixed doses of each component, which may not be suitable for all patients. Individuals with specific dosage requirements or those who require dose adjustments may not benefit from FDCs. For example, FDCs may not accommodate patients who require titration of individual drug doses to achieve optimal therapeutic outcomes.

- **Increased Risk of Side Effects**: Combining multiple drugs in a single dosage form can increase the risk of adverse effects compared to monotherapy. Patients may experience side effects associated with each component of the FDC, leading to a higher overall incidence of adverse reactions.

- For instance, FDCs containing multiple analgesics may increase the risk of gastrointestinal bleeding or renal toxicity compared to single-agent formulations.

- **Drug-Drug Interactions**: FDCs may increase the risk of drug-drug interactions due to the simultaneous administration of multiple drugs. Combining drugs with overlapping pharmacokinetic or pharmacodynamic profiles can lead to interactions that alter drug efficacy or increase the risk of adverse effects. For example, FDCs containing anticoagulants and antiplatelet agents may potentiate the risk of bleeding due to additive effects on hemostasis.

- **Loss of Individualization**: FDCs may not accommodate the individualized treatment needs of patients with complex medical conditions or unique drug response profiles. By combining drugs with fixed doses, FDCs limit the ability to tailor treatment regimens based on patient-specific factors, such as age, weight, renal function, or genetic variability.

## Conclusion:

- Fixed dose combinations offer several advantages, including simplified dosing, synergistic effects, and improved medication adherence.
- However, they also have limitations, such as limited dosing flexibility, increased risk of side effects, drug-drug interactions, and loss of individualization.
- Healthcare providers should carefully weigh the benefits and drawbacks of FDCs when selecting treatment options for their patients, considering factors such as treatment goals, patient preferences, and safety considerations.

**References:**

- Atkinson AJ, Abernethy DR, Daniels CE, Dedrick RL, Markey SP, editors. Principles of Clinical Pharmacology. 3rd ed. Amsterdam: Elsevier/Academic Press; 2012.

- Brunton LL, Knollmann BC, Hilal-Dandan R, editors. Goodman & Gilman's: The Pharmacological Basis of Therapeutics. 13th ed. New York: McGraw-Hill Education; 2018.

- Bushra R, Aslam N, Khan AY. Food-drug interactions. Oman Med J. 2011 Mar;26(2):77-83. doi: 10.5001/omj.2011.21. PMID: 22043389; PMCID: PMC3191675.

- Carpenter M, Berry H, Pelletier AL. Clinically Relevant Drug-Drug Interactions in Primary Care. Am Fam Physician. 2019 May 1;99(9):558-564. PMID: 31038898.

- Chandran J, Krishna B. Initial Management of Poisoned Patient. Indian J Crit Care Med. 2019 Dec;23(Suppl 4):S234-S240. doi: 10.5005/jp-journals-10071-23307. PMID: 32020996; PMCID: PMC6996652.

- DiPiro JT, Talbert RL, Yee GC, Matzke GR, Wells BG, Posey LM, editors. Pharmacotherapy: A Pathophysiologic Approach. 11th ed. New York: McGraw-Hill Education; 2020.

- Esseku YY, Mante PK, Dodoo ANO, Woode E. Drug Disposal and Ecopharmacovigilance Practices in the Krowor Municipality, Ghana. J Toxicol. 2022 Dec 30;2022:7674701. doi: 10.1155/2022/7674701. PMID: 36619292; PMCID: PMC9822764.

- Harpaz R, DuMouchel W, LePendu P, Bauer-Mehren A, Ryan P, Shah NH. Performance of pharmacovigilance signal-detection algorithms for the FDA adverse event reporting system. Clin Pharmacol Ther. 2013 Jun;93 (6):539-46. doi: 10.1038/clpt.2013.24. Epub 2013 Feb 11. PMID: 23571771; PMCID: PMC3857139.

- Hanlon JT, Perera S, Newman AB, Thorpe JM, Donohue JM, Simonsick EM, Shorr RI, Bauer DC, Marcum ZA; Health ABC Study. Potential drug-drug and drug-disease interactions in well-functioning community-dwelling older adults. J Clin Pharm Ther. 2017 Apr;42(2):228-233. doi: 10.1111/jcpt.12502. Epub 2017 Jan 22. PMID: 28111765; PMCID: PMC5336465.

- Hitner H, Nagle B. Pharmacology: An Introduction. 8th ed. New York: McGraw-Hill Education; 2024.

- Huang W, Percie du Sert N, Vollert J, Rice ASC. General Principles of Preclinical Study Design. Handb Exp Pharmacol. 2020;257:55-69. doi: 10.1007/164_2019_277. PMID: 31707471; PMCID: PMC7610693.

- Izzo AA. Interactions between herbs and conventional drugs: overview of the clinical data. Med Princ Pract. 2012;21(5):404-28. doi: 10.1159/000334488. Epub 2012 Jan 11. PMID: 22236736

- INTEGRATED ADDENDUM TO ICH E6(R1): GUIDELINE FOR GOOD CLINICAL PRACTICE E6(R2) Available at https://database.ich.org/sites/default/files/E6_R2_Addendum.pdf. Accessed on 16-Apr-2024

- Kang JS, Lee MH. Overview of therapeutic drug monitoring. Korean J Intern Med. 2009 Mar;24(1):1-10. doi: 10.3904/kjim.2009.24.1.1. PMID: 19270474; PMCID: PMC2687654.

- Li J, Wang Q, Xia G, Adilijiang N, Li Y, Hou Z, Fan Z, Li J. Recent Advances in Targeted Drug Delivery Strategy for Enhancing Oncotherapy. Pharmaceutics. 2023 Aug 29;15(9):2233. doi: 10.3390/pharmaceutics15092233. PMID: 37765202; PMCID: PMC10534854.

- Miller EJ, Lappin SL. Physiology, Cellular Receptor. [Updated 2022 Sep 14]. In: StatPearls [Internet]. Treasure Island (FL): StatPearls Publishing; 2024 Jan-. Available from: https://www.ncbi.nlm.nih.gov/books/NBK554403/

- Ofori-Asenso R, Agyeman AA. Irrational Use of Medicines-A Summary of Key Concepts. Pharmacy (Basel). 2016 Oct 28;4(4):35. doi: 10.3390/pharmacy4040035. PMID: 28970408; PMCID: PMC5419375.

- Singh S, Loke YK. Drug safety assessment in clinical trials: methodological challenges and opportunities. Trials. 2012 Aug 20;13:138. doi: 10.1186/1745-6215-13-138. PMID: 22906139; PMCID: PMC3502602.

- Rang HP, Ritter JM, Flower RJ, Henderson G. Rang & Dale's Pharmacology. Edinburgh: Churchill Livingstone/Elsevier; 2019.

- Saganuwan SA. Application of modified Michaelis - Menten equations for determination of enzyme inducing and inhibiting drugs. BMC Pharmacol Toxicol. 2021 Oct 11;22(1):57. doi: 10.1186/s40360-021-00521-x. PMID: 34635182; PMCID: PMC8507113.

- Tripathi KD. Essentials of Medical Pharmacology. 8th ed. New Delhi: Jaypee Brothers Medical Publishers; 2023.

- Trevor AJ, Katzung BG. Katzung & Trevor's Pharmacology Examination and Board Review. 13th ed. New York: McGraw-Hill Education; 2023.

- Tiwari G, Tiwari R, Sriwastawa B, Bhati L, Pandey S, Pandey P, Bannerjee SK. Drug delivery systems: An updated review. Int J Pharm Investig. 2012 Jan;2(1):2-11. doi: 10.4103/2230-973X.96920. PMID: 23071954; PMCID: PMC3465154.

- Udaykumar P. Textbook of Pharmacology. 4th ed. New Delhi Jaypee Brothers Medical Publishers; 2021.

- Whalen K. Lippincott Illustrated Reviews: Pharmacology. 8th ed. Philadelphia: Lippincott Williams & Wilkins; 2023.